Doubleday

NEW YORK LONDON TORONTO SYDNEY AUCKLAND

And Say Hi

to Joyce

AMERICA'S FIRST GAY

COLUMN COMES OUT

Deb Price and Joyce Murdoch

PUBLISHED BY DOUBLEDAY
a division of Bantam Doubleday Dell Publishing Group, Inc.
1540 Broadway, New York, New York 10036

Library of Congress Cataloging-in-Publication Data

Price, Deb.
    And say hi to Joyce : America's first gay column
comes out / Deb Price and Joyce Murdoch.
        p.   cm.
    Includes bibliographical references and index.
    1. Gays—United States.   2. Gay columns in
newspapers—United States.   3. Price, Deb.
4. Murdoch, Joyce.   5. Lesbian couples—United
States.   I. Murdoch, Joyce.   II. Title.
    HQ76.6.U5P75   1995
    070.4′493059′0664—dc20   94-24067
                                                CIP

Page 354 represents a continuation of this copyright page.

ISBN 0-385-47365-6

Dedicated to all the gay readers
who've put twenty-five cents in a newspaper box
and found nothing reflecting their own lives inside

Acknowledgments

IN THANKING THE MANY PEOPLE WHO'VE MADE WRITING THIS BOOK both possible and pleasurable, we naturally must begin by expressing our profound gratitude to *Detroit News* publisher Bob Giles and managing editor Christy Bradford for making Deb's column a reality. Assistant managing editor Julie Heaberlin graciously welcomed the column and Deb to the Accent section. Right from the start, Accent editor Marty Fischhoff has provided helpful guidance, and reporter Michael Hodges has dispensed much-needed moral support. The Accent copy desk, headed by Rita Holt, always humors Deb's desire to micro-manage even the tiniest change. A special hug goes to copy editor Ralph Finch, who can always be counted on to find ways to create room for a few extra words. Washington bureau stalwart Mary Lyle quickly established record-keeping procedures for Deb that kept chaos at bay. And the librarians at *The Detroit News* and *USA TODAY* routinely provide swift research assistance.

Gannett News Service editor Bob Ritter multiplied our blessings by making the column available to the entire Gannett chain. Thanks to the hardworking Los Angeles Times Syndicate team of Steve Christensen, Cathy Irvine, Grant Armendariz, Tom Griffiths and Jim Lomenzo, the column's reach continues to grow.

Several people and organizations played vital roles in generating early interest in Deb's column both inside and outside newsrooms: Sue Reisinger, a deputy editor of *The Miami Herald*, introduced us to the hundreds of members of the Associated Press Managing Editors association as well as to Hawaii by inviting Deb to speak there at the 1992 convention. For both gifts, we say, *"Mahalo."* Harriet Dart and Bob Bernstein, seeing that Deb shares the goals of P-FLAG (Parents, Families and Friends of Lesbians and Gays), very kindly helped her forge a strong connection to their group. Likewise, Ellen Carton, Donald Suggs, Cathy Renna and the other leaders of GLAAD (Gay & Lesbian Alliance Against Defamation) quite generously supported Deb's efforts to humanize gay issues. We are deeply thankful for the encouragement we've both received from P-FLAG and GLAAD since 1992.

Our thanks for making book writing seem like a viable option for Joyce go to best-selling author Leslie Walker. Our extraordinary literary agent, Charlotte Sheedy, deserves special thanks on two scores: First, for swiftly putting a halt to Deb's costly habit of weaving lyrics into columns. Second, for using her own matchmaking skills to marry us to a publishing house that shares our vision for this book. Thanks to Charlotte, we found our charming, skillful and exacting Doubleday editor, Renée Zuckerbrot.

Once the book was under way, Bob Giles' assistants, Ree Townsend and Lorraine Needham, steered Joyce to invaluable background materials at the *News*. Laurie Holloway, Diane Weiss, Emily Jones, Terry Murphy and Sally Weidler generously allowed Joyce to stay in their homes while conducting book interviews. Laurie Young helped us both stay on an even keel. Helen Gibson helped teach us the power of one. Cathy Rudder regularly administered much-appreciated doses of encouragement. Martha Nell Smith and Marilee Lindemann, wonderfully dear companions introduced to us by Emily Dickinson, ensured that our lives did not become all work and no play. Special thanks go to our little pal Raymond, who taught us to always try to look for the good in people. Deb's mother, Jane, and brother, Steve, gladly dog-sat our beloved Jazz and Eddie during all our book and column travels. Steve lent a steady hand to our publicity video. Deb's Mom helped bail us out when the computer ate the second draft of Chapter 7. And we especially appreciate the grace with which Deb's family and Joyce's Mother and Daddy handled essentially being outed as the relatives of lesbians by publicity surrounding the column.

On very short notice, Alison Howard, Cathy Rudder and Martha Nell Smith critiqued and substantially improved Joyce's first draft.

Many other people took personal or professional risks to push for inclusion of Deb's column in their family newspaper. This book tells the stories of some of them, but most are still strangers to us. We hope to meet and thank far more of you in the days ahead.

Finally, we thank our friend, our ally, our colleague, Gannett News Service managing editor J. Ford Huffman. He fanned the spark to make Deb's proposal catch fire. We are forever grateful.

—Deb Price and Joyce Murdoch
June 1995
Takoma Park, Maryland

Contents

And Say Hi

to Joyce

1

A GAY VOICE

THE LANDSCAPE OF MAINSTREAM JOURNALISM SHIFTED ON MAY 8, 1992, when *The Detroit News* profoundly shook up its readers. The *News,* the "conservative" paper in town, started the first gay column ever to run regularly in a daily newspaper. The Deb Price column "hit like an earthquake—8.5 on the Richter scale!" recalls Jan Stevenson, executive director of Detroit's gay community center.

Initial tremors of that powerful quake, which jostled assumptions of gay and straight readers alike, were felt hours before the main edition of the afternoon *News* landed on doorsteps and inside newsstands. At 6:15 A.M., when early copies of the *News* arrived, shock waves tore through the newsroom of Detroit's WJR radio. Within forty-five minutes the alarmed reverberations inside "the information station" had traveled 525 miles to my bedside phone: I was jolted awake.

Although I'm by no means a morning person, I caught enough of the words chipperly tumbling out of the receiver to understand that, while I slept, my life's terrain had forever changed: "Good morning! This is Rosanna Kelly. I'm calling from WJR radio in Detroit. I'm looking for Deb Price. I was hoping to talk to her and possibly do an interview with her on her new column that started in *The Detroit News* today on gay issues."

I'm not Deb Price, but the radio station had the right number. I'd crawled into bed with a fretful, expectant and obscure editor from the *News'* Washington bureau but woken up beside the mother of a groundbreaking newspaper column. The sleeping woman curled up beside me was the same; our world wasn't. Literally overnight, Deb had become "the most widely read gay journalist in the world," as *QW,* a New York gay magazine, soon noted.

On the night of May 7, Deb and I had exhausted ourselves with worry and anticipation: What if her column was canceled at the last minute? What if it really did run? Since we live in a Washington, D.C., suburb instead of Detroit, a *News* carrier didn't deliver answers to our door. Yet with the WJR call, I knew Deb's new column had indeed run as planned. The instant I realized the column was a reality I also realized I wasn't about to shake Deb, hand her the phone and risk her being immediately put on the air while still half asleep. Deb had never given an interview, never been asked.

We were both journalists, well trained at keeping ourselves out of our stories. Yet, Deb's private life and our life together suddenly had become very public. In my newfound public role as "wife of" a minor celebrity, I told Rosanna Kelly that Deb would call WJR back shortly. Anyone who wanted to speak with the gay voice that was rattling coffee cups throughout lower Michigan would just have to wait until the voice had downed her morning Dr Pepper.

By 7:50 Deb was on the air for a live, morning drive-time interview with Frank Beckmann, substitute host of the *J. P. Mc-Carthy Show,* a decades-old program that's a Detroit institution. The exchange was friendly, newsy, professional. Only years later did Deb and I learn that before we were even awake on May 8 the WJR newsroom had been shaking with hostility toward Deb's new venture. Kelly, the McCarthy show's executive producer, recalls with a laugh that Beckmann and the program's newscaster "were all up in arms about the column. They wanted to speak to

[Deb] because they were sort of outraged that this sort of column was going to be started."

What's so earthshaking about writing about life from a gay perspective?

Well, outside the gay press, no one in the entire newspaper industry was doing it. Not one of the regular columnists for the nation's fifteen hundred daily papers was devoted to writing about gay issues from a gay point of view. Even though voices within tens of millions of American families are gay, the chorus from the opinion pages of America's "family" newspapers was heterosexual or closeted. Gay readers felt frustrated and ignored; I know Deb and I did.

Then, on May 8, 1992, the newspaper industry lurched toward the twenty-first century. In a remarkable front-page letter to readers, *Detroit News* editor and publisher Bob Giles announced that he was

> pleased to introduce a gay issues column that is the first of its kind in a daily metropolitan newspaper.
>
> While newspapers across America, including our own, have increased news coverage of gay issues, no voice is regularly heard that looks at life from a gay perspective.
>
> The voice of this new weekly column belongs to Deb Price, news editor of our Washington bureau and formerly of *The Washington Post*. The column will be distributed to eighty Gannett newspapers nationwide.
>
> I invite you to journey with Deb Price each Friday in the Accent section as she explores our changing world. I think you will find her column provocative and enlightening. We invite you to share your thoughts with her and our editors at the *News*.

Mild-mannered Bob Giles probably could not have surprised his city much more if he'd announced that the Detroit Pistons were bouncing across the river to Windsor, Canada. That very day, the first Deb Price column appeared, stripped down the entire left side of the front of the *News'* feature section. From the first week, Deb's voice was heard within Gannett, the nation's largest newspaper chain, in daily papers from Rochester, New York, to Palm Springs, California. Soon her column was also being distributed through the Los Angeles Times Syndicate and appearing in such publications as the *San Jose Mercury News, Chicago Sun-Times,* Minneapolis *Star Tribune,* Atlanta *Constitution,* San Francisco *Examiner, The Key West (Fla.) Citizen* and *Liberal Opinion Week.* Seeing *The Detroit News'* example, a handful of papers launched regular gay columns of their own: Gabriel Rotello and Frank DeCaro write every week for *New York Newsday;* Victoria Brownworth and Mubarak S. Dahir appear in *The Philadelphia Daily News* on alternate weeks; Perry Deane Young's column runs every other week in the Chapel Hill, N.C., *Herald;* Leroy Aarons writes twice a month for *The New York Times* wire syndicate; Amy Adams Squire Strongheart writes a monthly column for the *St. Louis Post-Dispatch.*

Yet gay voices remain a rarity in mainstream journalism even though gay civil rights has finally broken into the news pages: During the historic gays-in-the-military debate of 1993, a tiny portion of daily papers published commentaries by an openly gay columnist. At more than 95 percent of American newspapers, straight columnists debated straight columnists on the future of gay people. Does that sound fair?

Fairness—or the lack of it—is a recurring theme in Deb's columns. But her first one didn't tackle discrimination head-on. A friendly round of introductions seemed a more fitting way to get acquainted.

Gay Partners Need to Make a Name for Themselves

MAY 8, 1992

There's no confusion when a woman says: "This is my husband." But how do I introduce the woman I've lived with for six years to my boss?

Is she my "girlfriend" or my "significant other"? My "long-time companion" or my "lover"?

Who says the gay-rights movement hasn't made a lot of progress? In just one hundred years, we've gone from the love that dare not speak its name to the love that doesn't know its name.

It sometimes seems as if we speak most clearly about our relationships once they are over:

"My ex."

The term is blunt with a lingering air of possessiveness.

No one thinks you mean ex-roommate or ex-business partner. They know ex-actly what your relationship used to be.

Documentary maker Debra Chasnoff brought this little dilemma of mine to world attention at the Academy Awards this year when she thanked her "life partner."

No sooner had she uttered these words than gay couples turned to each other on couches all across America and said, "Honey, did you hear that? That means she's a lesbian, right?"

Those of us who live in the land of the gay euphemism were pretty sure and won the bet. But to me, "life partner" sounds like what you become when you buy a health club membership.

Beyond that, if I break up with my life partner, do I have to refer to the next woman I live with as my "after life partner"?

But what are the alternatives?

"Significant other" sounds as though it should only be used by straight liberals who don't care who's doing what with whom —they just want to know how many people are coming to the barbecue.

"Longtime companion" sounds like the obituary-page creation that it is.

"Girlfriend" can be fun in the right crowd, but I feel pretty silly using it in mixed company to describe a thirty-eight-year-old professional.

"Domestic partner" always has a certain sarcastic ring to it for those of us whose dust bunnies breed like rabbits.

And then there's "spouse," "the woman I live with," and the psycho-babble guaranteed to land me on the couch for the night, "my relationship."

This vocabulary vacuum is a perennial problem for gay couples.

In *Borrowed Time: An AIDS Memoir,* Paul Monette said he and Roger Horwitz settled on "friend." They decided the most likely alternative, "lover," had a "beaded Sixties topspin."

But "lover" is the term Craig Dean uses to describe the man whose name he wants joined with his on a marriage license. Dean says "lover" underscores a vexing reality that "we're not legally married."

If he wins his lawsuit against the District of Columbia to marry, he says he'll call Patrick Gill his "husband."

The tabloids, on the other hand, have come up with "datemates" and "gal pals" to describe lesbian couples. And, for the first time ever in 1990, the Census Bureau counted us as "unmarried partners."

Yet most of the time, straight people and straight forms have no category to describe us.

"Check one. Are you married, single, widowed or divorced?"

Help me out on this one. Maybe I should cross out "single" and print in "double." Or, when things are really going great at home, "a party of two."

Let's face it, none of the terminology out there fits me—or us. Whatever phrase I use, I end up sounding like a foreigner who hasn't quite gotten the hang of American colloquialisms.

Do we need a unique word to describe gay coupledom? Maybe we should seize a word, as we did with "gay," and make it ours. Or is it simply part of gay culture to have a love that answers to many names?

Surely a little ingenuity will solve this problem. So tell me, America, how do I introduce Joyce?

———

Deb Price is the news editor of The Detroit News' *Washington bureau. Send your word suggestions to her at Gannett News Service, 1000 Wilson Blvd., Arlington, VA 22229.*

With those 634 words, Deb actually introduced me as well as herself and her disarmingly breezy writing style. Her upbeat tone, neither defensive nor hostile, unsettled some readers as much as her material. ("How dare you make your life seem interesting and worthwhile!" one reader demanded to know.) Deb was attempting to start a conversation with all her readers, signaling them that—regardless of their sexual orientation or attitudes toward homosexuality—she wanted to hear from them. We now have boxes and boxes of mail from readers eager to tell a lesbian exactly what they think. All those letters, even those warning that our travels together will include a trip to Hell, are encouraging. Nothing oppresses gay people more than silence—our own and that of heterosexuals understandably uneasy with the subject of homosexuality, which most Americans grew up believing simply wasn't discussed in polite company.

From the moment that she proposed a gay column to managing editor Christy Bradford, Bob Giles' chief lieutenant, Deb had no desire to become a gay George Will or David Broder writing with supposed detachment about the topic of the hour. Deb did not want to refer to gay people as "they" and "them," as even ardently gay-friendly Anna Quindlen must. Deb knew her column needed to be very personal, needed to capture how it feels to be gay in a society torn between its belief in civil rights for all and its worship of conformity.

The column Deb asked to write was the column she'd always wanted to read: She wanted to be entertained, not offended; talked to, not about; informed, not maligned; inspired, not demoralized. And she wanted gay readers, many of whom have little or no contact with gay publications, to be able to see a reflection of their own lives in the daily paper that they and their neighbors read. Eager for both gay men and lesbians to feel that they finally have a voice in mainstream journalism, Deb decided right from the start to use the inclusive term "gay" in describing her column. Since her picture and name make it clear she's female, Deb increases lesbian visibility while writing for and about all gay people. Deb's column pushes the national debate over gay civil rights forward by starting from the point that most Americans have yet to reach: Any form of discrimination against gay men and lesbians is wrong. Period.

Even before Giles and Bradford enthusiastically embraced Deb's proposal, Deb and I knew that our relationship needed to be an integral part of her column. We believe that humanizing gay issues is crucial. Our hope is that when straight folks read about our life together—how wonderful it was to vacation in a town where we felt free to walk hand in hand down main street, or how we bickered like any other longtime couple over whether Deb's new little convertible really needed air conditioning—gay people become just a bit less foreign, just a bit less frightening.

Deb began inviting readers into our home to show the sometimes exciting, often mundane reality of a permanent, monogamous gay relationship. Many of them have shared wonderful things in return: Our first anniversary card—ever—came from a sweet middle-aged housewife who had no one gay in her life until meeting us in the pages of the *San Jose Mercury News*. After years of feeling that the two of us were the only ones with a real stake in our relationship, we revel in knowing that folks all across the country expect us to spend the rest of our lives with each other. Their expectations and good wishes create a bit of outside pressure for us to stay together. I know this may be difficult for heterosexuals who've always been pushed to marry to understand, but a little external pressure to hang on even through the hard times feels mighty good when you're trying to survive in a culture that tells you in a thousand little ways that your relationship is, at best, meaningless. We hope Deb's column provides an oasis of encouragement for many of the other gay couples needing the support we unconsciously craved.

Deb and I are the first openly gay people that many of her readers have come to know. That's what her mail and national opinion polls tell us. Only 22 percent of the 1,154 adults surveyed in a *New York Times*/CBS News poll said they have a close friend or family member who is gay, the *Times* reported on March 5, 1993. Similarly, a *Newsweek* magazine survey published February 14, 1994, found that 47 percent of Americans said they don't know anyone gay—not even an acquaintance. Unfortunately, not knowing gay people doesn't stop most straight Americans from having strong opinions about whether we should be allowed to serve in the military, teach school or marry legally. The *Newsweek* survey also found most Americans (58 percent) support gays in the armed services but are far less accepting of gay elementary school teachers (47 percent) and "legally sanctioned" gay marriage (29 percent). When heterosexuals don't know gay people, their attitudes toward us—forged out of myths, stereotypes and fear of the unknown—tend to be quite negative. For example, among Anchorage, Alaska, employers surveyed in 1988 who said they did not have a gay friend or relative, a whopping 40 percent said they'd fire a worker for being gay *(Identity Reports: Sexual Orientation Bias in Alaska)*.

The good news for everyone who'd truly like this to become a kinder, gentler nation is that straight people who actually know gay people tend to like us. Of the Anchorage bosses in that 1988 survey who had a gay friend or relative, only 5 percent said they'd fire a gay employee. Poll after poll indicates that the fault line running through America on civil rights for gay men and lesbians doesn't divide gay people from straight, liberals from conservatives, young people from their elders or the religious from nonbelievers. That line of demarcation instead separates people who are well acquainted with gay people from those who aren't. Once we gay people step outside our dangerously cozy closets and find the courage to introduce ourselves, fair-minded straight people tend to realize that what unites us all as human beings is far more important than what sets us apart.

NOW, TO CONTINUE WITH THE INTRODUCTIONS: MY LAST NAME IS Murdoch, and when Deb's column began, I was thirty-eight and had been a *Washington Post* editor for almost a decade. Deb's millions of readers are on a first-name basis with me. We know that Deb's column is helping to shatter the stereotype of the lonely homosexual because so many letters to her end: "And say hi to Joyce." Since May 8, 1992, when the phone rang and our lives forever changed, Deb and I have become one of the best-known gay couples in America. Rather than being a cause for celebration, that fact indicates how very far there is to go in humanizing gay issues. Unfortunately, only a handful of the gay men and lesbians alive today have achieved any real name recognition—as gay people—within straight society. And most of the well-known gay people who are now in relationships have partners who are virtually invisible. Massachusetts Democratic Congressman Barney Frank's partner, Herb Moses, and rock singer Melissa Etheridge's partner, Julie Cypher, are two of the very, very few exceptions. No wonder "gay family" remains a concept that's difficult for many straight Americans to grasp. Meanwhile, the mainstream press continues to do very little to integrate gay couples into its coverage, whether it's of Valentine's Day or health insurance legislation.

Since 1992, Deb has been integrating bits and pieces of my life into a column read by countless friends and strangers. Now it's my turn. Whenever I've accompanied Deb on speaking engagements, audience members have asked the same questions whether we're in Toronto or Miami, Honolulu or Dallas: How did the column begin? Why was Bob Giles receptive to the idea of a gay column when similar proposals had gotten nowhere in other newsrooms? Does the column cause a ruckus every time a newspaper starts running it? Have outraged readers ever forced a paper to drop it? Have people come out because of the column? And how has the column affected Deb's life with me?

In answering those questions, this book traces the shock waves Deb's column continues to set off in city after city, newsroom after newsroom. Standing at the edge of a fissure—the bridgeable chasm separating people who know gay people from those who don't—has sharpened the focus of our lives. We are, at once, less naive and more optimistic than when Deb's column began. Much of my half of this book is devoted to exploring what we've learned:

♦ We gay people have far more allies than we tend to realize; we must risk asking for their support.

♦ Courage is as contagious as fear and much more rewarding. But fear is a habit that's hard to break. It imprisons even our dreams.

♦ Religion is a gay-rights battleground that must not be ceded to money evangelists, the pope or anyone else preaching that gay relationships are inherently sinful. The news media must stop perpetuating the myths that gay people are anti-religion and religious people are anti-gay. Many gay people are quite devout. And many of the strongest advocates of gay civil rights are deeply religious heterosexuals.

♦ In a world with problems so intractable that individual effort seems to count for nothing, one person can still make a tremendous difference by coming out as gay or gay-friendly. As Deb wrote during the gays-in-the-military debate, "Each of us holds the key to the freedom of all of us. Unlock the truth. Come out."

Deb's half of this book consists of her first year and a half of columns. They're grouped chronologically rather than under broad topics—as collections of columns tend to be—for two simple reasons. Just as life doesn't neatly separate itself into segments like "love" and "religion," each of Deb's columns is a jumble of laughter and tears, the personal and the political. They are designed to resist being categorized. Also, in a wonderful stroke of luck, Deb's column began just as gay issues gained the national spotlight as never before. To read her columns in their natural sequence is to climb back aboard a roller coaster and relive the promise of the Democratic National Convention of 1992, the outrages of the Republican National Convention, the exaltation of winning with the Man from Hope and the betrayal by President Clinton during the gays-in-the-military fiasco.

Deb prides herself on writing a column that's not only quite readable but rich with information. (One of the many joys of countering anti-gay prejudice is that the facts—historical, psychological, constitutional, even biblical—are on our side.) Her column quickly won professional laurels, most notably a 1992 "Best of Gannett" award. Honors have also come from the Associated Press of Michigan, the American Association of Sunday and Feature Editors, the National Lesbian and Gay Journalists Association, the Detroit chapter of Parents, Families and Friends of Lesbians and Gays (P-FLAG) and a national media watchdog group, the Gay & Lesbian Alliance Against Defamation (GLAAD).

Yet the column's quality is of very little importance when it first starts running in any newspaper. Readers respond very strongly to the knowledge that a gay columnist has become a regular part of their daily paper. What Deb actually writes is clearly secondary, at least in the first few weeks.

Soon after joining *The Detroit News'* Washington bureau in 1989, Deb began writing occasional long features on many of the gay topics later tackled in her column: the military ban, gay marriage, AIDS, openly gay public officials. Yet because the presumption of heterosexuality is so embedded in all our psyches, her byline might as well have been "Deb Price Presumed Heterosexual." Most of Deb's readers had no way of knowing they'd heard a gay voice. Her work caused nary a ripple.

(The presumption of heterosexuality is difficult even for a gay columnist, who spends her days telling the world "we are everywhere," to banish from her mind. Twice since starting the column Deb has attended journalism banquets and, between bites, gently instructed her tablemates on Gay Life 101—only to discover later to her embarrassment that her just-a-wee-bit-patronizing lecture had been delivered to a journalist as gay as herself.)

In contrast to her Presumed Heterosexual feature articles, Deb's column shakes up readers because they know she's gay. Deb compares her column's debut in any newspaper to what happens when someone comes out within a family: Some people respond with wholehearted acceptance, even delight. Some nervously withhold judgment and try to understand. Some wail in horror. And a few—whose ferocity magnifies their numbers—are so appalled that they shout "Shut up!" and cut off all contact, perhaps forever.

A daily newspaper, more than any other source of information, really does become part of the family. Readers have quite intimate, often lifelong relationships with their hometown paper. They bring it into their homes, hold it in their hands, eat meals with it and expect it to note with respect their departure from this world. Although many newspapers are having trouble picking up new readers, most current subscribers are deeply loyal—regardless of whether their newspaper is an interesting companion—and generally grow angry only when it fails to show up on time. Even adults who routinely channel-surf while watching TV or listening to the radio tend to stick with the same newspaper, year in and year out.

After spending so much time with their newspaper, readers naturally tend to think they know their paper's personality, know whether it's conservative or progressive, lively or staid. Most readers—gay and straight—also seem to assume their family paper is heterosexual. Inclusion of a gay column challenges that notion. From Motown to the Mojave Desert, the first wave of letters written in response to Deb's column expresses readers' tremendous surprise:

To Deb Price,

If it was up to me you gays would be locked up, not set free. If you want to advertise your obscene way of life, then do it through gay papers or gay radio, not through the San Jose Mercury News *that we normal people read.*

—Santa Clara, Calif.

Dear Mr. Giles:

A regular column devoted to issues of special interest to the gay community?! I'm shocked—and enormously delighted.

—a Detroit teacher

Lesbian Price:

I along with others have stopped liking The Desert Sun *newspaper because we are sick and tired of the trash you write about. . . . What good are you, you don't reproduce. . . . Stay in the closet. Shut up.*

P.S. Don't answer this letter like one faggot did that I wrote to.

—Palm Desert, Calif.

Dear Deb,

It is such a joy to see your column in our Rochester paper. I eagerly await each Thursday, with the greatest expectations, to see what you and Joyce have been up to! Reading your column gives me a feeling of connectedness.

—a gay man from "RaChaCha"

To Bob Giles:

At one time the News *was a family newspaper. No more. When you have columns on homosexuality, long feature stories on testing a female condom and every NAACP activity gets a headline, I find the* News *and I have nothing in common.*

—Dearborn Heights, Mich.

Dear Ms. Price:

I quit reading The Detroit News *twenty years ago because it was turning into a fascist, racist rag. It's still too right-wing for me, but I will buy it on Friday just to read your column. . . . Keep up the good work. Let the straights know what they're missing.*

—Mount Clemens, Mich.

Sir,

I grew up with The Detroit News. *As a young boy I recall cutting out articles from the* News *for a class assignment or cutting out my hero's* [sic] *from the sport pages. When I was in the Army during World War II my family sent me copies of the* News *that I would read over and over, it was a touch of home.*

Now for the first time, I will not have a Detroit News *to read. I have canceled my home delivery.*

Your weekly column by Price on behalf of the gay groups has gone one step beyond what I consider a respected newspaper should be. . . .

This past Sunday I went with my family to a golf club for a Mother's Day dinner. The families there were a great American mixture, different races, different religions. You may like to know the main topic of conversation was not the '92 elections or the L.A. riots, it was the Detroit News' *new column. People were totally discusted [sic] with the paper. . . .*

In my entire sixty years, I have never written a letter to the News, *but I am hurt and disappointed that an old friend has forgotten the true meaning & importance of a strong American family newspaper.*
                                                  —*Macomb County, Mich.*

Although Deb's column rattles assumptions every time a newspaper begins running it, the column jolted Detroit readers especially hard because *The Detroit News* had long been considered the conservative paper in town. Old friends and old enemies of the *News* were far more startled than they'd have been if a gay issues column had debuted in the "liberal" *Detroit Free Press.*

Just as most of us resist radically changing our relationships with family members, readers' loyalties die hard. Again and again, dedicated *Free Press* readers exclaimed that because of Deb's column they'd now be buying the *News* regularly—on Fridays. On the other side were people like the Detroit couple who declared their son would no longer be allowed to deliver the *News*—on Fridays.

Jan Stevenson, who gave up a career managing a $300 million loan portfolio as a corporate banker to become a full-time gay activist, long viewed *The Detroit News* as the "white male elite business paper. When I was a banker, I never saw the *Free Press."* Now executive director of Affirmations, Detroit's gay community center, Stevenson first met *News* publisher Bob Giles in March of 1992, when his paper honored her as a Michiganian of the Year. The connection to Giles came in handy. Stevenson recalls getting an urgent plea from a tipster at 8:30 A.M. the day Deb's column started. A friend told her, "Bob is going crazy because the paper is being flooded with all this anti-gay stuff. People are canceling their subscriptions. Do something!"

"So," Stevenson says, "I called Bob." Understanding that a paper's currency is subscriptions, she told him, "I really admire your guts for doing this. Like any good leftie, I would never subscribe to the *News*. But I'm subscribing now, and I'm going to get twenty-five friends to subscribe [because of the gay column]."

Stevenson says she was impressed with Giles's response to the hostile reactions to Deb's first gay column. "He said, 'You know, this just underscores why we have to do this,' " Stevenson recalls. "I still didn't have total faith in the *News*," she adds. "What I thought was going to happen was they might run [Deb's column] for a month or two and then, after it had gone through its initial splash: 'Deb Price has moved to Manitoba.' But the fact that it hasn't happened has been really wonderful. . . . It would be impossible to overstate the impact [Deb's column] has had here. People talk about the column all the time."

When strong aftershocks continued for weeks in Detroit, Deb worried that her column would be canceled. Giles insists there was never any danger of that happening. But Stevenson wasn't the only gay Detroit reader sharing Deb's trepidation. They'd grown so used to having nothing inside a daily paper to call their own that they had trouble believing they would keep hearing a gay voice. One Detroit lesbian told us she saved the first twelve columns, then realized "they're not going to take it away."

Gradually, 99.9 percent of *Detroit News* readers adjusted to the presence of a weekly gay column. During the May that Deb's column began, 157 subscribers responded by canceling. But column-related cancellations quickly trailed off, dropping to 46 in June, hovering between 30 and 40 in each of the next four months and plunging to 6 in November, the last month the paper tracked them.

All told, the *News* recorded 353 cancellations over its addition of a gay issues column. Giles, a generally calm man in a panicky profession, notes with satisfaction: "That really isn't very many. Is it?" No, it's really not—353 represented less than one-tenth of 1 percent of the *News'* circulation, 434,181 in the audit immediately before the column began. For editors who doubt their city is ready to accept a gay voice, that number should be looked at another way: For every Detroit reader who severed ties to the *News* because of its gay column, 1,230 did not. Similarly, when the Minneapolis *Star Tribune,* a paper with a far more liberal reputation, picked up Deb's column in mid-1993, it lost 475 of its 410,920 subscribers, or just over one-tenth of 1 percent, according to its ombudsman.

Despite their bravado, most editors and publishers are notoriously timid about any innovation that could scare away even a tiny group of readers. Thus, it's worth noting that the *News'* cancellation figures, low as they are, don't tell the whole story. The liberalism of the *Free Press* left anti-gay readers with nowhere to turn comfortably. Undoubtedly, some drifted back to their old friend, the *News.* Also, the *News* failed to track the number of new subscribers, like Stevenson and her friends, that it gained because of the column.

WHEN DEB AND I STRUCK UP A FRIENDSHIP, ALMOST IMMEDIATELY after she became a *Washington Post* editor in late 1984, I never would have dreamed that she'd become the first nationally syndicated gay columnist and cause such a commotion. I couldn't have imagined that she'd be interviewed about her work as a gay journalist by *The New York Times, Chicago Tribune, People* magazine, *Editor & Publisher, The Washington Post,* CNN, the Voice of America and even the British Broadcasting Corporation. Since she adored Charles Dickens, I wouldn't have been surprised to learn that in eight years she'd be devoting her tremendous energy to penning captivating newspaper tales about society's problems and what can be done about them. That she'd design those tales to be read aloud—like each installment in a Dickens novel—wouldn't have surprised me either. But I wouldn't have guessed Deb would write a gay column because I didn't guess she was gay.

How could I not have known, since she regularly attached mildly flirtatious postscripts to the work-related computer messages she sent me? Well, embarrassing as it is to admit, Deb violated my own lesbian stereotype: She had long hair. Finally, I told my dearest colleague, a straight woman who'd attended the same Washington, D.C., girls' school as Deb, how puzzled I was. "Does Deb Price flirt with you? Maybe she's just one of those people who flirt with everybody. She doesn't look gay," I said. With an amused look that said, "Gay people surely can be bumpkins," my friend replied, "Everyone who went to National Cathedral and looked like that was gay. Trust me, Deb Price is gay."

Even armed with that information, it took me a bit longer to trust Deb enough to come out to her. Being closeted at work back then, I was careful to tell only co-workers—even gay ones— who'd be discreet. But once Deb and I stopped being coy with each other, we quickly began sharing things that had brought joy into our lives: Deb risked ruining the transmission of her ancient and beloved Triumph by teaching me to drive a stick shift. I returned the favor by teaching her to delight in—not merely accept—being gay.

Back at the *Post,* Deb and I were working nights and spending our 9 P.M. "lunch hour" endlessly discussing how our newspaper was failing all its readers by refusing to integrate gay people into its day-to-day coverage and to deal forthrightly with AIDS. (When in 1985, as a *Post* editor, I sought permission to replace the confusing AIDS-transmission euphemism "exchange of bodily fluids" with a clear explanation of what behavior could put our readers at risk, the conversation-ending reply came swiftly: "No, this is a family newspaper!") Gradually, as the vision Deb and I had of fair gay coverage evolved, so did our relationship. We stopped being just good friends.

By 1989 Deb was tired of trying to pretend the *Post* would soon become the progressive, well-managed paper many of us wanted it to be. She was sick of looking up and jamming her nose against a very low glass ceiling. She jumped at the chance to become second-in-command of the ten-person Washington bureau of *The Detroit News.* As part of Gannett's newspaper chain, the *News,* despite its conservative reputation, prided itself on paying more than lip service to hiring and promoting women and racial minorities.

Deb quickly blossomed at the *News.* Her talent and hard work were noticed and rewarded. Her prospects within Gannett seemed almost limitless. When she talked of someday becoming a managing editor, I encouraged her. But when she talked of trying to become mainstream America's first gay columnist, I panicked. Ironically, by then I was one of the few openly gay people at the *Post* and Deb wasn't truly out to anyone at Gannett, even though she'd taken me to company dinners. But I was suffering from *Washington Post* traumatic stress syndrome. I didn't regret coming out at work, but I'd been burned professionally for offering suggestions—most of them ignored, most of them made at the request of upper management—about how the *Post* could improve its gay coverage. I couldn't imagine that the *News* would ever start a gay column. Deb would be risking her future for nothing, I warned.

Luckily, Deb ignored my fears as well as her own. When managing editor Christy Bradford came to town and started a what-do-you-want-to-do-when-you-grow-up conversation with Deb, my wonderfully energetic partner found the courage to launch into an hours-long fugue about the tremendous potential of a gay column, of throwing open a window to a little-known world.

Bradford, a brusque but enormously kind woman, thinks the cardinal sin of U.S. newspapers today is that they're "really, really boring." Newspapers underestimate readers' intelligence and put them to sleep (or, as an ex-boss of mine loved to say after editing a real snoozer, "We'll have 'em facedown in their Cheerios in the morning"). Bradford knows gay people, likes gay people. She was intrigued by Deb's idea.

But, Bradford wondered, who would be the target audience? What imaginary reader would a gay columnist in a mainstream paper keep in mind? Deb said she'd be thinking of herself at sixteen.

Photographs show that sixteen-year-old Deb Price looked very much as she does today—tall and lanky. They don't show that she already knew that only her hair was straight. At sixteen Deb was young and in love—and paranoid and tormented. As much as she and a classmate at the National Cathedral School for Girls tried to hide their high-octane romance, they were "too close" to suit the school's teachers and counselors. The misguided staff, intent on stamping out homosexuality without ever uttering the word, scarred Deb just as permanently as American teachers a generation earlier had marred the left knuckles of students who didn't naturally fit in a right-handed world. Rather than being able to celebrate her own sexual awakening, Deb spent endless hours fretting over the rumor that she and her girlfriend would be ridiculed in their yearbook as "Campus Cuddlers." Deb still shudders at the thought.

Teenagers horrified at their inability to feel heterosexual in a world where they're led to believe that homosexuals are immoral and miserable account for a disproportionate number of teenage suicides and suicide attempts, research indicates. Obviously, Deb managed to survive high school. But the next decade of her life almost certainly would have been smoother if she hadn't been taught at National Cathedral that being gay was something to hide. Her experience makes me thankful that I was oblivious to my sexual orientation until college.

What Deb needed to hear in high school—and what she wanted to share with her imaginary sixteen-year-old gay reader—was quite simple: "Don't let fear choose your path." Between the lines of every column Deb is saying, "You'll be fine. You can be gay and have a good life. Don't let anyone make you ashamed of being true to yourself. Treat your heart with respect." The assurances she offers by writing about our solid but playful relationship, about the productive lives of proud gay men and lesbians, and about our many heterosexual allies couldn't be found in any daily paper when she was struggling to grow up.

Deb's "imaginary" reader turns out to be quite real.

He's a gay sixteen-year-old who wrote Deb that he was "totally overwhelmed with joy when I spied your article" one Sunday in the Springfield, Mo., *News-Leader*. He was happy to find, "finally, an article in a newspaper in the heart of the Ozarks that treated gays and lesbians with respect and talked about what went on in their world." He added, "I was inspired by seeing your gay world column. It reminded me that there is a gay-tolerated world out there." Before meeting Deb through her column, he had shared the secret of his sexual orientation with no one. "At least now I know," he wrote, "that SOMEBODY out there knows the real me."

The imaginary reader also turns out to be a gifted eighteen-year-old lesbian who dreams of becoming an English professor. Kim Casey came out to her parents in La Quinta, California, because Deb's column had taught her about the struggle for gay civil rights. "It was your article," she wrote Deb, "that gave me the reasoning behind my request for the love and support of my parents."

One of the readers grateful for the message Deb herself had needed to hear as a teenager wrote from New York State to say, "Thank you from the bottom of my heart for what you are doing." The reader's father discovered her lesbianism by reading her diary at sixteen. "From then on, he made my life a living hell," she said. She closed by asking, "Please keep my secret. I do not have the courage to come out of the closet yet." She is a retired teacher, then seventy-three years old. Letters such as hers made Deb and me quickly realize that the once-imaginary gay reader, the one yearning for a positive message to be slipped under the closet door, is as likely to be sixty as sixteen. Some of Deb's older, very real readers have been encouraged by the column to make their final break with the stifling closet: Dal Turner, a psychologist and former Hollywood socialite in his mid-fifties, finally came out to his parents, who are in their eighties.

Because Deb's column has a special resonance for gay people of all ages, some editors assume it is meant just for their gay readers. Others, like Giles, primarily see the column as a way to educate straight subscribers. Actually, even though Deb thought of herself at sixteen when first asked to describe her target audience, the bridge-building reality is that she writes for all newspaper readers, the majority of whom are straight.

Most of us who are gay spend years, even decades, scouring libraries and bookstores for information to help us accept ourselves and understand how homosexuality came to have such a place of dishonor in our society. Then, comfortable with ourselves, we turn around and expect heterosexuals who've never seriously studied homosexuality to accept us automatically. Of course, a great many can't respond so quickly. They aren't necessarily people who hate everybody. Most of them are fair-minded folks who've been failed by the news media and other major American institutions—our schools, our churches, our government. They've never been properly educated about homosexuality or, in most cases, sexuality of any sort beyond the rudiments of reproduction. They walk through their lives carrying myths, lies and scary stereotypes about gay people without ever consciously acquiring that cultural baggage. Most heterosexual American adults know little more about homosexuality than they did when they were getting sex education lessons in the playground from kids who very likely thought frogs cause warts. No wonder so many parents initially react with horror to the news that their daughter or son is gay.

Detroit News publisher Bob Giles always emphasizes the educational value of running a gay issues column in his metropolitan paper. Deb shares that attitude and writes not just for her archetypal gay reader—herself at sixteen—but also for Harriet Dart as she was in 1983. Harriet, then a fifty-one-year-old Rochester, New York, homemaker, personifies all the fair-minded, good-hearted heterosexuals failed by the very institutions that should be helping them to understand a diverse world. What Harriet didn't know about homosexuality almost killed her. Literally.

Harriet grew up in northern Minnesota in the small town of Proctor and was raised mostly by her grandmother because her mother worked full-time. Yet her mother took charge of Harriet's sex education. "I can remember my mother coming home one time and saying to me, 'We've got to talk.' And we went out on the front porch, and she says, 'There's some things, when you get older, things you should know.' And she stammered and stuttered. . . . Never said a thing. And I'm still waiting for my mother to tell me the facts of life," Harriet recalls with a chuckle. Harriet's grandmother got a little more specific. Never get involved in a "mixed" relationship, she warned. Translation: Stay away from Democrats and Catholics! In high school, where Harriet was sweet on a boy named Bill, sex education was taught by the gym teacher. "You didn't know anything when you came out of there," Harriet says with disgust.

After graduating with the forty-seven-member Class of 1950, Bill and Harriet married. Figuring out heterosexuality for themselves, they became the parents of two girls and a boy. Decades passed. By the early Eighties, all three kids were married. Harriet and Bill became grandparents, thanks to their older daughter. Then their son, Kevin, divorced. Newspapers were beginning to run a few small stories about "bizarre" homosexuals but never anything positive, Bill recalls. Homosexuality just didn't seem to be part of the Darts' world. "So when Kevin came out to us, he might as well have told us he was going to be a Chinaman. I didn't know anything about it. . . . I just knew it was bad," Harriet says.

Kevin, then twenty-seven, broke the news to his parents in a phone call nine months after moving to San Francisco. Harriet recalls her son telling her to "try to remember I am still the same as you remember me, only now I feel like the weight of the world is off my back." As soon as they hung up, Harriet and Bill "cried like there had been a death in the family," Harriet recalls.

Harriet, an iron-willed woman, had no doubt Kevin wasn't really gay: He was just upset about his divorce or had fallen in with the wrong crowd. That's what she told her son in the three-page letter she now refers to with embarrassment as "almost hate mail."

After getting his mother's letter, Kevin called back, angry this time. "His parting words were, 'There's nothing wrong with me. But if you don't get help, we're not going to have anything to say to each other.' And he hung up on me," Harriet says.

Desperate, she called the Rochester crisis line and was referred to a woman who'd been a friend for years. Their husbands worked together at Eastman Kodak headquarters. Shocked to learn that her friend's son was also gay, Harriet agreed to attend a meeting of Parents, Families and Friends of Lesbians and Gays (P-FLAG). But P-FLAG's message that homosexuality is a natural human variation, much like left-handedness, initially was lost on Harriet.

She consumed pack after pack of cigarettes, and self-pity consumed her. "Because I didn't know, or at least didn't think I knew, any homosexual persons, I thought only the worst scenarios possible. I grieved so for myself. . . . Why has God done this to me! Why me? I didn't deserve to have this burden placed on me," Harriet thought then. Her asthma was worse than it had been since childhood. Even being hospitalized for four days didn't help her breathing for long. Neither did loading up on pills. At a P-FLAG conference, a nun saw Harriet gulping pills and suggested that she was taking too much medication. A Methodist who still didn't have much use for Catholics, Harriet snapped,

"Sister, you take care of your religion, and I'll take care of my health!"

Eventually, Harriet became friends with the nun and took her advice that she change doctors. The nun also insisted that Harriet tell her new physician that she'd recently found out her son is gay. Stubborn as ever, Harriet grudgingly agreed. Her new doctor's immediate response was to ask, "How are you taking this news from your son?"

"I'm trying."

"And how is your son?"

"He tells me he's never been happier."

"Then what you have to do," the doctor told Harriet, "is, the very next person you see, you walk up to them and say, 'Guess what! I have a gay son.' And if they have an asthma attack, it's going to be their problem. But if you have another one, it will kill you."

Once the burden of trying to hide her son's homosexuality from most of the world was off Harriet's chest, she breathed easier. She joined a college speakers' bureau and began to talk about being the mother of a gay man. And she inhaled every book she could find about homosexuality and human sexuality in general. She gave herself the thorough sex education that she'd failed to get elsewhere. She finally understood that Kevin really is gay, and she pitied neither him nor herself.

Harriet went on to found Detroit's 150-household chapter of P-FLAG. Her dynamic activism also won her a spot on P-FLAG's national board for eight consecutive years.

Kevin Dart, whose longtime partner, Dan, is treated as a son-in-law now by Harriet and Bill Dart, says he's "very, very pleased" with his parents. "Sometimes I'm a little surprised at how far they've gone. They seem to take that extra step and that extra mile," he adds. Sharing his mother's stubborn streak, Kevin says that if his parents had not changed their attitude toward homosexuality, "I don't think I would probably be talking to them. It would be sad." Mother and son still tussle over how Kevin lives his life. But, my, how the battlefield has changed! Their annual tug-of-war is over whether Kevin will take a few days off from work to join his parents at the P-FLAG national convention.

Harriet Dart believes her journey toward understanding Kevin's sexual orientation "absolutely" would have been easier if Deb's column had been around in 1983. Now that the column is around, Harriet uses it in coming to the rescue of other parents reeling from the news that their son or daughter is gay. "They may not want to read a book. They may not want to come to our [P-FLAG] meetings," Harriet explains. "But we can say, 'If you get *The Detroit News,* be sure to read Deb's column on Fridays.' It's a non-threatening way of getting the education into a house because it's coming with *The Detroit News.*

"The whole reason for the column is to show how normal [gay] life is: You still have to pay taxes and cut the grass and go grocery shopping, and that isn't anything that ever crosses people's minds when they hear the word 'gay' or 'lesbian,' especially when they've heard it for the first time in their own family. Believe me, grocery shopping and taxes are not on their minds!"

Since Deb always writes with the hope of helping other parents avoid the extended agony of Harriet Dart, she's especially gratified when a mother or father drops her a note or takes her aside after a speech to tell her that she's succeeded. But what difference does it really make whom Deb has in mind when she begins crafting each column? She can't reach readers who don't want to be reached, can she? Well, newspaper surveys indicate that perhaps she can. Fifty-four percent of adult newspaper readers report that they "generally read every page" of their daily paper, regardless of the topics or authors, according to the Simmons Market Research Bureau's 1992 Study of Media & Markets. And Deb's mail suggests that even some of her staunchest critics read her column regularly and, sometimes, are changed by it. After Deb tore into then-President George Bush for his gutless opposition to gay rights, a regular correspondent from Lathrop, California, wrote: "Against my better judgment I've continued to read your articles. . . . Before criticism, why don't you tell us how many combat missions you have flown? How many aircraft have been shot out from under you?" (He managed to ignore that as a woman and a homosexual Deb was doubly barred from flying combat missions. Besides, her eyesight is terrible.) But having read another week's column about an anti-violence squad patrolling a gay neighborhood, Deb's critic gave her a little credit: "You did tell us how you volunteered for Q Patrol in Houston. . . ." He certainly didn't cross the bridge of understanding that Deb is attempting to build between the gay and straight communities, but for perhaps the first time he set foot on it. That's an important start, just as it was when a Missouri man kept reading the column long enough to find out that Barry Goldwater, Mister Old-Style Conservative, supports gay civil rights. The Missouri reader called the Springfield paper to say he'd been on the verge of canceling his subscription because of Deb's column but had had a change of heart: If Barry Goldwater supports gay rights, he said, maybe I'd better rethink my opposition.

ONE OF DEB'S PRIMARY OBJECTIVES AS A COLUMNIST IS TO CORRECT distorted impressions inadvertently created by the news media about the nature of the opposition to gay civil rights. In the name of balance, newspaper reporters and editors consistently insert hateful quotes into even the most innocuous feature article about gay people. These days no reputable U.S. newspaper would gratuitously add anti-Semitic remarks to a mundane story about a Jewish family celebrating Hanukkah or let a Ku Klux Klan grand dragon flap his sheet in a routine article about a black family's reunion. The subtle, if often unintended, message behind those editorial decisions is that it is more normal, acceptable and commonplace to despise gay people than to harbor other prejudices. Hating gay people comes to seem like what it is not—one of the most popular heterosexual pastimes. We gay people tend to respond by developing an inordinate fear of being ourselves anywhere that's not explicitly gay turf. And many heterosexuals, who Congressman Barney Frank points out usually aren't as homophobic as they think they're supposed to be, hesitate to say anything gay-friendly for fear of seeming unusual, unheterosexual.

In attempting to reflect national attitudes, the news media contort themselves into a carnival mirror, making homophobia appear larger than life and quite separate from forms of bigotry they consider less fashionable. In fact, national polls have repeatedly found that three out of four Americans oppose job discrimination against gay people. And while most heterosexuals may not yet be ready to grant gay people full equality, nearly one-third of the nation already supports gay marriage, an idea seldom discussed even in the gay press just a decade ago.

Yes, some heterosexuals are rabidly anti-gay, but their attitudes need to be viewed in context. There is a narrow mean streak running through our society. Twenty percent of Americans, Deb and I have come to believe, are like Mikey in the old Life cereal commercials: They hate everything! Their vile, barely literate letters to Deb start by attacking homosexuals and move quickly to blacks, Jews, working women, anyone with AIDS and, since Clinton's election, "the president and her husband, Bill." Often, in the rush to spew venom, these misanthropes trip over their own epithets: "Every time I see your queer, sissy, faggot, lesbian, ugly, dyke face in our local paper I want to puke." Sitting down to read several of their letters is like being forced to watch reruns of the 1992 Republican National Convention. These name-calling letter writers are the same sort of people—in many cases, I believe, the very same ones—as the 20 percent of whites who, according to a 1991 National Opinion Research Center survey, believe interracial marriage should be illegal. One needn't be a psychologist to diagnose that they're deeply insecure, terribly threatened by anything the least bit different from themselves and not the sort of people that most of us would want to get stuck with in a stalled elevator. Their homophobia is inseparable from their other Neanderthal views. Rather than crawling into caves in search of anti-gay quotes, journalists should be helping fair-minded heterosexuals to better understand gay people.

The only time the press doesn't leap at the chance to publish anti-gay remarks is when they are part of a hateful diatribe against other groups. For example, when Nation of Islam official Khalid Abdul Muhammad's anti-Semitic, racist, anti-Catholic speech made headlines in 1994, its virulently homophobic passages went almost unmentioned in the mainstream press. Newspaper readers need to see viciously anti-gay remarks where they exist in reality —right alongside other expressions of prejudice most Americans consider flatly unacceptable. Extreme anti-gay prejudice rarely exists in isolation.

One message Deb tries to send fair-minded but insufficiently informed readers is that homosexuality isn't a tragedy. Through the column, millions of readers meet gay and gay-friendly people with much to teach us about having courage, being humane and savoring life. The awe-inspiring Christine Burton, founder of Golden Threads pen-pal club for older lesbians, springs to mind. When Deb expressed surprise that the eighty-seven-year-old Burton was dating a fifty-eight-year-old, Burton retorted: "If you're going to blame me for robbing the cradle, I'm going to say, 'What do you want me to do—rob the grave? Everybody my age is dead!' " Burton's tendency to grab life by the ears and kiss it on the nose is shared by the never-say-never P-FLAGers who make clear that the gay fight is their fight, too. As one San Jose P-FLAG mother's button declared: "I'd rather have a bigot think I'm a lesbian than a lesbian think I'm a bigot."

SHATTER THE SILENCE. ADDING AN OPENLY GAY VOICE TO A MAIN-stream newspaper certainly does that. Just as Americans of the 1940s had to learn to utter the dreaded word "cancer" before they could begin pouring significant sums into trying to conquer the disease, we cannot break homophobia's stranglehold on our society without first learning to talk more freely about homosexuality. From a proper emotional distance, the noisy expressions of fear, prejudice and hostility that quickly follow the debut of Deb's column in any city almost seem musical. They are the painful, opening words of a long-overdue national conversation. Until people can put their amorphous negative attitudes into words, they've little chance of understanding the origin of those attitudes enough to outgrow them. Most people—except for that truly hate-filled 20 percent or so—can outgrow them. But they won't if gay and gay-friendly people keep silent. Fortunately, the people who have no qualms about signing anti-gay letters to the editor always spur other readers to find the courage to counter those attacks by speaking the truth about sexual orientation.

For too long we gay people kept silent in hopes of avoiding abuse, only to find we'd actually avoided any possibility of real freedom. "I have come to believe over and over again that what is most important to me must be spoken, made verbal and shared, even at the risk of having it bruised or misunderstood," the poet

Audre Lorde wrote in *Sister Outsider*. "My silences had not protected me. Your silence will not protect you," she warned after finding the strength to talk of her experiences as a black lesbian fighting cancer.

Dangerous demagogues like Pat Buchanan and Pat Robertson have frightened decent people—straight and gay—into silence about homosexuality. At the very least, Deb's column always succeeds in getting people talking. Within newsrooms, the challenge to newspaper editors is to find ways to acknowledge the uproar Deb's column initially causes without backing away from the decision to let a gay voice be heard. No paper has ever run Deb's column regularly and then dropped it. When the column began in *The Detroit News*, "the Diversity Committee thought it would be a good idea to defuse the hostile reaction," recalls Julie Heaberlin, an assistant managing editor known for her cowboy boots and boldness. Her solution—as head of both the Diversity Committee and the Accent section—was to keep Deb's two-week-old gay column stripped down the left side of Accent's front on Friday, May 22, 1992, and to devote four-fifths of the remainder of the page to a heterosexual readers' forum assessing it. Under a huge headline, DIVIDED WE STAND, an unsigned editor's note told readers:

> When Deb Price's column debuted two weeks ago, it became the first in a major metropolitan newspaper that regularly looks at life from a gay perspective. We knew it would produce a response, but even we are surprised at the attention it is receiving. Reader opinions have ranged from congratulatory to grateful to strongly opposed. Even the national media is picking up on the story. This week, *The Washington Post* and *USA TODAY* ran interviews with Price. . . . Today, we decided to turn our page over to three readers with varying opinions, who agreed to share their impressions of this groundbreaking column.

Cast in the role of middle-of-the-road heterosexual was Sally E. Stanton, identified as a Birmingham, Michigan, real estate agent and mother of three. She began by asking in seeming dis-

may, "What's all the excitement about, anyway?" In assessing the
still-wet-behind-the-ears column, Stanton concluded:

> I really don't believe that Ms. Price's rather innocuous
> column is going to do much damage to the all-American
> family. Some of the material on daytime TV gives me a
> lot more pause than her pieces. I also don't believe it's her
> purpose to proselytize, but rather to provide a degree of
> insight and understanding. I think she, along with all mi-
> nority groups, ought to be given a forum. Bias and big-
> otry just aren't working. I vote for knowledge and en-
> lightenment.

The forum's lone vote against knowledge and enlightenment
was cast by state Representative Dave Jaye, who describes himself
as a conservative Republican. "Competition from electronic media is causing some newspapers to degenerate into titillating tabloids. A weekly homosexual column is one symptom of this de-
cline. Will bondage columns be next?" Jaye asked.

"High-priced adult bookstores, nude bars and over-twenty-
one drinking laws protect innocent teens from early exposure to
sex," wrote Jaye, sounding like a recent arrival on planet Earth.
"However," he added, *"The Detroit News* is available for twenty-
five cents to any teenager. . . .

"Long ago, *The Detroit News* stopped carrying advertisements
for X-rated entertainment. A homosexual lifestyle column is also
inappropriate for an easily accessible family newspaper," he concluded.

A year and a half later, Jaye, then thirty-five, had come around
a bit, much like the people who mellow after reacting very nega-
tively to news that a relative is gay. Jaye represents suburban Ma-
comb County, a Polish, Italian, and Ukrainian enclave often
viewed as a national political barometer. And he wrestles with
contradictions.

He doesn't know quite how he'd react to having a gay employee in his legislative office. "What I do insist on," he says, "is a
clean-cut professional conservative workforce. I don't allow any of
my lady workers to run around without a bra." Yet he says he'd

fire anyone who told him how to run his own life, anyone who said, "I don't like the fact, Dave, that you dated your wife for five years before you married, or I don't like the fact, Dave, that you use birth control with your wife."

Jaye says he's "an old-fashioned Polish Catholic . . . brought up in a family where it was very important to have a father and a mother." Important, perhaps, but eventually unworkable: His parents divorced. The trouble his mother then had establishing credit and earning a living wage opened his eyes to the hurdles placed in the path of women.

The Michigan lawmaker reads Deb's work occasionally. And if the decision had been his to make, he now says, he would have run a few of her columns. He singles out ones on anti-gay violence—"That's abhorrent"—and AIDS prevention. "I'm not for censorship," adds the man who in 1992 favored canceling Deb's column.

By no stretch of the imagination has Jaye become a gay-rights advocate. While granting gay men and lesbians "their due-process rights," he'd keep us out of the military, teaching jobs, the Boy Scouts, and health professions. Also, gay couples, he says, "shouldn't have the same rights as your traditional heterosexual couples as far as adoption or marriage." Yet his agreeing that a "homosexual column," at least now and then, has a place in his family newspaper constitutes real progress. Perhaps if he keeps reading, he'll come to understand that we gay people deserve fair treatment just as much as his mom did when she joined the workforce.

The third voice in the *News'* heterosexual forum spoke clearly of the difficulty and importance of coming out as gay-friendly. "I am writing this only because I am afraid to do so," began J. B. Dixson, the woman who heads Dixson Communications, a Detroit public relations firm. "Afraid that congratulating *The Detroit News* for running Deb Price's column will (a) hurt my business, (b) make people think I'm a lesbian, (c) make me a target for all the nutcases out there.

"But if people like me are silent, then whose letters to the editor will be printed?" Dixson asked, identifying herself as a "middle-aged heterosexual woman with no particular ax to grind on gays." In fact, the *News'* editorial page quickly printed nearly a full page of letters, most of them negative. Supporters of Deb's column wrote to the publisher or to the editorial page but tended to be too fearful of possible repercussions to allow their names to be published. The *News,* like many newpapers, prints letters only if it may also print the author's name.

Dixson's own fear of being publicly identified as gay-friendly remains vivid. "I literally had visions of people coming up and killing my dogs," she recalls. That imagined horror, like most of those we gay people conjure up to keep ourselves from finding the courage to speak, was never realized. In fact, nothing truly rotten happened. None of the corporate clients Dixson feared upsetting said a word about her supportive essay. But several parents of gay people called to say thanks.

Speaking up for inclusion of a gay column in the *News* was difficult for Dixson, a feminist now in her early fifties, even though she's defended gay people since the 1970s, when lesbians were under attack within the women's movement. Coming out as gay-friendly is very hard, she says, because "you figure I have enough problems of my own that I have to take care of. Why should I throw myself into what is not 'my issue'? It's always been one I've been supportive of, but it has frankly always been difficult for me to do."

Anyone who stands up for gay rights risks being accused of being gay, notes Dixson, who lives with a man. "Your instinct is to say, 'Oh, no, I'm not.' A long time ago I told myself I wasn't going to do that . . . it was a disservice to lesbians. But it's very difficult, quite frankly," not to reach publicly for the protective cloak of heterosexuality, as she did in her *News* essay. "You want to proclaim [your heterosexuality] to the skies. And you bullshit yourself by saying, 'Well, it'll have more credibility coming from a straight person,' " Dixson says with a hearty laugh. "But what it really is, is fright."

She also knows that, in important ways, homophobia actually is her issue. "It works very well," she notes, to keep all women in line, to keep them from challenging sexism. Every woman knows that if she is independent and outspoken, she'll likely be accused of being a lesbian. Many choose complacency instead.

Dixson's defense of Deb's column ended with an anecdote about being invited to the housewarming party that friends were throwing for their granddaughter. "She's gay, and they've known it for a long time. Grandma is sixty-eight; Grandpa is seventy-two and an ex-cop. (Honest.) If those two suburban, Republican retirees can stare down the world on behalf of their granddaughter, maybe the rest of us ought to at least stand up for Deb Price's once-a-week column."

Soon after Dixson's defense was published, people who'd read that very sketchy description began calling the grandmother to ask, "Is that you?" One elderly woman, someone the grandmother had grown up with and resembled in many ways, told her, "Gee, I had no idea you had 'one of those' in your family." Just as the grandmother was about to cut off the conversation with a curt reply, the caller started crying. "It turned out her daughter was 'one of those,' " Dixson explains. But because of "the schism that had been caused when they found out, the daughter moved to San Francisco. And there had been absolutely no communication. It was just a complete cutoff." The distraught mother talked with her old friend, the supportive grandmother, for a long time, Dixson says. "And at the end of the conversation she was going to call her daughter.

"If Deb wrote for a thousand years and just that happened," Dixson adds, "it would have been worth it."

Deb's column sets off shock waves strong enough to change the landscape of lives. After making all the appropriate introductions the first week, Deb began depicting slices of life. Most of the topics—a class reunion, a trip to Paris, wedding gifts—are newspaper standards, but the old familiar tunes sound quite different when sung by an openly gay voice.

Again and again, in interviews for this book, straight journalists and their straight readers singled out one of Deb's earliest pieces as the column that struck the strongest chord with them personally. Each of them talked of having their perspective altered by Deb's column about an all-American ritual, the high school prom.

Chapter

2

COLUMNS

MAY 15–OCTOBER 2, 1992

AT PROMS, TEENS SHOULDN'T
HAVE TO DANCE AROUND
THE FACT THAT THEY'RE GAY

MAY 15, 1992

American high schools are extraordinarily adept at teaching Compulsory Heterosexuality. The final exam is Senior Prom.

Viewed by most teachers and parents as a gentle rite of passage that helps students ease their way into adulthood, the prom looms as a treacherous rite of passing for gay teens.

Although prom committees spend weeks trying to pick the dance's theme, there is truly only one: Noah's Ark. Boy-girl, boy-girl, boy-girl. Board the ship of life as a mixed couple or don't board at all. Gay boys and budding lesbians have two options: sink or swim.

If you're eighteen years old and the hand you want to hold

belongs to someone of the same sex, learning to "swim" often means learning to deceive, to hide, to be secretive. My first girl-friend and I went to our Senior Prom disguised as heterosexuals. Each of us had the one essential accessory: a boy.

Our teachers and the counselor prone to lecture on "The Dangers of Being Such Good Friends" must have felt so proud that night to see that we had straightened up our act. From all outward appearances, the notorious Campus Cuddlers were well on our way to trapping some other naive boys into marrying us and giving us permanent heterosexual credentials.

Several years and hundreds of miles away, Barney Frank, who now represents Massachusetts and all gay people in Congress, also passed his Compulsory Heterosexuality final. He took a girl to his prom. "I was gay at the time, but I didn't tell her," he says.

Now Frank takes his lover, Herb Moses, with him to White House dinners. "The point we're trying to make is that we want to socialize like everybody else. . . . I think that helps people get over their prejudices."

For most of us who knew or suspected in high school that we were gay, the prom was one more reason to feel isolated, left out, invisible and unwanted. Those feelings can translate themselves into a deadly lesson in conformity when gay teens believe the future holds no comfort for them. A heartbreaking number of children come out in suicide notes.

Aaron Fricke chose instead to come out in a lawsuit. In 1980 Fricke, then only eighteen, made history and national headlines by fighting to take the date of his choice to his school prom.

"The prom is this hallowed, sacred ground," says Fricke, "which I think is really quite hysterical because it's just a dance. But it means so much."

In the years since Fricke's prom victory, boy-boy or girl-girl couples have braved prom night here and there. They are the rare exceptions to the rule of heterosexuality.

But last Saturday night, two hundred gay adults held a take-back-prom-night extravaganza at the Washington Court Hotel on Capitol Hill here in D.C. It was billed as "the prom you never had, with the date you always wanted." Barney was there with Herb. And I was there with Joyce.

The crowd roared with approval as names were drawn and the King and Queen both happened to be men. And as the doctors and lawyers and military officers danced, I wished I could have videotaped the scene and shown it to every lonely gay teenager.

The dance was a fund-raiser for a Washington group called the Sexual Minority Youth Assistance League. SMYAL throws life preservers to gay teens. Gay kids beyond SMYAL's reach can call this toll-free number for an understanding ear: (800) 347-TEEN (Thursday through Sunday, 8 P.M.–1 A.M. EST).

Prom chair Greg Greeley, a native of Temperance, Michigan, said, "A lot of people in mainstream society refuse to admit that gay teenagers even exist. I remember in my teenage years fighting the fact that I was gay and really having no one to turn to."

Greeley and the rest of us at Saturday's prom have learned the truth in the gay anthem from *La Cage aux Folles: Life's not worth a damn 'til you can say, I am who I am.*

NON-TRADITIONAL U.S. FAMILIES DON'T UNDERMINE VALUES; THEY ADD TO THEM

MAY 22, 1992

Is it love that makes a family? Or is the crucial element a free toaster?

For most gay couples, the benefits of domestic bliss are intangible. We watch our siblings get eight silver trays, twelve pickle forks, a fondue pot and a trip to Hawaii for settling down. And then our relatives give us a hard time or nothing at all.

So I've wondered about the free toaster.

Many politicians who claim to be defenders of so-called family values sound as if no one would ever marry without special enticements. And that the smallest step toward helping others imperils the entire existence of traditional marriage. Somehow they make an incredibly durable institution seem like a shimmering soap bubble that could be burst by the gentlest wind of change.

Take Congressman Clyde Holloway.

This Louisiana Republican is trying to derail the District of Columbia's effort to make it easier for all sorts of families to pay for health insurance. The law, which the federal government is reviewing because the District is America's Last Colony, allows single city employees to register adults they live with as their domestic partners and buy them health insurance at group rates.

A lesbian teacher could register the woman she loves. But the relationships don't have to be romantic. A trash hauler could sign up his elderly mother, for example, or a firefighter her out-of-work sister.

The District also plans to give tax breaks to private employers who extend health benefits to non-traditional families.

What could be more reasonable than making it easier for loved ones to take care of each other, especially in a nation with 34 million uninsured? Millions of other Americans are paying through the nose for obscenely expensive private health insurance simply because their family configuration isn't nuclear.

What could be the fallout of helping these folks a bit, as the District law would do? Well, Holloway told his House colleagues that "this act represents just one more reason not to enter into the commitment of marriage."

Congressman Holloway, who calls himself a "family man," rightly points out that what happens in Washington, D.C., the nation's capital, is symbolic of the nation's values. But is he correct that the Health Care Benefits Expansion Act—and similar efforts in a few pioneer towns across America—would "radically alter" those values?

This is a nation that values family life. I know I do. But it's gotten so that I cringe when I see a restaurant that advertises itself as a "family" place. The word "family" has been twisted into a weapon to be used against anyone who doesn't fit into the household of Ward and June Cleaver.

As a nation, we've struggled to understand that American families come in all different colors. Now we need to recognize they come in all shapes and sizes.

The folks next door to Joyce and me are a friendly young married couple and his mom. Close by, my mother and brother share a townhouse. All of us are families—and could benefit from laws similar to D.C.'s.

The author of the District's plan, D.C. Chairman John Wilson, who is an atom in a traditional nuclear family, points out that we all share a "common commitment to the people we love."

When it comes to families, married couples with kids under eighteen are a minority. Those folks are about one-quarter of American households.

Yes, they should get benefits to strengthen their families—but so should the rest of us who are the all-too-silent majority.

Two centuries ago when our forebears squabbled about forming a more perfect union, they came up with an enduring blueprint. It said nothing about marriage—or toasters, for that matter. But they wrote of "insuring domestic tranquility." And isn't that what we still want to insure?

BEING REPUBLICAN IS NO PARTY FOR MANY OF AMERICA'S "LAVENDER ELEPHANTS"

MAY 29, 1992

Over three decades, Marvin Liebman labored to remodel the Republican Party, helping transform its conservative wing into the dominant force in presidential politics.

The Goldwater and Reagan campaigns, Young Americans for Freedom, anti-Communist crusades, multimillion-dollar fundraising letters. He had a hand in it all.

Now he wants a word with the party workers who'll hammer together the 1992 GOP platform. But they say they just don't have time to hear about his latest cause: gay rights.

"The right wing doesn't want us," says Liebman, one of several gays told they couldn't speak at a recent GOP listening post in Salt Lake City. "We've replaced the communists as the evil people."

Two years ago, Liebman wrote in the *National Review* that he was sickened by fellow conservatives' vulgar and self-serving attacks on gays. And he came out at age sixty-seven in an open letter to longtime pal William F. Buckley, Jr. Now Liebman and other gay Republicans are trying to wrest their party away from the Radical Right and get it back to the founding principles of Abe Lincoln.

"These 'traditional family values' people make the Puritans look like hippies," Liebman complains.

Had he been allowed to speak, Liebman would have urged that the GOP platform oppose the military's ban on gays, back equal rights for gay couples, endorse civil rights laws for gays and demand more attention to AIDS.

But it's not just the Republican Party that treats "lavender elephants" with dismay, if not scorn. Many gay Republicans say they feel as if they need to live in a double closet—hiding their sexual orientation in political circles and their political orientation in intolerant gay circles.

A recent poll by Overlooked Opinions confirmed the lock the Democrats have on the gay vote: Only 13 percent of gay men and a tiny group of lesbians identified themselves as Republican.

Yet Rich Tafel, president of the Log Cabin Federation, a national gay Republican group, says the gay community is selling the GOP—and thereby itself—short. He argues that the party of Lincoln is the natural home for gays because it emphasizes individual liberty.

"The gay community has been very blind in saying, 'We're going to put all of our eggs in the Democratic Party basket and they're going to take care of us someday.' Well, what's happened is we've been taken for granted by the Democrats," he says.

But Tafel is not predicting that George "no leadership" Bush will suddenly do great things for gays if re-elected. No, Tafel and others see hope in the rise of William Weld, Massachusetts' Republican governor.

Weld has created a commission on gay teens, appointed a gay

Republican to head the state's civil rights panel, named Tafel to a key health post and lobbied fellow GOP governor Pete Wilson of California to sign a measure banning bias against gays.

Massachusetts is one of six states with such a law. "An important message has been sent that discrimination against gays . . . is quite simply wrong," Weld wrote Wilson.

Also pushing were California's Log Cabin chapters, which had helped elect Wilson. As "Torch the Log Cabin" buttons began appearing on some GOP lapels, Wilson vetoed the bill.★

"Political parties only understand power," says Liebman. "And until we [gays] have some power, they'll ignore us. And we'll have power only when we force ourselves in."

The GOP has yet to live up to its billing as a "big tent" with room for diversity. But gay Republicans needn't despair. As an Arabic proverb says, "If the camel once gets his nose in the tent, his body will soon follow."

And no one is better prepared than Liebman to teach young activists how to win by a nose.

★ In October 1992 Governor Wilson signed into law a narrower measure that bans employment discrimination based on sexual orientation.

MARTINA'S EX TAKES CENTER COURT WITH BOOMING SERVES OF HER OWN

JUNE 5, 1992

It's the oldest country and western song: She done me wrong. Only this time, the busted-hearted Texan isn't disappearing into the sunset. And she's as fiery and strong as the one who's gone.

Judy Nelson, Cotton Bowl beauty queen and Fort Worth society wife, met her first lesbian nearly a decade ago and fell in love. Deeply. Completely. Permanently—or so she thought.

And because that lesbian was tennis superstar Martina Navratilova, the love affair attracted an international spotlight. When Martina vaulted into the stands to hug Judy after winning at Wimbledon in 1990, millions of viewers felt the electricity.

"For those eight years, it really was that happy," recalls Judy. "It was good, it was healthy, it was happy. And what happened, I may never know."

> *Strange, how you stopped loving me*
> *how you stopped needing me*
> *when she came along.*
> *Oh, how strange.*

But what was it like to be with the woman who haunts other lesbians' most athletic fantasies?

"She's extremely attentive when she's involved with you," Judy explains. "And when she's through with you, she's through with you. I mean, she's gone."

But unlike the late country great Patsy Cline, who popularized "Strange," Judy will never be mistaken for a doormat.

"I was willing to say, 'Wait a minute, Martina. You can't do it this time. You've walked out on everybody else.' "

Striking a "Don't Mess with Texas" pose, the green-eyed blonde sued. Exhibit A in the multimillion-dollar palimony case was a videotaped relationship contract. We're "partners if we win; partners if we lose," Judy had said on the videotape with a beaming Martina beside her.

"I believed that she needed to honor the agreement—that she shouldn't be able to walk away just because she's a woman."

But despite years of playing a traditional wife role in their relationship, Judy slammed into the difference between married and gay couples: legally recognized rights and responsibilities.

"If the two of us had been married, there would have been no question about how things would be," she says of her trailblazing effort to persuade a Texas judge to enforce the agreement.

But after a high-decibel battle that made them look a helluva lot like other divorcing couples—only richer and cuter—the women settled out of court.

Now Judy is putting the finishing touches on her account of their love gone wrong. Her co-writer wanted to call it just *Nelson vs. Navratilova,* but Judy insists on a less combative subtitle. Maybe *Love, Set, Match.*

On Judy's side of the net, the memories of "the love of my life" still linger.

> *Strange, you're still in all my dreams.*
> *Oh, what a funny thing*
> *I still care for you.*
> *Oh, how strange.*

Here Judy parts ways with Patsy. Martina is no longer in *all* her dreams. They've begun to star *Rubyfruit Jungle* author Rita Mae Brown, who ironically was also left in the dust by Martina.

Is the love affair serious?

"I don't do flings," Judy playfully drawls after a morning horseback ride on Rita Mae's three-hundred-acre estate near Charlottesville, Virginia.

And now Judy feels political. She's watched her children, parents, much of Fort Worth and even her ex-husband change their minds about gays because of her openness about the two women she's loved. But she says more of us need to come out.

"Then the people who are so heterosexual, so afraid, wouldn't be afraid anymore. They'd say, 'These are people I know, I work with.' "

She'll help where she can. "If I can make a difference, that's what I want to do. I must have come this path for some reason."

Jukebox king George Strait laments that *Cold Fort Worth beer's just no good for jealous.*

Judy's new tonic is warm Southern Comfort.

SOCIAL CLUBS ARE A BRIGHT SPOT FOR THOSE USED TO THE DARK BAR SCENE

JUNE 12, 1992

Has your gal pal been spending her Saturday mornings with an Early Girl? Has your boyfriend been heeding the demands of a Beefmaster?

Then you, too, must be living with a compulsive gardener, who darts from bed to mulch, weed, fertilize and water the tomatoes. You, meanwhile, are left under the covers wishing you were a tiny bit greener and leafier so you could get a little attention.

Joyce brought this compulsion with her into our relationship. I had to get used to a basement filled with wire tomato cages, thirty-pound bags of cow manure and an array of tools that would delight any grave-digging mad scientist: stakes, shovels, five kinds of trowels, vicious-looking bulb planters and a baby rototiller.

Joyce takes a Tom Sawyer approach to sharing her hobby: I am transformed into the Human Mule, spending my weekends hauling huge sacks of cocoa mulch to the garden. (Chocoholic gardener logic: "It's worth paying twice as much because it smells like a Hershey bar.")

Joyce, meanwhile, busies herself transplanting vegetables and composing lettuce songs. (Lyrics not available upon request.) And at sunset, after watching a mudslide go down the bathtub drain, she innocently says: "I love it when we do couple things."

But, sensing I'd rather read Virginia Woolf than duplicate her lover Vita Sackville-West's white flower garden, Joyce has turned to the gay Four Seasons Garden Club. Plants that Joyce doesn't even know by first name get introduced there in Latin.

Gay social groups of all sorts are sprouting up nationwide. There are clubs for fiction writers, fliers, bowlers, intellectuals, square dancers, business owners, amateur radio buffs, film buffs, even in-the-buff buffs. While gay bars are deeply rooted in our culture and history, clubs are quickly becoming the preferred way to have fun.

In the early Fifties, just about the only place gays could find privacy and romance was a bar. Even in the Sixties, "for the most part there was no other gay culture than bar culture," says gay historian Eric Marcus.

In 1969 the modern gay-rights movement exploded at a bar —Greenwich Village's Stonewall Inn—when gays rioted after a routine Vice Squad raid.

Long gone are the days when gays danced in mixed couples out of fear. Also gone in most cities is the era when a bar was the only safe place to meet other gays.

Yet bars still offer something hard to come by in this world: a public place where we can hold hands, be affectionate and dance.

But usually, most of us prefer being out and about in the sunshine with like-minded people.

"Bars are probably the least conducive place to meet some-body you really want to meet," says one rower in D.C. Strokes, the first gay crew club. "You can develop friendships in athletic clubs; cruising isn't the objective."

"It's like a progression from [anonymous sex] tearooms to bars to running clubs," agreed Mark Willocks, who jogs with the D.C. Frontrunners.

Rochester, New York, lesbians now have Alternatives to Bar Scenes. "With the summer, we're thinking of going canoeing, miniature golf, just stuff where a bunch of women can hang out together and not be drinking," says a founder.

And getting sauced has new meaning for Palm Springs, California, gays who take a cooking class.

Moving away from bars and into groups based on shared interests is a healthy evolution.

But being a literature major, I have to tell you that I'm glad lilac-loving Walt Whitman missed out on the Four Seasons Garden Club. Somehow "When *Syringa vulgaris* last in the dooryard bloomed" lacks a certain poetry.

TIM AND SCOTT ADOPT A NEW FAMILY AS COURTS ADOPT A NEW ATTITUDE

JUNE 19, 1992

It might seem an unlikely home for two gay men, what with the giant wooden choo-choo train edging the swimming pool, the closet filled with Walt Disney videos, the colorful secret playroom with pint-sized table and chair, and the stuffed-animal collection, bountiful enough to rival any zoo.

But Tim Fisher and Scott Davenport are not your typical gay male couple.

Tim and Scott are raising two children brought into their lives with the help of surrogate mothers. Already, a Washington, D.C., judge has recognized their parental relationship over Kati, who at two is a puzzle maniac and Disney fan. Soon a judge will be asked to extend legal recognition over silky-haired Fritz, born May 18.

All this makes Tim and Scott quite remarkable. They are believed to be the first gay male couple who through "co-parent adoption" are now acknowledged as the parents of a child conceived through surrogacy.

"Modern technology has made a lot of dreams possible, and that is totally true in our case as well," says adoptive parent Scott, thirty-four, a vice-president of a major consulting firm.

The couple met at the University of Pennsylvania and will celebrate their fifteenth anniversary this fall. They always wanted kids. While they considered traditional adoption, surrogacy held out a bonus card—the biological link.

"I like that she looks like me and my family," explains Tim, thirty-three, the biological father of Kati and Fritz. "I asked to be selfish, and Scott had no problem with that."

After placing an ad in a D.C. gay paper, they worked out surrogacy contracts with two women, which included financial support. (Michigan and sixteen other states, according to *The New York Times,* ban surrogacy contracts involving money.)

Like many moms, computer consultant Tim has temporarily shelved his career to stay at home until the kids are in school. "Being a househusband is great when the kids are there, but frankly your brain atrophies when you don't talk to anyone who can construct three-word sentences," he jokes.

Modern reproduction techniques—including surrogacy and alternative insemination—have brought bouncing, smiling joys into the lives of all kinds of couples, including many of the nation's 2.3 million married couples otherwise unable to conceive.

Of course there's nothing new about gay couples raising kids. In the not-so-distant past, the children almost always came from a previous marriage. But now it's increasingly common for gay and lesbian couples to have children together. That is raising cutting-edge legal questions.

Some judges have proved themselves ready for the challenge. New York's Eve Preminger, for example, in January extended parental recognition to two moms:

"A child who . . . receives the love and nurture of even a single parent can be counted among the blessed. Here this Court finds a child who has . . . two adults dedicated to his welfare, secure in their loving partnership, and determined to raise him to the very best of their considerable abilities. There is no reason . . . to obstruct such a favorable situation." Yet, Judge Preminger and farsighted judges in the seven other U.S. jurisdictions that have granted "co-parent adoptions" are rare lighthouse beacons. And for gay couples, family law courts remain largely uncharted and unpredictable waters.

To help gay parents and their children, the Gay and Lesbian Parents Coalition International was formed in 1979. For details on the group, call (202) 583-8029.

All this talk about judicial wisdom and turbulent waters has got Kati yawning and Fritz needing a fresh diaper. "Poppa" Scott takes Kati up for a nap, while "Daddy" Tim sprinkles baby powder on a wiggling Fritz.

This is the home of doting parents.

GETTING A HANDLE ON IT: FINALLY, JOYCE HAS A MONIKER, IN THE NAME OF LOVE

JUNE 26, 1992

I s she my "queer friend" or my "better half"? My "lady lover" or my "quiet light"? My "partner in perversity" or simply my "partner"?

My, my, who would think so many folks would reply to a plea for help in introducing the woman who puts the bounce in my sneakers?

Don't tell Dan Quayle, but since making that simple request, I've regularly met Joyce for lunch on a bench outside the White House. There, with mayonnaise-coated fingers, we sort our mail into love letters and sex letters.

People who read "G-A-Y" as "S-E-X" apparently also misread my question: I didn't ask people to call Joyce names. "Sodomite." "Partner in sin." "I think you should call her sick." A Detroit reader who forgot to sign his name added: "When the breakup comes, you could describe it as 'queered out.'" Better that than straightened out.

But, as we suspected all along, most of you are true romantics.

"Writing this note on our twenty-second anniversary is a perfect way to celebrate our twogetherness!" wrote a Livonia, Michigan, lesbian couple. They introduce each other as "my cov"—short for their covenant with each other.

Twenty-two years? Joyce and I thought we deserved a "good traveling companions" award for passing milepost No. 7 last month. But the real long-distance runners are the Palm Springs, California, guys who call themselves the Desert Rats.

"What I wouldn't have given in 1957 to take my lover in my arms at college and not feel we're some 'queers from outer space,'" one of them wrote. Thirty-five years later, they're still embracing. Call them inspiring.

But what should I call Joyce? Using words originally intended for mixed couples makes me feel like an imitation heterosexual.

As one Belleville, Michigan, grandfather said of using "spouse" to describe the man he has loved for a decade: "I feel very much like I am living in somebody else's house. I, too, would like words that are unique to our lives, giving us a validity all our own, instead of copying other lifestyles that don't quite fit."

But what feels comfortable? *Partners* magazine surveyed 1,749 gay couples and found women are most likely to call each other "partner" or "life partner," while "lover" ranks first among the fellas. But no term won a majority vote, and many folks complained that none fits all occasions.

Our own confusion leaves our gay-friendly co-workers tongue-tied. As one lesbian put it: "Almost any term would be an improvement on being known as someone's 'ummm'! As in, 'Say hi to your . . . ummm . . . Barb.'"

One solution was offered by a Royal Oak spinster who said she too feels like an outcast in many social situations. She suggests "mate"—"It implies lifelong bonding, and it is already part of the English language." And co-opting "mate" could cause "delightful repercussions amongst a few macho types in Australia and New Zealand!"

But a linguistically concerned Farmington Hills, Michigan, reader who cringes at being labeled "straight" deems "mate" more suitable for "unemotional, offspring-bearing relationships typical of animals."

Instead, she suggests "lovemate," which "has the advantage of connoting both tenderness and togetherness. . . . After all, you are housemates and lovers."

Let's put "lovemate" to the test. Is it confusing? No. Did Ozzie use it to introduce Harriet? No. Would I be mortified to have it shouted across the office? "Your lovemate is on the phone!" No.

A bit cutesy? Unfortunately. But it gets bonus points for sounding like a winning chess move: Queen captures queen. Lovemate.

I'm game. I'll try subbing it for "And this is Joyce." And if you're one-half of a gay couple, tell me how it works when at the next Xerox dinner in Rochester or PTA meeting in Des Moines you say, "I'd like to introduce my lovemate."

NEW VISIBILITY OF "GAY PAREE" OWES A DEBT TO AMERICANS PAST AND PRESENT

JULY 4, 1992

Much of gay history is maddeningly debatable. Is it significant that Shakespeare wrote his sonnets to another man? Was Emily Dickinson in love with her sister-in-law?

But self-proclaimed geniuses Oscar Wilde and Gertrude Stein indelibly carved their own names on the gay family tree. That's why Joyce and I were fiercely drawn to Père Lachaise Cemetery during a recent trip to Paris. The grave of Wilde, who once quipped that he was dying beyond his means, lies under an elaborate winged sculpture. A few hundred yards away is the simple headstone of Stein and Alice B. Toklas. (Toklas—polishing Stein's image even in death—had the stonemason chisel her own name on the back.)

Putting flowers on those graves is a rare opportunity to pay tribute to our gay ancestors. Tokens of appreciation left by others showed we were not alone in being grateful to two writers who help us to feel—not simply to know—that we are not a people without a past.

The first time we visited France, the graveyard and a brief photo opportunity outside the apartment where Stein held court for decades were our only contact with Gay Paris. The bohemian capital of the 1920s and '30s, which freed so many artful Americans to experiment with their lives, eluded us.

But our trip this summer was quite different, thanks to Lindsy

Van Gelder and Pamela Robin Brandt, a lesbian couple we've traveled with for more than a year—yet have never met. In prose as light and rich as a Parisian croissant, they wrote the invaluable *Are You Two . . . Together? A Gay and Lesbian Travel Guide to Europe.*

Reading the chapter on Paris is like watching a master magician: One minute you see a wonderful, enchanting city. Presto! It's transformed into a wonderful, enchanting and gay-friendly city.

Suddenly we were staying in the Left Bank hotel where Gertrude and Alice put up their friends and biking in the park where "naturally unnatural" writer Natalie Barney swept women off their feet and into her carriage.

We easily found a lesbian bar bursting with long-stemmed pink roses—and might have had some wonderful conversations if my language skills had been stronger or Joyce had stepped more softly on that dog's tail.

But in a truly bizarre coincidence, we did have a wonderful conversation in a tiny restaurant in the gay-centric neighborhood of Les Halles with two Miami guys. It turned out they had met another American lesbian couple the last time they were in Paris: Lindsy and Pam. They'd even secured a bit part in the travel guide with the campy quote: "We're in true love because we're both trash."

Ever diplomatic (NOT), I realized who they were and shrieked, "Oh, you're 'trash'!"

Ah, Americans in Paris.

We had returned to that fabulous city to revel in the bygone era when our English-speaking ancestors showed the world that same-sex lovers can live without apology or shame. We also found our modern-day French cousins.

Three flights up a dingy staircase just off an unremarkable street, we found La Maison des Homosexualities. Everywhere was proof that we Americans no longer must leave home to find the center of the gay universe. Our Parisian counterparts are embracing gay rights American style without even stopping to translate it into French. Until recently the *"maison"* was known as the "Gay Center." Its members march in the "Gay Pride" parade on the anniversary of Stonewall. ACT-UP Paris is the most controversial —and most visible—gay group.

As an out-of-work gay banker told us, "Always, your country is a symbol of liberty."

France has granted its gay sons and daughters job protection but little more. Most still live, as one put it, "with the blinds closed." Domestic partnership legislation is under consideration, but the route to passage seems even steeper than the *maison*'s spiral staircase.

The path to gay rights has always been rugged. As he headed for prison, Wilde wrote his lover: "Our love was always beautiful and noble . . . the nature of that love has not been understood."

In Paris, the posters say *"Silence = Mort."* Our dead on both sides of the Atlantic still speak to us. Now we must speak up for ourselves.

NATION'S ATTITUDES TOWARD GAYS AND OTHER MINORITIES AREN'T POLLS APART

JULY 10, 1992

Anyone looking for fresh evidence that gays are the most despised minority in America can point to the fact that Ross Perot wasn't hounded out of the presidential race for declaring that only heterosexuals need apply for his Cabinet.

But divining the place of gays in the hearts and minds of our fellow Americans isn't that simple. Even having a presidential candidate say "homosexual" and "Cabinet" in the same sentence was unheard-of before this year.

Pollsters report each tiny shift in Perot's popularity. But what have they found out about gays?

Well, two-thirds of Americans oppose gay marriage (National

Opinion Research Center's annual General Social Survey, 1988). But perhaps we shouldn't take that too personally. Just last year, two-thirds of whites said they'd object to a close relative marrying a black person. And 20 percent of whites still think interracial marriage should be illegal (General Social Survey, 1991).

Lesbians may now take it on the chin with that old familiar punch line "But I wouldn't want my sister to marry one," but clearly we're not alone in the ring fighting against intolerance.

So while the Archie Bunkers of America might not want to dance at my wedding, they remain darned discriminating about where else they'll kick up their heels as well.

Strains of intolerance run deep in our national psyche. Eleven percent of non-blacks would "object strongly" to a family member bringing a black friend home for dinner (General Social Survey, 1985). And 40 percent of gentiles say Jews should "stop complaining about what happened to them in Nazi Germany" (Yankelovich, Skelly and White, 1981, for the American Jewish Committee).

Appalling as those numbers are, polls show intolerance declining. Anti-gay bigotry is again shrinking after ballooning in the wake of AIDS in the mid-Eighties.

Americans are taught "all people should be treated equally. . . . it's part of our moral code," says Hoover Institution political scientist John H. Bunzel. So most of us feel an internal tug toward accepting diversity.

For example, Maureen Fiedler of Catholics Speak Out, a church reform group, says polls show that the "evolving opinion" among Catholics is that "the sin . . . is not being homosexual; the sin is discriminating on that basis."

Few polls directly compare gays with other designated outsiders. But the 1985 General Social Survey found more acceptance for allowing "a homosexual" to teach college than letting a communist, a racist, someone "against religion" or someone advocating a military government do so.

In fact, 80 percent of Americans now oppose job bias against gays and discharging soldiers solely over their sexual orientation (Penn and Schoen Associates, 1991, for the Human Rights Campaign Fund).

And, in one of the first solid indications that anti-gay rhetoric can cost politicians, most adults surveyed recently by *The Washington Post* said they would be less likely to vote for a presidential candidate who'd bar gays from the Cabinet.

Perot has issued a statement promising he wouldn't allow anti-gay bias as president. So we've seen how quickly a sixty-two-year-old Texas billionaire can backpedal.

Gay-rights surveys confirm that "acceptance is increasing—and very quickly," says gay pollster Jeffrey Vitale of Overlooked Opinions. "Unless our community plays its cards very foolishly, we have the winning hand."

Our straight flush is that most heterosexuals already know and like us. Unfortunately, only 29 percent of Americans realize they have a gay friend or acquaintance (Gallup, 1987). Clearly, quite a few introductions are long overdue.

In the meantime, here's one more figure to ponder. Fifty-one percent of American voters told the *Los Angeles Times* in 1985 that it wouldn't matter to them if a presidential candidate were gay.

Well, let me tell you, it'd matter to me.

DEMOCRATS HAVE FINALLY INVITED THE GAY COMMUNITY TO COME TO THE PARTY

JULY 17, 1992

The ultimate grassroots political campaign is the gay-rights movement. And, appropriately, many of us were pretty darn green when we started paying our dues.

As Ohio State University law professor Rhonda Rivera wryly puts it: "Honey, if you wake up in the morning and the person next to you is the same sex, you *are* political."

So, it's not surprising that most of our victories have been close to home. Scores of gay people now hold local office around the country, and many, many more elected officials are pro-gay.

But gay politics has never been presidential politics. Until now.

What a difference four years can make.

In 1988 Republican Senator Orrin Hatch of Utah labeled the Democrats "the Party of Homosexuals." And Democratic nominee Michael Dukakis did his best to make Hatch a liar. Instead of championing our cause, Dukakis treated gays as the uninvited guest at a private party.

But this year, gay activists shoved gay issues onto the national agenda. Suddenly, the terrain of presidential politics shifted.

"This is the start of a new era in national politics," says Tim McFeeley, the executive director of the gay Human Rights Campaign Fund. "We're not being taken for granted anymore. We're seen as a political force and we see ourselves as a force."

Gay Democrats were OUT in force at the Democratic National Convention. The gay caucus—a record 108 people—was larger than the delegations of thirty-four states. And their caucus meetings in New York City were electrified with a sense that profound change—in the form of the first gay-rights president—is not only possible but within reach.

Under the leadership of nominee Bill Clinton, the Democratic Party is vowing to work for our civil rights, abolish the military ban and fight "homophobia." And two openly gay people—San Francisco Supervisor Roberta Achtenberg and Clinton staffer Bob Hattoy—addressed the nation from the convention podium.

"The distance we have traveled is enormous," says gay Representative Barney Frank (D-Mass.). "Gay voters will have the clearest choice they've ever had."

Clinton's unflinching embrace of gay people sets his campaign far apart from the gay-baiting tactics of Bush-Quayle. "I have a vision, and you are part of it," Clinton told gays at a California fund-raiser.

Unfortunately, the Arkansas governor's promises sparkle more than his record. He only recently publicly voiced opposition to his state's gay-only sodomy law. And he has yet to protect the jobs of gay state employees.

Similarly, running mate Al Gore of Tennessee—whose voting

record is praised by national gay groups—is not a sponsor of either major gay-rights measure before Congress: One would lift the military ban and the other would outlaw discrimination against gay workers.

Nonetheless, gay Democrats in the Big Apple were positively shining over the prospects of the Clinton-Gore team, contending that both candidates' understanding of problems facing gays has evolved.

As Clinton's longtime gay friend David Mixner comments, Clinton and Gore "aren't saints. But they are of a generation that knows openly gay people and knows our issues."

And ever-pragmatic Frank asks, "If you aren't going to give people credit, what's the incentive for people to change?"

When will gay rights become American reality? Paul Tsongas had this answer for gay voters:

"Never under George Bush.

"Next year under Bill Clinton."

The Democrats deserve credit for the way they've changed. Clearly, the party and its presidential nominee have figured out a few things:

"Gay" is an adjective, a wonderful modifier. But we're people first. And that's what the red and white Clinton signs all over Madison Square Garden proclaimed:

People First.

City-Living Gay Transplants Are Taking Root in Small Places

JULY 24, 1992

Remember Norman Rockwell's painting of two men holding hands as they watched the fireworks at the county fair?

Well, among all his depictions of the casual joys of small-town

America, that scene actually is nowhere to be found. Gay life has long been invisible on Main Street.

Many of us who grew up in a reasonable facsimile of Thornton Wilder's Our Town felt we were trapped in Their Town: a saga with no role for any self-respecting gay person. That's why Act II of the lives of so many gays could be entitled "Escape to the City."

"The options were very few and very stark," recalls John Preston, editor of Hometowns: Gay Men Write About Where They Belong. "Get to a big city and save yourself, go insane, commit suicide or lie."

That feeling of having been hatched in the wrong nest was captured by the late Merle Miller who joked in his autobiography that by the time he was two years old he was packing to leave his little Iowa hometown. "Either they ran you out of town or you left before they got around to it."

As World War II ended, migrating gays began creating safe places in cities to spread their wings. Now some of the nation's most vibrant urban neighborhoods are gay. And quite a few close-in suburbs have a lavender tinge.

But Joyce and I recently learned about a new gay exodus—this time to the smallest of small-town America.

Deep in a misty valley, light-years away from the nearest parking meter, we found the weekend farmhouse of a lesbian couple we know in Washington. Ever urban, we'd brought along our sound machine so the silence wouldn't keep us awake.

Green we expected, as in the nuclear-sized vegetables in the garden and the circling hills. But never would we have expected two dozen gay couples to live in this valley community, where the big draw on summer Saturdays is a flea market with free watermelon.

This is no Fire Island or Provincetown or Key West. In this Gaysville, gay couples blend into the landscape.

"What I'm after isn't something you can find in a gay bar or a gay bookstore," one of our friends told us. "What I'm after isn't a gay thing; it's a country thing."

The gay settlers trickled into this valley over the last decade as word spread from couple to couple that a peaceful life was possible. Some built rustic mansions; others renovated old farmhouses with an eye toward early retirement.

And there seems to be a pact with the valley's old-timers that some things are better left unspoken.

"We haven't done anything to make them feel threatened or uncomfortable," our friend told us, "and they haven't done anything to make us feel uncomfortable."

The gay settlers live in a "parallel universe." She and her lover of thirteen years socialize with other valley gays "right alongside this other world of straight, basically white and Christian people who are real conservative and Republican. . . . It's like we're ghosts. They don't really see into our world."

The only folks who talk about the influx of gay couples are the gay couples, explains one lesbian who grew up there. "You would get the same kind of treatment if you beat up on your wife —everybody'd mind their own business."

What would get folks riled up? Stealing someone's wife?

"That'll do it," she says, speaking from experience.

The gay newcomers—although agreeing that even their state should remain anonymous—generally say they feel safest when chickens outnumber cars. As one put it, "There's no gay bashing here."

Their out-of-the-way haven is the unlikely offspring of the city neighborhoods where gays—having left Norman Rockwell behind—found the strength to be themselves.

A gay identity, once embraced, travels well.

HIGH SCHOOL CLASS REUNION
SHOWS CHILDHOOD PALS
ARE HARD TO SURPRISE

JULY 31, 1992

A bully bulldog used our Eddie, a dyed-in-the-fur pacifist, as a chewy toy last year. Long after his wounds had healed and his attacker had moved away, Eddie quaked whenever we walked him near the scene of the crime. Speaking on Eddie's behalf, I'd tell Joyce: "The fear still hurts."

Lingering fear of rejection popped up in Joyce's own path this summer when she looked at the RSVP form for her twentieth high school reunion: "Name of Spouse."

Since we're already out to our mothers, our bosses and several zillion newspaper readers, I don't know what she was afraid of. Perhaps that the reunion organizers would tear her reservation check into tiny pieces and send it back with a nasty note, or that we'd show up for the party and be pummeled with rotten fruit from the stinko ginkgo trees that lined her elementary school playground.

Fear of the unknown threatened to throw her off stride. But she gritted her teeth and forged ahead, crossing out "Spouse" and writing in "Partner" and my name.

After that, putting a "7" after "Years Married" came easily. And, as it turned out, so did everything else about our night in Macon, Georgia, with Central High School's Class of '72.

I trooped along because, like many other thoroughly modern lovemates, I'm finding it increasingly hard to duck out of Almost Certainly Boring events to which mixed couples have always dragged their spouses: the office Christmas party, for example. Small talk is a small price to pay for life outside the closet.

Quite a few of the folks I met at the reunion had known Joyce since the first or second grade. And nobody seemed really surprised about how any of their classmates had turned out. The one question Joyce fielded all night had nothing to do with me: "Well, did you become an editor?"

Her "yes" helped earn her a few votes for "Least Changed Female." I suspect that having me in tow was also a vote-getter, since she'd always voiced dismay at the fuss girls made over boys.

But for consistency, no one could compete with the guy who had spent his grammar school years drawing warplanes. He showed up with a chest full of ribbons and an Army dress uniform that actually included spurs. Grown-up occupation: helicopter pilot instructor.

The passage of two decades had left most smiles and personalities recognizable, Joyce found. But a lot of rough edges had been rubbed off. Life Happened. And Joyce thinks she's not the only one who is the better for it.

The twentysomethings tending bar thought life had taken me for a pretty wild ride, though. "You don't look a thing like you did in high school," one earnestly told me. Should I have told her that I had swiped my girlfriend's photo/nametag and back in 1972 was a lowly eighth grader?

But the question I'll not soon forget was put to us by one of the women Joyce insists on calling the MNOPs, a group who became friends while being seated together in class after alphabetized class.

"Now I want to ask y'all this, and I hope y'all won't be offended." In unison we caught our breath. This was the friend Joyce had most counted on seeing. I feared we were about to be hurt.

"Now, why haven't y'all had children together? You seem to like kids so much."

We burst into goofy grins and babbled on about truly loving dogs best. And I knew exactly what Joyce had always seen in her friend Kathi Moxley.

Sometimes we get so caught up in trying to control other people's reactions to our being gay, in trying to avoid yet another painful encounter, that we miss the pleasure of being loved for exactly who we are.

The world is changing in delightful and unexpected ways. We

have options the earliest gay trailblazers could never even have envisioned.

Don't let fear choose your path.

TOWN HAD A PLACE IN ITS HEART FOR A LESBIAN COUPLE AND FRIED GREEN TOMATOES

AUGUST 7, 1992

Juliette, Georgia. "Two women's names—how perfect for the town where they filmed a romance without a Romeo," Joyce remarks as we fill up on corn muffins and fried green tomatoes at the Whistle Stop Cafe.

This tiny river community was snatched back from the brink of extinction by the popularity of *Fried Green Tomatoes*.

Although the stars jetted off last year, their story lives on through the cafe and half dozen souvenir shops transformed from the movie's old sets. Fans from seventeen countries have come to taste the cafe's secret sauce and snap up green tomato T-shirts, aprons and coffee mugs. Seems like everybody wants to celebrate the film's much-loved lesbian couple.

Lesbian couple?

In this tiniest of towns, this line of inquiry raises no eyebrows. Clearly, everybody's thought—and gossiped—about the relationship of Idgie and Ruth.

"Some people thought they were *like that*," says El Binion, waving his hand in the "like that" signal as he barbecues pork slabs for the cafe. "I really don't know. We can all look at the same thing and see it differently."

Shopkeeper Jane Langston recalls chatting about it with novelist and screenwriter Fannie Flagg. Langston says Flagg "danced around the question," as did others. "They wanted you to use your own judgment."

Well, when the film opened, *The Washington Post,* in an assessment echoed by other reviewers, declared "they are not lesbians, just really, really good friends."

Did Joyce and I misunderstand the entire flick? I don't think so. Here's the movie we remembered as we walked along Juliette's railroad tracks:

Little Idgie Threadgoode, an adorable baby dyke who looks silly in a fancy dress, insists on wearing a suit and tie to her big sister's wedding. Just a few years later, she's spending her evenings at the River Club—called the "den of the Devil" by the town's preacher—smoking cigars and beating the fellas at poker.

While her mother sees Idgie's strange ways as a ten-year bout of depression over her brother's death, those of us who've worn her boots know she's just keeping a healthy distance from heterosexual roles that don't fit her.

Enter Ruth. A sweet, Southern lady. Although she sets out to clean up Idgie's act, she finds herself swept away.

"You're just a bee charmer," Ruth says after Idgie reaches deep into a honey tree to please her. (Sigmund Freud, are you getting this?)

The charmed bee accompanies Idgie to the River Club, where after a fair amount of whiskey sipping, the two lounge on the riverbank. Ruth sloppily kisses Idgie, saying she's had the best night of her life . . . but, by the way, she's going home to get married.

Idgie, reacting just like any other really, really good friend, vows never to see Ruth again. But Ruth eventually dumps her husband and tells Idgie to come get her. The summons, torn from the Bible, is an old standby at Protestant weddings: "And Ruth said, 'Whither thou goest, I will go.' "

The two women live together, raise a son and support themselves by running their Whistle Stop Cafe. Years later, Idgie reassures Ruth, "I'm as settled as I ever hope to be."

Sounds like a lot of lesbian couples we know. No public announcements, just a lot of ordinary love and affection.

But apparently the proof reviewers needed is a hot sex scene. Or maybe they would have gotten it if the KKK had scrawled "Go Back to Lesbos" on the cafe door.

Yet Idgie and Ruth caused no stir in the 1930s. And they

could just as quietly run the cafe in Juliette today as open lesbians, shopkeeper Langston says. "They'd be accepted because there are people like that who live here."

This month Idgie and her honey are moving into video stores. Invite them over for the evening, if you'd like to be charmed.

GAY COUPLES FIND THAT PROVINCETOWN AND TOLERANCE GO HAND IN HAND

AUGUST 14, 1992

The handlike tip of Cape Cod, a mighty arm of land reaching into the Atlantic, beckoned the Pilgrims ashore in 1620. Their first haven from intolerance and rough seas was the stretch of woods and sand dunes now known as Provincetown, Massachusetts.

The Mayflower Compact, simple rules for trying to live in harmony, was signed there. The Pilgrims soon sailed onward, settling in Plymouth. But the land where they first found refuge continues to welcome people who yearn to breathe free.

In the Pilgrims' wake have come poor Portuguese fishermen, painters, poets, bohemians, playwrights such as Tennessee Williams and Eugene O'Neill and, especially in recent decades, gays. Every photograph of the hordes of summer people strolling along P-town's well-named Commercial Street could be captioned "Diversity for Fun and Profit."

For centuries this seafaring town's economic ship periodically came in—and sank. The demand for salted fish soared, then plunged. Sea captains became wealthy on lamp-lighting whale oil; then the market extinguished itself. But gradually P-town has come to make a comfortable living by sharing its gentleness.

Gentleness, as in the muted gray of so many houses' wooden shingles. As in the swaying of the boats that line the bay. And in the way townsfolk and tourists alike treat people who are visibly different from themselves.

"I really like the mix—gay, lesbian, straight. It's wonderful," says a gay man from England.

"Provincetown is the way the world should be," says Gillian Drake, author of *The Complete Guide to Provincetown*. "It's simply not an issue whether you're gay or straight." She's one of many residents who came for a vacation but ended up unpacking for good.

Provincetown's first tourists, William Bradford recalled, had "no friends to welcome them, nor inns to entertain or refresh their weather-beaten bodies." Too bad for the Pilgrims.

But hooray for what we gay tourists find waiting to welcome, entertain and refresh us as we step off the ferry from Boston. Gay-friendly inns. Gay movies. Gay T-shirts ("I Can't Even Think Straight" or my favorite for guys, "Nobody Knows I'm a Lesbian"). The gay flag's rainbow flying alongside the Stars and Stripes. And time-share condo pitchmen who target lesbian couples.

It's a joy to have our gay dollars openly courted, to have comedians listen for our laughter instead of making us the butt of their jokes. But the siren song that pulls Joyce and me back to Provincetown is much more simple. The Beatles sang it, but outside of P-town it has a hollow ring for most gay couples: "I Want to Hold Your Hand."

We return for the intoxicating freedom to meander along Commercial Street with our fingers intertwined. Mixed couples take for granted touching each other casually in public. An arm around a shoulder. A hand smoothing down a windblown strand of hair.

But in our hometown and every other place we've traveled, Joyce and I generally act as if we're separated by a thin, invisible wall as soon as we leave the privacy of our quarters. Even within the darkness of theaters, we never hold hands without silently analyzing potential costs and benefits. And when the risk is taken, our self-consciousness dilutes the pleasure.

But in P-town, caution takes a holiday. And very quickly the act that should be second nature to every loving couple comes to *feel* natural. We hold hands.

P-town is not yet paradise. Over the years there have been instances of intolerance: Methodists had fish heads thrown at them in the early 1800s. And now sometimes there are anti-gay aberrations.

"Whenever there are problems with discrimination," Drake writes, "it invariably stems from a lack of understanding as to how the community functions."

Her diverse community functions very well indeed. Joyce and I like to think we have visited the future and it is Provincetown.

ON EQUAL RIGHTS, TRUMAN GAVE 'EM HELL, BUT BUSH CAN'T STAND THE HEAT

AUGUST 21, 1992

Despite warnings he was committing political suicide, President Truman put himself at the forefront of the dominant civil rights struggle of his time: equal treatment for black Americans.

As president, Give 'Em Hell Harry couldn't "sit idly by and do nothing in the face of injustice," writes David McCullough, author of the new biography *Truman*.

Even as he struggled uphill in his 1948 re-election campaign, Democrat Truman single-handedly integrated the armed forces and pressed Congress to make lynching a federal crime.

Eventually, a friend from Missouri wrote to ask the president to ease up on his push. Truman responded with a graphic account of racial violence against blacks and concluded, "I am going to try to remedy it; and if that ends up in my failure to be re-elected, that failure will be in a good cause."

That is leadership—defending those without power, rising

above the hatreds of the day to do the right thing for the America of tomorrow.

Forty-four years later, we have a president who likens himself to Truman. But George Chameleon Waffle Bush—whose moral compass always points to Expediency—is no Harry Truman.

Lacking serious solutions for serious national problems, Bush hopes to divide in order to conquer.

This is how our "Family Values" president is responding to one of the major civil rights movements of his time:

♦ On the military ban on gays that he could lift with a Trumanesque stroke of his pen: "I support our policy on that, and everyone knows my adherence to traditional family values."

♦ On gay parents: "I can't accept as normal lifestyle people of the same sex being parents."

♦ On the possibility of a grandchild coming out to him: "I would hope he wouldn't go out and try to convince people that this was the normal lifestyle, that this was appropriate lifestyle."

♦ His running mate, Dan Quayle, has weighed in ominously that "homosexuality is not the preferred option."

♦ Bush's platform denounces gay marriage, gay soldiers, gay adoption and gay Boy Scouts. And his campaign has big plans for Pat Buchanan, who worked conventioneers into a frenzy by attacking gays.

"The strategy of the campaign is fatally flawed," says Representative Bill Green (R-N.Y.). "Their arithmetic will lose votes."

That's already happening.

Banned from any role in their party's convention, the gay Republican Log Cabin Federation voted against endorsing Bush/Quayle.

"There's been a clear movement in the Bush campaign against us," says Log Cabin President Rich Tafel. ". . . The Religious Right keeps pulling them in that direction and I think they're going to pull them right off the cliff."

As Bush searches for leaders to model himself after, he should listen to the architect of Republican conservatism: Barry Goldwater.

"Under our Constitution," he recently said in support of a Phoenix gay-rights ordinance, "we literally have the right to do anything we may want to do, as long as the performing of those acts do not cause damage or hurt to anybody else. I can't see any way in the world that being gay can cause damage to somebody else."

It's the 1964 GOP presidential nominee—not the current one —who is in touch with Middle America on gay issues. A recent *USA TODAY*/CNN/Gallup poll found 55 percent of voters agree with Democrat Bill Clinton's support for "equal rights for homosexuals." Only 27 percent said he goes too far.

President Truman said he felt it was his duty under the Constitution to push for equal rights for all Americans. If George Bush can't follow that example, perhaps someone should let him know that advocating gay rights just might be the most expedient course this year.

Our nation is ready for change.

HOUSTON'S MONTROSE DRAWS PARTY LOVERS—AND UNINVITED, DEADLY MENACES

AUGUST 28, 1992

It's the weekend in the Montrose. The neon is bright red, the music is loud and everywhere is the laughter of folks who've left their workday costumes at the office.

This is the heart of Houston's gay neighborhood, where in ten minutes you can step into a dozen bars with just as many personalities. The Mining Company throws Full Moon Madness, a monthly party for guys whose moods swing with the lunar cycle. And over at Pacific Street, Saturday night cowboys can lasso a free admission by showing up in chaps.

The Ripcord has just collected three hundred stuffed animals for children with AIDS. The winners of "Butchest Bear" and "Nelliest Bear" were stripped of their leather and pearls before being sent on their way.

"The managers of bars are constantly looking for new ways to draw people in, so they look for something theme-oriented and timely," says Tad Nelson, party columnist for the local gay paper.

For years running, the biggest hit has been the Garden Party, whose theme this year was Queens of the Nile. As three thousand guests piled out of limos and Rolls-Royces, four hundred spectators held up scorecards rating their Egyptian garb.

"It was just as much fun outside as inside," Nelson recalls.

The gay bars' playful energy gives the entire Montrose a carnival magnetism on weekend nights. Unfortunately, that magnetism also attracts some people looking for trouble.

"If we see a pickup truck with three males, nine times out of ten we've got a problem," says Houston native Mark Gartner.

"A problem" ranges from taunts to shootings.

Last year, on the Fourth of July, twenty-seven-year-old investment banker Paul Broussard and two friends were jumped as they left a Montrose bar. Two carloads of youths from thirty miles away attacked them with nail-studded two-by-fours and a knife, police say.

Broussard died.

Four months later, Phillip Smith, twenty-four, was fatally shot in the eye as he left Heaven, another Montrose bar.

Finally, according to oil company worker Annise Parker, "the whole community said that we don't have to put up with that anymore. . . . Not only are we not going to put up with the physical bashers, we're not going to put up with any of it."

Out of the community's sense of outrage and anger and fear came Q Patrol. Each weekend night Q Patrol members—unarmed and sober—keep tabs on traffic through Montrose, some of it drunk and armed.

The Houston police—having had an undercover officer posing as a gay man badly beaten with baseball bats—now stand ready to help Q Patrol try to keep situations from getting out of control.

"Those kids come down one week to yell at 'queers.' The

weekend after that to throw eggs at 'queers,' the weekend after that to beat them with boards with nails. It just escalates," says Gartner, a Q Patrol founder.

"And now we have the opportunity to catch them on the first weekend that they're down there."

Donning a Q Patrol tank top on a recent Saturday night, I felt like a lightning rod for all the hate in Texas. For the next three and a half hours, obscene gestures and vile comments were directed at those of us on foot patrol as Q Patrol vans followed closely. Every license plate number was jotted down.

Q Patrol sends postcards to the vehicle owners—often letting Mom and Dad know how Junior and his pals spent Saturday night. After describing a hateful incident, Q Patrol writes: "If this vehicle belongs to your son or daughter, we strongly recommend that you have a talk with him or her before this situation becomes a problem."

The life of Paul Broussard cannot be brought back. And the life of the eighteen-year-old sentenced to forty-five years in prison for knifing him is forever ruined.

But Q Patrol aims to save other lives. As the Q Patrol postcard says, "Gay bashing is no longer a sport in Houston."

Report hate crimes to the Justice Department at (800) 347-HATE.

THEIR GREATNESS LIVES ON,
THANKS TO A LITTLE HELP
FROM THEIR FRIENDS

SEPTEMBER 4, 1992

Playwright Charles Ludlam, historian Michael Lynch and authors Robert Ferro, Michael Grumley and Christopher Cox died of AIDS before completing their life's work.

Yet the "symphonies" of these gay men will not remain unfinished. As each man has fallen, a lover or friend has stepped in, gathered up the pieces of his artwork and carried it forward.

"Fine artists of any stripe are exceedingly rare. And a disproportionate number of them are being taken from us," notes Steven Samuels, who compares rescuing half-formed artistic creations to saving the rain forests. Both preserve diversity.

When Ludlam died in 1987, he left behind two dozen unpublished plays, boxes of essays and the aptly named Ridiculous Theatrical Company. His longtime friend Samuels has pulled together his work in *The Complete Plays of Charles Ludlam* and *Ridiculous Theatre: Scourge of Human Folly*.

And Ludlam's lover Everett Quinton has done what many thought impossible: kept Ludlam's madcap genius alive by taking over the theatrical company and its wonderfully ludicrous leading roles.

Most of us missed our chance to ache with laughter as Ludlam played the dying Camille. But in Greenwich Village, his lines still work their magic.

Camille, now played by Quinton, tells the maid: "Nadine, I'm cold. Throw another faggot on the fire!"

"There are no faggots in the house."

Camille (looking plaintively at the audience packed with gay men): "No faggots in the house?"

Ludlam was not simply a gay playwright; he was the writer of supremely *gay* plays. His fallen comrades had also directed their energies toward casting more light on what it means in this culture to be homosexual.

When Michael Grumley died in 1988, he left *Life Drawings,* a novel about a modern gay Huck Finn that he'd desperately tried to finish in his last months.

Grumley's lover Robert Ferro, author of *Second Son,* outlived him by only ten weeks but spent that time making the necessary changes in Grumley's book. "Robert died the day after a typed version of *Life Drawings* was completed," says scholar David Bergman.

But even with their heroic efforts, they left behind trunks of unpublished literary treasures.

"You never know what you're going to find when you start going through these papers," says Bergman, who spent his summer doing just that.

Grumley, Ferro and five other gay New Yorkers formed the Violet Quill in 1979 to critique each other's writing. Its members —four of whom are now dead of AIDS—produced some of the most memorable gay literature of the 1980s.

As he began to put together a Violet Quill anthology, Bergman searched for the unpublished works of the late Christopher Cox, author of a gay guide to Key West and the group's least famous member. The search led him to Cox's sister, who exclaimed, "I've been waiting four years for this phone call!"

But Michael Lynch was more fortunate. He died knowing that his fragmentary history of Walt Whitman's New York was in capable hands. Historian Bert Hansen says his friend was able to let go once he knew the project wouldn't die. "And he had a much more peaceful last five months."

"Michael partly searched out and partly stumbled on some very unusual documents" that detail the daily lives of ordinary homosexual men before 1860, Hansen says. "These are the jewels that I want to polish and arrange and share with the world."

Gradually Hansen has learned "not to get hung up on trying to figure out what Michael would have wanted. . . . Michael trusted me . . . and I have to trust myself to make the best decisions."

Although AIDS continues to rob us of the mature work of a generation of gay artists, our inheritance is far richer because of the community-spirited decisions of their closest fans.

HAPPINESS IS WHEN GUEST LISTS AND EMPLOYEE BENEFITS ADMIT ALL PARTNERS

SEPTEMBER 11, 1992

The Bouquet Barometer is a reliable gauge of worker comfort. It's usually activated by a simple question: "So, what's the occasion?"

When Joyce surprised me two years ago with flowers, a co-worker asked the obvious question. The words "our fifth anniversary" were not about to pass my lips. I cut off the conversation with a brisk "it's personal."

One of the joys of my life these days is that I no longer feel compelled to build an eight-foot wall between my work life and my personal life.

But I'm just one of the many gay workers whose Bouquet Barometer now points to "Share the Happiness" after being stuck for years on "Ill at Ease." Personal photos are popping up on desks that for far too long were strictly business. And summer vacation stories are more likely to include mention of a travel companion.

The quickest way for companies to make gays feel welcome is to add sexual orientation to the anti-discrimination policy. Such policies rarely appear magically.

"Nothing happens unless the employees band together and decide that something needs to be done," says Ed Mickens, editor of *Working It Out,* a newsletter on gays in the workplace.

In other words, gay employees need to ask. And that's exactly what's happening. Gay workers are asking for anti-bias protection, for recognition of gay workers' groups and for equal benefits.

Levi Strauss & Co., the world's largest clothing maker, eventually said "yes" to Cynthia Bologna, a lesbian who wanted her lover covered by the company health insurance. Levi's is now the largest U.S. company to offer health coverage to the domestic partners of its unmarried employees.

"It makes good business sense," says Bologna, explaining that the inclusive approach boosts worker loyalty.

Levi's supports a gay workers' group, forbids bias based on sexual orientation and sponsors a gay awareness week. Recently its philanthropic arm stopped contributing to the Boy Scouts because of its ban on gays and atheists. (The Girl Scouts, who realize that people come in as many flavors as cookies, still get funds.)

While few companies could boast they are as gay-friendly as Levi's, several have similarly extended health benefits to unmarried workers' partners—whether gay or not. Others—Lotus Development Corp., Montefiore Medical Center and MCA Inc.—have solely added gay couples, who don't have the option to marry.

The first victory of Gays and Lesbians at Xerox, the worker group known as Galaxe, was a special computer link that allows gay Xerox workers anywhere to communicate with each other.

"Out of that support network people have become more confident," says David Frishkorn, a Xerox accountant in Rochester.

While not yet shooting for the stars, Galaxe asked for—and won—an agreement that the company will help relocate members of a transferred employee's household, not just a "spouse," notes Al Lewis, a Xerox marketer in Los Angeles.

Flora Piterak, a software engineer at Digital Equipment Corp., says that to start a gay workers' group, "all you need is one person who's willing to stand up and say, 'This is who I am,' and put something on a bulletin board. Eventually, you will find people willing to come out and work with you."

Digital's gay group has educated managers to include "significant others" in invitations to company parties. That's the sort of thing that makes gay employees feel as if they're finally one of the gang.

Once we're sure our company really wants us, we no longer have to play hide-and-seek about our personal lives. Friendly gestures are no longer threatening.

My Bouquet Barometer recently swung to "Delighted" even though there wasn't a flower in sight: The office manager was revising the spouse list and asked how to spell Joyce's last name.

LEARNING FROM THE SLOW, PAINFUL TRANSFORMATION OF TWO EX-CONGRESSMEN

SEPTEMBER 18, 1992

In the lives of Bob Bauman and Jon Hinson, the 1980s were the years of metamorphosis.

When the decade began, both were conservative Republican congressmen. They were also married, self-destructive and deep in denial about their homosexuality. By the end of the decade, they had lost their House seats in scandals, divorced and finally accepted being gay.

"My freedom in the sense of accepting who I am is an enormous help," says Bauman, now a Florida attorney. "But . . . it means that I stand across an enormous chasm now from a life that most people would have found to be rewarding, of great achievement."

Bauman, a brash wizard of parliamentary procedure, represented Maryland until he lost his 1980 re-election bid four weeks after revelations he'd solicited sex from a young male hustler.

"It was like I was another person. That was another life," Bauman recalls of the netherworld he lived in as a closeted member of Congress. Resisting the truth spun him out of control, winding him up in seedy bars searching for one-night stands, not long-term solutions.

Hinson, who now manages family property back in Mississippi, remembers that as a congressman "I was so profoundly determined that I would not be a gay person that I would have fought someone who had the temerity to suggest that I was."

Mostly, though, he warred with himself, torn between his

inability to face the lie he was living and his inability to continue living it. He began to do "incredibly risky, stupid things."

In 1981 he was caught trying to have sex in a House men's room. "I knew the minute I was arrested that my career was over. . . . I look back now and see that I was a gay man trying to lie to myself."

Recently the gay press has been on a binge of outings: a sensitively placed Bush official, a GOP speechwriter, the son of a well-known anti-gay crusader, and a "family values" congressman. Branded hypocrites, these people have had their private lives publicly vivisected. More unanesthetized surgery on political litmus-test flunkers is threatened.

I suspect some of these targets are privately struggling with their sexuality, as Hinson and Bauman did. The experiences of those ex-congressmen offer to teach us much as a community.

We can never know what's inside another's heart. But that's not my primary concern about outing. When being gay is turned into an accusation, the result—regardless of the intent—is to make homosexuality seem shameful, a blackmailable offense.

And attempting to undermine an anti-gay congressman by saying he has slept with men simply reinforces the mistaken idea that gays deserve to be punished.

Sexual behavior and identity can take a lifetime to align. And some unlucky souls never allow themselves to face being gay in a society where that may mean losing a career and family.

As Bauman puts it: "I didn't accept being gay myself until two or three years of therapy and counseling—religious and psychiatric—after I lost the election."

Congress may not be short of furtive sex of any sort, but those of us who feel good about being gay are definitely under-represented. We need to turn our attention to electing and keeping gay and gay-friendly people in Congress.

We have two openly gay congressmen: Barney Frank, who is expected to be re-elected easily, and Gerry Studds, a leading foe of the military's gay ban who now finds himself in jeopardy after redistricting.

And all across the country, openly gay candidates are running for traditional springboards to Congress—school boards, city councils and state legislatures.

Expanding Congress' Gay Caucus is a frustratingly slow process. But we can no more increase its membership by exposing the private lives of lawmakers than we can get a butterfly by cruelly slicing into a cocoon. A thing of beauty has its own timetable for coming out.

As Cancer Assaults Lesbians, They Can Learn to Fight Back

September 25, 1992

Cancer was stealing the life of Mary-Helen Mautner. But as she lay perfectly still for a bone scan, she thought about how lucky she was to have someone who cared waiting outside.

It was August 1989. Her cancer had returned and spread since her mastectomy seven years before.

" 'I've had this great idea,' " her lover Susan Hester recalls Mautner saying after the test. "She said, 'We have to do something for lesbians with cancer. We have to make sure people don't go through this alone.' "

Three weeks later she was dead, leaving behind Hester and their little girl. She also left a single page of notes.

From that rough outline, Hester—who shared her partner's ardent feminism and belief in confronting problems head-on—created the Mary-Helen Mautner Project for Lesbians With Cancer.

The Washington, D.C.–based project helps ill lesbians and their families cope. Volunteers lend a hand with grocery shopping, provide rides to chemotherapy appointments or just listen.

Lesbians used to fending for themselves often find it hard to ask others to shoulder part of their burden. Hester recalls how long it took for her and Mautner to realize they could no longer manage alone.

"We came to a crisis point and had to ask for help," she says. Fortunately, the couple had a supportive network of friends and co-workers. That's what the Mautner Project offers other lesbians now. There's no other group quite like it, even though the need is tremendous.

Breast cancer now strikes one American woman in nine. And the rate may be three times that high among lesbians. Our rates of cervical and ovarian cancer also may be unusually high.

Dr. Suzanne Haynes, chief of health education at the National Cancer Institute, has tried to piece together why breast cancer seems so common in the lesbian community. She pinpointed four risk factors more prevalent in our community: not giving birth, obesity, alcohol abuse and sporadic gynecological exams.

"It's all speculative," she said, "because there are no studies."

But Susan Hester wants to change that. The Mautner Project has asked for a $70,000 federal grant to study breast cancer screening among lesbians. This landmark proposal could give cancer specialists the early data they'll need for the next step—reducing risks.

Already a few medical articles exploring health care experiences of lesbians suggest troublesome areas.

It is known that early detection of cancer or precancerous conditions is the key to survival, yet most lesbians—who don't need birth control and are unlikely to have sexually transmitted diseases—go to a gynecologist only when a problem arises *(American Journal of Obstetrics and Gynecology, 1981)*.

Part of lesbians' reluctance to get regular checkups stems from the well-grounded fear of giving a doctor a vital bit of information: sexual orientation. Seventy-two percent of women who come out to physicians report negative responses *(Image: Journal of Nursing Scholarship, 1988)*. And 40 percent of physicians admit feeling uncomfortable with gay patients *(Western Journal of Medicine, 1986)*.

But cancer won't stop its brutal attack on our community simply because we've got good excuses for ignoring our health.

After years of being strangers to doctors' offices, Joyce and I now visit our gynecologist together right after filing our tax returns, getting two unpleasant chores out of the way at once.

So, pick someone who'd miss you if you were gone. Get your annual exams together. Then go celebrate your good sense.

And consider helping those women now fighting for their lives by setting up a lesbian cancer project in your hometown. As Hester says, "All you have to do is call a meeting, and it will happen."

————

For more information on the Mautner Project, call (202) 332-5536.

Quilt Panels for AIDS Victims Help Survivors Keep the Thread of Love Alive

OCTOBER 2, 1992

B illy's Mom. That's what other volunteers at the NAMES Project office in Washington, D.C., call LaVerne Yost. A year into her grief over her youngest son's death to AIDS, she now helps others create Memorial Quilt panels for their lost loved ones.

"We teach them to thread the needle, tie a knot," Yost says with a laugh of the sewing disasters who wander into this bustling workshop.

Colorful spools of thread, yardsticks and scissors cover the walls. Donated sewing machines wait to link panel to panel. And Yost and other Quilt maestros buzz about helping those who still aren't quite certain they can start a tribute when the grief feels so new.

"After they've picked the fabric and they've decided what kind of letters they want," you can see the relief in their faces, Yost says.

"I remember one fellow who had been so torn up. He was

cutting out his letters like he was in kindergarten, and he started humming. That was one of my nicest moments," she adds.

Each panel tells the story not just of a death, but of an irreplaceable life—one of the 1 million already claimed by this global plague.

On October 9–11 the AIDS Memorial Quilt will blanket fifteen acres around the Washington Monument. Within sight of the White House, more than 20,000 grave-sized panels will bear testimony to the 152,000 Americans who have died as Presidents Reagan and Bush looked the other way.

It is not too late to make a panel for this massive display. A special section will be reserved for late arrivals.

◆ Figure out a design that includes your loved one's name. You may want to include dates of birth and death as well as a hometown.

◆ Choose a durable material, such as cotton, for the background. The final panel must be three by six feet, so leave a few extra inches for the hem.

◆ Try to capture your loved one's personality, perhaps by attaching a favorite object: a teddy bear, a feather boa, a merit badge, a wedding ring.

◆ Write a brief letter about the person and take it and the Quilt panel to the Washington Monument grounds.

William N. Rosenthal—"Our Billy" as the Quilt panel reads —was a flight attendant based in Denver who prided himself on getting a private pilot's license. He also loved being gay and was "very good-looking and knew it," recalls his mother.

He died at 9:31 P.M. on June 19, 1991. He was thirty years old.

Billy had visited the Quilt once. "He thought it was such a wonderful way to express memories of people," Yost says. "I think he knew his mother would do that for him."

When other survivors—friends, lovers, sisters—have come to the workshop, Yost has shown them "Billy," as she refers to her panel.

Its colors are blue and khaki, like the preppie clothes his

brothers remember Billy wearing. His aunt added a needlepoint of the West Virginia cabin where he loved to stargaze. On the bottom is a pocket closed tight around letters from family and friends.

In sewing a Quilt panel, Yost says, "You work through a lot of emotions, but it's a peaceful thing."

But now she has had to part with the Billy panel.

"It was another saying good-bye, of letting go," she says. "And then seeing it stitched with seven other panels and realizing, yes he is dead, because those other seven people are dead."

Like other American quilts, the AIDS Quilt is an artwork to be handed down to future generations. Everyone who snips a thread for it helps piece together a legacy of grief turned into action, of love that confronts bigotry, of respect for a common humanity.

If Billy were the only AIDS casualty, it would be one death too many. When you see the Quilt—or pictures of it—remember his name. Remembering is the least the rest of us can do.

————

For information about the Quilt, call the NAMES Project at (415) 882-5500.

Chapter

3

THE POWER OF ONE

"Is bob giles gay?"

The question came from an Atlanta lesbian, one of two hundred who'd just heard Deb's speech describing the birth of her column and how her publisher's wholehearted support had made it possible. The question also came from *Detroit News* readers who called or wrote Giles to protest his addition of a gay voice to their paper. The column's critics tended to phrase the query a bit less politely.

Deb's Georgia audience roared with delight when she told them the answer. "My publisher also belongs to a widely stigmatized group—straight white men."

In letters to his gay-baiting attackers, Giles writes, "It is a pity that you are led to suggest that anyone who believes in tolerance for gays and lesbians must himself be a homosexual. My wife and children would find that suggestion hilarious."

Gay people and those who despise us easily slip into the same false assumption: Real heterosexuals aren't willing to go out on a limb on behalf of anything gay. By "balancing" gay quotes with those of anti-gay heterosexuals, newspapers stoke the wrong-headed notion that gay men and lesbians have no straight allies, except perhaps for a few parents. The press's unconsciously divisive approach fuels gay paranoia, making it more difficult for us to ask for support, and fuels heterosexual fear, making it more difficult for them to be supportive in public.

A rumor that circulated inside the *News* when Deb's column was nine months old illustrates the persistence of the gay vs. straight myth. Still struggling to make sense of Giles' enthusiasm for a gay issues column, a gay reporter latched onto the idea that the publisher's sister, Lois, is a lesbian. She's not. But when the rumor reached Giles, who tends to be amused when he's called gay, he was a bit disheartened by it. He says he wishes gay people would take his acceptance at face value rather than feeling there "ought to be some excuse for it." Giles adds that he just tries to operate from a basic sense of fairness. And he asks, "Why should I treat someone who is different from me any different from people who are like me?"

Giles never lost sleep over whether to give a gay column the go-ahead. Instead, when managing editor Christy Bradford first told him what Deb was suggesting, he reacted with characteristic decisiveness: "That sounds like a terrific idea! Why don't we have Deb put together some sample columns so we have a better idea of what she's proposing to do."

"Once I saw the [sample] columns," Giles recalls, "I was very enthusiastic. I didn't have any concept in my own mind about what a column about gays would or should be like, but I was very receptive to what Deb was thinking. It just struck a good tone. It was educational." He told me he especially liked the way Deb's prototype columns challenged stereotypes by "talking about the parts of your lives together that are just like everybody else's." And he believed that Deb, whom he considers "very gentle and very thoughtful," was the right person for the task. "I thought," he recalls, " 'This will work. She knows how to do this.' "

(It was Bradford's response to the prototypes—"I like it when you're funny!"—that gave Deb psychic permission to cut loose with her writing and sidestep the Op-Ed trap of ponderous pontification.)

Looking back, Giles says, "My reaction [to Deb's proposal]

was influenced by the fact that a number of people that I care a great deal about in our newsroom are homosexuals. And I have seen them be the butt of jokes." He saw a gay column as one more way for his newspaper to carry out its duty to educate readers about "our changing world."

The birth of Deb's column illustrates two points crucial to the immediate future of the gay civil rights movement.

First, we gay people must let go of our fear of rejection long enough to risk asking for what we need. Our potential straight allies aren't mind readers. We can't expect them to sit around thinking, "Gee, I must have some gay employees [or friends or readers or church members]. Let me try to guess how they'd like me to show my support." In fact, as the story of P-FLAG mother Harriet Dart shows, we gay people often don't even cross the radar screens of heterosexuals until after we shun stealth and properly introduce ourselves. Once we say hello, we have a real chance of getting our needs met—eventually. Deb's column never would have existed if several gay journalists hadn't found the courage to ask Giles and Bradford for what they needed. Obviously, only one of them was Deb.

Second, the Bob Gileses of the world run the world; we gay people aren't going to advance very quickly without their cooperation. That means we can't write off straight white men. We can't afford the childish luxury of assuming they are the enemy. We have to approach them as potential allies. The situation inside the newspaper industry is particularly telling. In 1992, the year Deb's column began, 91 percent of the publishers of daily newspapers were male and 99 percent were white. When Deb proposed a gay column, not one publisher of a daily newspaper was openly gay. (That's still true today.) Ideas don't go far within the newspaper industry unless they can win straight white male support. Without gay-friendly heterosexuals, Deb's column wouldn't have gotten beyond her own computer. It runs in dozens of papers from Guam to Vermont only because high-ranking straight journalists, most of them white men, said "yes" to adding a gay voice to their newspapers. Of course, the one essential nod of approval came from Bob Giles himself.

Okay, so Giles was vital to a small but important change in

American journalism and symbolizes the kind of person who must be reached if social progress is to be made quickly. If he's not gay, what is he? Well, "straight white male" barely begins to describe how much Giles personifies what in the Sixties was called "the Establishment." He's a Reagan-Bush voter who lives in posh Grosse Pointe Farms, runs a newspaper with one of the most conservative editorial pages in America and was just a month shy of fifty-nine when he announced Deb's column. He's married to an outspoken liberal, a child psychologist who wept in disgust when her husband received one of George Bush's famous thank-you notes after the '88 election. ("We do not talk politics," Nancy Giles flatly declares when discussing her relationship with her husband, whose ex-lifeguard good looks enhance his image as one of society's golden boys.)

Professionally, Bob Giles' establishment credentials are also impeccable. He literally wrote the book on *Newspaper Management*. Having directed the *Akron Beacon Journal*'s Pulitzer Prize–winning coverage of the 1970 Kent State shootings, he now stands in the top ranks of his field. In addition to being editor and publisher of *The Detroit News,* twenty-second largest paper in America, he is a past president of the Associated Press Managing Editors, president of the Accrediting Council on Education in Journalism and Mass Communications, founding president of the Associated Press Managing Editors Foundation, and a trustee of the University of Kansas' school of journalism. Now secretary of the American Society of Newspaper Editors, he is in line to become ASNE vice president in 1996 and president a year later. He's been a Pulitzer Prize juror six times.

Giles' stable, midwestern boyhood brings to mind a Norman Rockwell painting. Dad was the breadwinner, an electrical engineer in charge of movie theater sound systems. Mom taught Presbyterian Sunday school. The young Bob was a Boy Scout, baseball player and sports editor of his high school paper. Although his Cleveland upbringing wasn't nearly as silver-plated as those of Bush and Quayle, Giles is now the kind of man our society revolves around. Straight white men are a widely stigmatized group in part because they're so often both in power and insensitive to anyone who doesn't fit society's model for success quite so neatly as they do. What makes Bob Giles different from that stereotype? Or, reducing the question to the level of a political button, why is he straight but not narrow?

Three experiences were crucial in molding Giles into a publisher willing to put his considerable reputation on the line for a gay column. Together, they helped him cherish human diversity, respect gay people and not shrink from potential criticism.

The first of those experiences may be the most important: As an ambitious young journalist, Giles gradually realized that he just didn't fit in. Yes, he was straight, white and male, but there his resemblance to the newspaper editors he was expected to emulate stopped. Giles, a gentle and somewhat shy man, just wasn't a cigar-chomping, floor-spittin', "Get me rewrite, Sweetheart," kind of guy.

In the preface to his newspaper management book, Giles recounts what he learned about being a boss from his very imposing chief editor at the *Akron Beacon Journal,* Ben Maidenburg. "His impatience with the seeming stupidities of his staff could boil into action quickly, and we all dreaded the moment when a mistake or misjudgment would capture Ben's attention and ignite his temper. At those times, he would stride across the newsroom, a copy of the offending story in one hand and an unlit cigar in the other, his eyes dark and angry. You could feel him coming, a towering giant. The power of his voice guaranteed that the message would not be missed," Giles wrote.

After watching colleagues become city editor only to get chewed up and spit out, Giles' turn came. Almost every afternoon Maidenburg grilled him, then gave him the same tip on how to handle reporters: "Bob, you've got to learn to be a son of a bitch." The lesson wasn't lost on Giles, who wrote, "Unwittingly, I think, he reinforced my basic instinct that there are other ways to run a newspaper than by being a son of a bitch."

Today the soft-spoken Giles usually oversees the *News* with what author Tim Kiska aptly described as a "Zen-like calm" in *Detroit's Powers & Personalities.* "I don't get riled up easily," Giles says. "If I get angry, I've taught myself not to respond immediately . . . because I've found that I'll regret it the next day." He quietly supervises what he hopes is a humane workplace, where journalists who aren't straight, aren't white, or aren't male feel as valued as those who are. "Our newsroom is close-knit," he says. "I want everyone to feel comfortable."

After starting her column, Deb introduced me to Bob Giles at a national journalism conference in Honolulu where she was the lunchtime speaker. As soon as I realized that Giles wanted to help me feel at ease during my first official public appearance as "gay spouse," I was struck by how kind he seemed. I remember thinking how uncomfortable he'd be in a newsroom crackling with "creative tension," the term former *Washington Post* executive editor Ben Bradlee coined for the dog-eat-dog atmosphere he deliberately fostered. Now I know Giles, too, is a survivor of S.O.B. journalism and remembers exactly how it feels not to fit in.

The second experience that molded Giles was directing the *Akron Beacon Journal*'s coverage of the Kent State shootings. Dispatched to the university campus to quell demonstrations sparked by the U.S. invasion of Cambodia during the Vietnam War, the Ohio National Guard opened fire on unarmed students on May 4, 1970. Four people died; another nine were wounded.

Even after the killings, "the town-gown tensions were extraordinary," recalls Giles, then managing editor of the *Beacon Journal*. "And in the little town of Kent, which was about twelve miles away from Akron, there was a very strong belief that there was a conspiracy to cause the students to riot, that communists and the Students for a Democratic Society were behind it all and the National Guard should have shot the students.

"A lot of the reporting that the *Beacon* did was focused on revealing how badly the National Guard handled their responsibilities and how the governor of Ohio came in and made some bad decisions about closing the campus and restricting the students. So we got an enormous amount of mail criticizing us," Giles says.

What Giles doesn't volunteer is that the paper also got death threats, some targeting him and his family. His wife, Nancy, vividly remembers one terrifying phone call: "You tell your husband we're going to blow your goddamn head off!" She recalls asking herself then, at age thirty, whether "it would be worth dying" for journalism, for "the freedom to express your ideas." Mulling the question alone, "I finally concluded that, yeah, it would." Her husband, who later wrote *Editors and Stress,* reached the same conclusion. The result was what he calls his proudest professional achievement, the *Beacon Journal*'s winning the 1971 Pulitzer Prize for local reporting.

Giles risked persevering on an editorial course that he believed was morally right. And, ultimately, he was rewarded. That experience helped steel him for the criticism that he knew would follow inauguration of a gay column. "I've been through it before," he says mildly. "The number of letters I got critical of the column was greater than any other subject I had dealt with, with one exception." The exception, of course, was his Kent State coverage.

The third factor that molded Giles into a publisher willing to be the first to run a gay column was that he already respected his gay colleagues and had been given opportunities to support them on lower-profile issues.

Giles went to graduate school at Columbia University in the mid-1950s but was oblivious to New York's gay subculture. He became good friends with a gay person for the first time decades later while in charge of both Gannett newspapers in Rochester, New York, the morning *Democrat and Chronicle* and afternoon *Times-Union.* The managing editor of the *Times-Union* was a man Giles respectfully calls "such a lovely person," J. Ford Huffman. Listening to both men's accounts of that era, I think Giles probably realized Huffman (who goes by "J. Ford," never "Jay") was gay before Huffman admitted the truth to himself. When Giles moved on to Detroit in 1986, he took with him the goodwill toward gay people that knowing Huffman had engendered.

As publisher of *The Detroit News,* Giles gradually came out as gay-friendly. One of his first opportunities arose when he heard that his gay assistant managing editor for graphics, Dierck Casselman, had been upset by an anti-gay wisecrack made by a Metro desk editor during a "budget meeting," a planning conference for the next day's paper. Giles assembled his senior editors and told them that "I just wasn't going to tolerate any kind of comments that make people feel uncomfortable." He added that when a news story dealing with homosexuality needs to be discussed,

"We've got to do it on a professional basis, and we've got to do it without making any homosexuals in the room feel uncomfortable, intimidated, or unwilling to talk about it." Then in the fall of 1991, features reporter Michael Hodges, who is gay, asked why the newspaper's extensive anti-discrimination policy didn't include sexual orientation along with the many characteristics, such as race, religion, and gender, already explicitly covered. "And I said, 'I don't have a good answer for that, but let me look at it and I'll get back to you,' " Giles recalls. "I went back to the office and looked at it and said, 'There's no reason why it shouldn't be in here.' So I just put it in the typewriter and rewrote it and reposted it."

Deb was ecstatic when she spotted a copy of that rewritten policy on the bulletin board by the water cooler in the *News'* Washington bureau, where she was the deputy chief. She'd been writing long feature articles on gay issues for more than a year—all the while fretting over whether she was jeopardizing her future. While at *The Washington Post,* Deb had watched me be branded "political" by then-managing editor Len Downie for complying with his request for a report on how the *Post* could improve its gay coverage. Deb had always hoped the *News'* management was more gay-friendly. Seeing Giles's memo, she became a believer. She suddenly felt protected—free to pursue her interest in gay issues wherever it might lead. She was still grinning when she came home that night and handed me a photocopy she'd made of Giles' memo.

About the time of that memo, Gannett launched News 2000, a program that encouraged editors and reporters at all its newspapers to think more seriously about the readers they are supposed to serve, to offer different voices, to reflect their community's diversity and to be on the cutting edge of journalism. Deb noticed that News 2000 materials focused on race and gender while largely overlooking sexual orientation. She decided it was time for a gay voice to be heard. (When Deb's column began, News 2000 director Mark Silverman dropped Giles a congratulatory note calling a gay column "long overdue.") Yet if Giles hadn't already signaled that it was safe to come out, Deb would not have proposed writing a gay column. And she would have never known that, although he didn't quite realize it yet, Giles was very ready to say "yes."

Even though some of Giles' peers have applauded his decision as courageous and wrenching, he says it was neither. "It was an easy decision because it was a good idea," he explains. Some editors would like to run a gay column but can't get the publisher's approval, Giles says, noting with a chuckle that he's in the enviable position of being both editor and publisher. Many other editors, he thinks, would like to pick up Deb's column but "don't want to be bothered with the reaction. I think they're being oversensitive. . . . You lose readers for a lot of different reasons. . . . The paper doesn't get there on time or the printing is lousy or because you didn't cover their high school team the way they wanted." He believes newspapers must be willing to risk a few cancellations as the price of attempting to "inform and enlighten" readers.

The wave of hostile reactions that hit Giles immediately after starting Deb's column convinced him that "what Deb was writing was absolutely essential because there was so much misunderstanding and so much mean bias being conveyed in these letters and phone calls." At first, no matter how rude the reader, Giles' standard reply letter was conciliatory: "I urge you to follow Deb's column for a while and read it with an open mind. Then let us know whether you think it has an appropriate place in your newspaper." But before long he was sending angry readers copies of news articles explaining the growing evidence that sexual orientation has a genetic component. And by the fall of 1992 Giles had stopped suffering fools gladly. In response to an Eastpointe man who argued, "This great nation of ours was built on traditional family values and a strong belief in God. Not with queers & lesbians," Giles wrote, "Thank you for your letter. The ignorance it conveys about homosexual lifestyles is a reinforcement to me of the importance of continuing to publish Deb Price's column."

Giles contends that *News* readers who object to adding a gay voice to a "family newspaper" understand neither the diversity of families nor of their newspaper. Yes, the entire *Detroit News* used to be quite conservative and the editorial page still is. But after

Gannett bought the paper in 1986 and Giles became publisher, he made the rest of the paper much more progressive, much more dedicated to exploring social issues. "If you read our stories," Giles says, "you see we're not trying to titillate but educate and explain what often are very difficult changes in society." Part of that educational process is teaching people that loving families often don't fit what Giles calls the *"Saturday Evening Post* family image." He believes, "Gay families are just an extension of the family concept." Giles says he's been struck by how obsessed many heterosexuals are with the purely physical side of gay relationships: "They don't think of it as love; they think of it as sex."

Giles was prepared for most of the criticism he received for starting Deb's column. "The letters I guess I didn't expect were from parents and ministers talking about having teenage children or counseling teenage children who were struggling with their sexual identity and how helpful the column was. I think one of those letters made up for 150 of the others," he says.

He also didn't expect that he wouldn't be able to escape the harsh initial criticism of Deb's column even during a weekend at his country home. Bob and Nancy Giles became embroiled there in what he calls "long talks" with their adult children. Being less circumspect, Nancy Giles exclaims, "God, it was like World War III!" Gradually, though, Bob Giles says, "They came to appreciate my perspective."

Bob Giles isn't a crusading journalist in the style of the late Ralph McGill, who in the 1960s persistently railed in his front-page column in the Atlanta *Constitution* against the evils of racial segregation. The footsteps Giles is following are more like those of his own sound-engineer father: He's working behind the scenes so someone else's voice can be heard. "What I tried to do," Giles says, "was facilitate the ability of someone who had something to say out of her own experience to have a forum in *The Detroit News*. And I think in some ways that's more effective than anything I could write on the subject even if I wrote it on Page One. What I've tried to do is set a good example for other editors to follow."

Once a gay column carried the imprimatur of Bob Giles and *The Detroit News,* other Gannett editors were eager to run it. Bob

Ritter, head of Gannett News Service (GNS), immediately began distributing Deb's column to all eighty-plus Gannett newspapers through the chain's own wire service. Two of the column's first permanent homes were in Rochester, New York, and Palm Springs, California.

J. Ford Huffman, GNS managing editor for features, graphics and photography, pitched the column to an old friend from his Rochester days, Keith Moyer, the editor of both Rochester dailies. "J. Ford was a helluva salesman for it," Moyer says. "He certainly played a role in getting it into this paper." Knowing that Rochester has a sizable and active gay community, Moyer was quickly sold on the idea of a regular gay column. "Some of the very best people I have working for me are gay or lesbian, some of the most talented people I have. So how could their editor say, 'Well, I'm not going to run that'? How hypocritical that would be!" Moyer, a straight white married man who was in his late thirties when he picked up Deb's column, jokes, "I don't know where I went wrong, but the fact that somebody is gay or lesbian has never meant anything to me. If I like them, I like them. If I don't, I don't."

Since Deb's column is more personal than most traditional Op-Ed pieces and more overtly political than most features columns, editors often puzzle over where to run it. Because Moyer wants it to be viewed as an integral part of the *Democrat and Chronicle,* he runs it next to Ann Landers. "I thought it was important to get it off the editorial page so that it wasn't like 'These are not the opinions of management,' " he explains. Through the column's placement, he says, he was signaling readers, "Hey, this is mainstream. This is part of some people's lives. This is there if you want it." Some readers, many of them straight parents, quickly replied they wanted no part of it. Moyer recalls parents who complained that their daughters always read Ann Landers and " 'here you have this lesbian writing right above it. How dare you do this!' "

"My response is basically that 'the newspaper needs to reflect all sorts of people. Certainly your daughter is not going to become a lesbian or not become a lesbian based on what she reads in this column.' The more calls I got, the more I saw the need for the column. There's an educational process that needs to take place. I don't get any negative feedback now," Moyer says. Overall, Moyer took less heat than he'd expected. The worst of it came from two unidentified male callers who predictably asked, "Are you some faggot? You must be a queer."

A continent away, Moyer's counterpart at the much smaller Palm Springs *Desert Sun* made a snap decision to use Deb's column every week and to run it on the Op-Ed page. "It seemed like a natural. We'd have to be really dumb not to notice you have a very large gay community here," explains executive editor Joan Behrmann, now in her early fifties.

Shortly after moving to California and taking charge of *The Desert Sun* in 1987, she instituted a weekly AIDS-education column with a question-and-answer format. Behrmann, who has quite a few gay male friends, saw Deb's column as a reasonable next step in serving readers in a town that's becoming a magnet for gay tourists. Forty motels and bed-and-breakfast inns in the Palm Springs area cater primarily to a gay clientele. And tens of thousands of women swamp the desert valley for what's become an international lesbian rite of spring, the Nabisco–Dinah Shore women's professional golf tournament.

Life has an unusual rhythm in Palm Springs. The tourist industry rises and falls with the migration of the "snowbirds" who spend the winter there. Thirty percent of year-round residents are what Behrmann calls "active seniors" at least sixty-five years old. Many somewhat younger residents also are retired or—to use a favorite Palm Springs term—"semi-retired." They populate the valley's seventy golf courses. (Deb, who is allergic to grass, made the mistake of scheduling a Palm Springs speech for the week all the courses were reseeded.) Exploring Palm Springs can seem like traveling into the Twilight Zone because so many thoroughfares honor yesterday's celebrities. For example, *The Desert Sun*'s shiny new headquarters sits on Gene Autry Trail. And anyone asking directions in Palm Springs hears something like, "Turn right at the intersection of Dinah Shore and Bob Hope, and just keep going until you meet Gerald Ford. If you hit Frank Sinatra, you've gone too far."

The initial reaction to Deb's column in Palm Springs, a town always a bit different from other places, wouldn't have registered on the Richter scale. A few people stopped Behrmann's husband, Nick, on the street or in the supermarket to praise the column. And Deb received several wonderful letters from gay couples who'd been together for decades—forty-one years, in one case. But that was about the extent of the early comments.

If this were a newsreel playing before a Gene Autry western, I'd continue the Palm Springs saga by ripping pages off a calendar: 1992 ended, Clinton took office and the firestorm over gays in the military broke out. With the national media spotlight directed at gay issues, Deb's weekly column finally caught the attention of a great many readers who'd never noticed it or hadn't realized it was a regular feature of *The Desert Sun,* Behrmann says. Suddenly the town with plenty of firsthand experience with earthquakes began rocking over Deb's column. Crockery began to rattle and phones to ring. Finally getting in sync with the general pattern elsewhere, the letters to the editor registered a lot of opposition, then a lot of support.

Just over a year after she added a gay column to her paper's mix, Behrmann announced in an opinion piece headlined "All views have place in the Sun" that Deb was the "columnist most likely to upset valley readers." Nosed out of first place was steadfastly progressive Bill Edelen, a retired Congregationalist minister who enjoys tweaking the Religious Right.

"Judging from the mail here, we do have people from fundamentalist backgrounds who deeply believe that gay people . . . are going to burn in Hell and that they do somehow live different, maybe twisted, lives in which maybe Satan is a component," Behrmann told me in an interview. "And for other people, I think, the whole idea [of homosexuality] makes them nervous and makes them want to giggle."

Unlike Bob Giles, Behrmann and Moyer don't enjoy the luxury of being both editor and publisher. Yet neither had to take flak from a publisher over Deb's column. Shirley Ragsdale, opinion page editor of the *Muskogee Daily Phoenix,* wasn't so fortunate. Although Deb loves to say "a newspaper doesn't have to be pro-gay to run my column, it just has to be pro-news," she was as surprised as I was when her column began running in Muskogee,

Oklahoma. We figured an editor there must have courage. Shirley Ragsdale certainly does, but she didn't realize she was being gutsy by wrapping Deb's column around a gay-friendly cartoon and popping them both onto her page. One delightful Joel Pett cartoon that Ragsdale ran shows a heterosexual symbol (made by combining the medical symbols for male and female) ranting: "Repent ye perverts or suffer eternal damnation in Hades!" Finally, the lesbian and gay male symbols reply: "But you won't be there, right? Do they take reservations?"

A woman who hasn't lost her sense of humor, Ragsdale takes the slow, scenic route in describing how she started using a gay column and sent a shock wave through her own career: "I'm just like every other woman—well, not every other woman. Most women don't plan these things. We just kind of think it's the right thing to do at the time. And it seems so logical, and we can't imagine why anyone would oppose it. So we do it. Then it all blows up in our faces.

"Gannett had a gay and lesbian writer. She wrote pretty. She wrote about stuff that had never been on my page before. So I figured if Gannett liked it and the Detroit newspaper liked it, shoot, who am I to say it's not a good column? And I liked it. Then we had this big News 2000 plan with Gannett: diversity—all segments of your community—old people and young people, straight people and gay people, blacks and whites and Hispanics and weird religions. You're supposed to reflect your community. And although I didn't have anybody who would fess up to it, there had to be one or two gays or lesbians in the community. And, besides, this is stuff non-gay people have never read; I imagine they'll just be fascinated. So I put it on the page. And, my God, the publisher got phone calls that we were promoting homosexuality and bestiality, [asking] was he a Christian or some kind of pervert?

"He called my boss's office, and then my boss called me in. And they said, 'Cool it on Deb Price's column.' And I thought, 'Well, what's 'cool it'? If you don't want me to run it again, you say: 'Never run that again.' 'Cool it.' So I waited another month, and I ran another one. And it just so happened that the publisher was out of town. It wasn't because he was out of town. It had been a month, so I ran another one. Well, he thought I went behind his back. You know men. And that's how I got into all the trouble I got in."

Ragsdale, then in her early fifties, found herself being treated like a naughty little girl. Her publisher began requiring her to make printouts of everything she planned to use on her page and get his authorization, she says. Even after she got a new publisher, the humiliating prior-approval rule (virtually unheard-of in daily journalism) stayed in effect.

Some journalists take Ragsdale's story as a cautionary tale. A woman who is a top editor of a leading California paper once remarked to Nancy Giles that she'd never have the nerve to use the Deb Price column after hearing how Ragsdale fared. Ragsdale herself is not so easily intimidated. She kept running Deb's column occasionally, just as before. And she dropped Deb a note to say that even her publisher liked the July 16, 1993, column about teenagers and safe-sex education. Sometimes small victories are the sweetest.

Ragsdale's been in Oklahoma since 1979 but grew up in Ventura County, California, where her eighth-grade science teacher was lesbian. "She and another 'old maid' lived alone in a home in the best part of town. It was just no big deal. And out here it's a sin. And that's a big deal. And I just never bought into that," Ragsdale says.

Anti-gay columnist Cal Thomas, once the Moral Majority's vice president for communications, never causes a ripple when he runs in the *Daily Phoenix*. "He's right-on for Muskogee," according to Ragsdale. Deb, of course, always kicks up dust. "You can bet they read every word she writes—to see what 'that lesbian' said," Ragsdale says, adding that, as usual, "the longer we ran [Deb's column], the less they protested." But in the beginning, a few of Deb's loyal readers addressed some innovative, unsigned notes to the married Ragsdale: "I know you had to be conceived in a petri dish, not by two loving parents. You wouldn't know anything about a male-female relationship or offspring from the old-time way of impregnating. . . ."

Even at conservative papers in one of the fifty conservative states, we gay people have a growing number of allies: straight journalists willing to put up with personal insults to add a gay voice to their newspaper's chorus. There remain countless exceptions, of course, including some who apparently think they're clever when they sing the song of homophobia. Take Ed Plaisted. Please. When Deb's column started in Detroit, Plaisted was executive editor of the *Times-Herald* in nearby Dearborn.

The gay column was just five days old when the weekly *Times-Herald* printed Plaisted's rejoinder, which began by claiming that Deb's column was a circulation-building ploy. He continued:

> Although such a column may offend the traditional religious and moral values of God-loving Americans, the *News* is gambling that normal readers will not react. If this is successful, can we not expect the liberal press to follow with columns about other obscene sexual practices from bondage to beastiality [*sic*]?
>
> There are many rapists, child molesters and other perverts who could be attracted to the *News* by columns aimed at their sexual preference. How about a column on date rape by Mike Tyson? But who am I to argue with a publisher of such high moral statue [*sic*] as Bob Giles of the *News*.
>
> I, too, have been pondering a gay love advice column for *Times-Herald* readers. You know, sort of a "Dear Dykeann" column for the homosexuals. I'm sure they must have some of the same romantic problems as normal people.

Plaisted followed with six question-and-answer exchanges from an advice column he dubbed "Dear Lesie" *(sic,* yet again).

Dear Lesie:
I am heartbroken and have tried to drown my unhappiness in booze and drugs. My true love, Mary, deserted me after a seven-year relationship. She left me for a man! A man. . . . What could any woman see in any man? . . .
When I confronted Mary she admitted everything. She said she

wanted to get married to this man and live a normal life. I'm devastated. I know there are lots of gay joints in Detroit but I don't like the bar scene.
                                                              —Martha, Dearborn

Dear Martha:

Any real woman who would leave you for a man isn't worth getting upset over. There are plenty of real women out there. Get out of the house and start attending NOW and Bill Clinton for President rallies. Good hunting.

In his "Dear Lesie" column, Plaisted asked readers to "please let me know your thoughts." This lezzie considered sharing a few of mine, then decided not to bother.

Allowing blatantly anti-gay diatribes into print regardless of how many falsehoods they perpetuate isn't the only major flaw in the newspaper industry's handling of gay issues. Just as serious is the newsroom heterosexism—much of it unconscious—that produces coverage rendering gay men and lesbians almost invisible or completely alien. Even today, newspapers rarely attempt to depict how thoroughly we are woven into the fabric of American life by including us in stories that are not specifically gay. Ever see a gay couple and their children included in an ordinary back-to-school feature, for example?

AIDS, more than anything else, exposed the dangerously unprofessional way the press covered—failed to cover—gay issues. The AIDS crisis has prodded the press to begin writing more realistically about gay lives and forced many editors to think, perhaps for the first time, about whether they are truly serving gay readers. Now, despite nationally syndicated columnists like Patrick Buchanan, who refers to gay men as "sodomites," and William F. Buckley, Jr., who once proposed that gay men with AIDS be tattooed on the buttocks, daily newspapers are less overtly hostile to gay people than they were a dozen years ago. A great many newspapers have added "sexual orientation" to their in-house anti-discrimination policies, more than a dozen run announcements of gay couples' commitment ceremonies and a few, including *The New York Times,* extend family health benefits to gay employees' partners.

Inside newsrooms, where more and more gay journalists are speaking up, there's a growing awareness of what a poor job the press still does in covering gay issues and gay people. One of the many heterosexuals aware of the problem is Tom Bray, a Gannett editor. "I've seen coverage of the gay community botched over and over again," he says. "I think a lot of us, in our attempts to be sensitive and thoughtful, have an awful lot of heterosexual confusion," he adds.

Except for calling himself a "clumsy heterosexual," Bray reaches for very traditional touchstones to describe himself: "I'm a small-town guy with a wife and a daughter. And I'm Catholic and go to church every Sunday." He quickly adds, "I really do try to be compassionate. And I really do try to be enlightened."

In early 1992 Bray was assistant managing editor of the Palm Springs *Desert Sun*. "What I wanted at that time very badly was a thoughtful, regular presence [in the *Sun*] that dealt with gay issues," he recalls.

"What kind of regular feature can we run that would be a thoughtful analysis of how issues are addressed differently in the gay community?" Bray popped that question to J. Ford Huffman of Gannett News Service in February during a mini features summit in Reno for Gannett's western papers. Bray recalls, "He said, 'You've asked me that question, and I'm going to get you an answer.' I think he had the answer in mind before I ever asked." Huffman suddenly saw the opening he needed to help Deb get a gay column started.

In *Slaughterhouse Five*, Kurt Vonnegut, Jr., floats the idea that a child has at least seven biological parents—some of whom never meet. As I gradually pieced together how many people played essential roles in the conception and birth of America's first gay column, Vonnegut's silly theory began to seem pretty close to reality. The abbreviated version of the column's creation—that Deb asked and Bob Giles said yes—is absolutely true. But it absolutely ignores that if Tom Bray, J. Ford Huffman, Christy Bradford, Michael Hodges, Dierck Casselman, *News* assistant managing editor Julie Heaberlin, crusty Ben (S.O.B.) Maidenburg or the *News* editor who made the anti-gay wisecrack had behaved differently, the column might never have been born.

Deb had broached the possibility of a gay column in late fall of 1991 during one of Bradford's trips to Washington, D.C. Bradford, the *News'* managing editor, liked the idea but didn't pass it along to Giles when she returned to Detroit. A short while later Deb casually mentioned the idea to Huffman, just to bounce it off a respected gay journalist. She didn't realize Huffman was Bradford's sometime traveling companion. Huffman deals with even his closest friends as if they were soufflés: Timing and delicacy are of the utmost importance. If he were going to encourage Bradford to act on Deb's column idea, the moment would have to be perfect. Tom Bray's question provided that moment.

"J. Ford called me one day and said, 'Palm Springs is interested in a gay column. Could *The Detroit News* do that for GNS?' " recalls Bradford. "And I said, 'Sure.' " The old friends talked briefly about Deb's interest in writing such a column. Because Bradford works a late shift for the afternoon *News,* she was still at home. She didn't want to wait any longer to push the idea forward: "I called up Bob [Giles] from home and said, 'J. Ford wants a gay column. Can we do it?' He said, 'Sure,' and that was that. Giles is fabulous like that. . . . There was no agonizing, hand wringing, carrying on."

Once Giles saw Deb's sample columns and gave the final go-ahead, everything happened quickly. Julie Heaberlin embraced the notion of running a gay column in her Accent section. Giles visited Deb's immediate supervisor, the *News'* quite traditional Washington bureau chief, to notify him that Deb's duties were expanding to include a weekly gay column. (In less than a year, Deb was allowed to turn most of her attention to the column.) Deb was summoned to Detroit to spend an entire day—excruciating for someone who never primps—with a column-photo specialist determined to capture the image the *News* and Huffman wanted Deb to convey: serious yet subtly feminine. (The photograph, which makes Deb appear to be a Breck Girl with a Mona Lisa smile, challenged lesbian stereotypes head-on. As one straight commentator wrote, "Funny, she doesn't look dykey. Or is it butch? No moustache, no leathers, no visible tattoos." Even gay publications felt compelled to comment on Deb's "cascading blonde hair." And one New York State paper that regularly runs

Deb's column actually called GNS to ask whether a different photo was available—"one that looks like a lesbian.") With Deb's this-is-what-a-lesbian-looks-like color photograph selected, the column came out.

The birth of Deb's column flooded our lives with so much hope and joy that it forced Deb and me to let go of much of our protective cynicism. Most of society's problems are so intractable that one person's courage or determination can seem to count for nothing. Yet, each of the people who pushed to make a long-overdue gay column a reality demonstrated the power of one person to do good. Whether they just asked a crucial question that got the ball rolling or had enough power to turn Deb into a gay issues columnist, each played an important role. But nobody, including Bob Giles, demonstrates how much one person can do to encourage goodwill between gay and straight people better than J. Ford Huffman.

If, like some lucky children, Deb's column has two fathers, Giles is one and Huffman is surely the other. Time after time, when I interviewed heterosexuals who had key roles in the early days of Deb's column, I asked them why they were willing to take professional risks on behalf of something gay, why they had such good feelings about gay people. And, time after time, the answers revolved around one name, "J. Ford." Personally liked and professionally respected, Huffman lived for more than a decade in a glass closet, mistakenly thinking his sexual orientation was his secret. As mentioned earlier, Giles assumed in the Seventies that Huffman was gay and began harboring good feelings toward other gay folks because of him. Similarly, it's largely because of knowing Huffman well that Bradford flatly declares gay people "are no different from non-gay people." Bray and Moyer both talked about trusting Huffman's judgment when he began pitching Deb's column. "He doesn't sell a bad product," Bray commented.

Within mainstream newspaper journalism, Huffman was without a doubt one of the highest-ranking openly gay people when Deb's column began in May 1992. Neither his journey toward openness nor his journey toward self-acceptance was easy.

J. Ford Huffman calls his childhood "unhappy." But that word is far too mild for the tale he tells. "Miserable," "devastating," "ego-crushing" seem closer to the mark. "From Day One, I didn't like myself," he recalls. His father was a Wheeling, West Virginia, grocer with an eighth-grade education. His mother stayed home to raise him, his three brothers, and his sister. Theirs was a world in which boys were rough and tough and athletic. Sensitive, artistic, creative J. Ford just didn't fit in.

Everywhere he turned, he recalls, he was pounded with negative messages: "You're abnormal; be ashamed." If we're fortunate, childhood's bumps are cushioned by belief that somebody loves us unconditionally—a father, a grandmother, maybe just Santa Claus. But J. Ford didn't get lucky. He got insulted. Even now he recalls the sting of being a second-grader and meeting Santa Claus during a Christmastime festival at school. "Santa Claus called me a 'sissy.' He asked me what the 'little girl' wants for Christmas," Huffman says.

Year after year, the idea was hammered into him that masculinity was a test that he was failing by not being athletic. "I remember going into my bedroom crying in junior high because my mother so very kindly told me she wished I would play basketball like other boys—it would really make my father happy," he says. Later, in high school, he prayed, "Please, God, let me be a man." Looking back, Huffman says, "I spent my childhood and adolescence wanting to be the high school jock."

Huffman, who's now in his early forties, finally discovered his athletic side after joining a gay sports group in 1990. Gradually, he became a runner—a jock who ran in the 1994 Gay Games five- and ten-kilometer road races wearing the D.C. Frontrunners' T-shirt he designed. He gave a team shirt to Bob Giles for his sixtieth birthday.

When J. Ford was growing up hating himself, he only knew he was "different." He had no gay role models and no way to see that being gay was a possibility for himself. He was twenty-eight and working in Rochester before he first tentatively told a friend, "I think I'm gay." But in his nine years at the Rochester paper, he didn't once date. Not once. For a long time he felt that having a gay social life would somehow conflict with being a good journalist. "What I was really hiding behind," he says, "was this myth of objectivity. . . . I had to realize I can be gay and I can be a journalist, too." Slowly, he realized he was expecting himself to be detached from the world in a way that he'd never expect of a heterosexual colleague. After moving to Washington, D.C., in 1986, he stopped shackling his personal life. Yet he remained closeted at work. "I'd make story suggestions and say, 'We should do a story on gay literature and how that's really grown.' I'd never once say, 'I know this for a fact because I go to Lambda Rising and buy books,' " he says.

Listening to straight colleagues discuss gay story ideas stemming from the AIDS crisis nudged Huffman into coming out professionally in 1990. "I turned to my deputy one day and said, 'You've probably figured this out, but . . . I'm gay. And I'm tired of hiding myself. Feel free to tell anyone you want,' " he recalls.

"I don't believe in having regrets," Huffman continues. "I think things happen when they're supposed to happen in the flow of life. I wish I had come out long before this, but I guess the time just wasn't right. And I think that I've probably had more effect this way. I was able to establish a reputation in journalism for lifestyle coverage and [graphic] design so that a lot of people want the information I have. Now I can sort of say, 'Okay, on top of all that expertise you think I have in design and features and entertainment coverage, you get a gay person, too. You win the bonus on this one!' "

Huffman understands the importance of gay visibility, especially within the news media. "Too many of our friends are living unjustly unhappy lives. We have to do whatever we can to help them," explains the quietly persuasive editor who remembers all too well how unhappiness feels.

Huffman is proud of having helped to father America's first gay column. "As you know, I've always thought of Deb's column as my own," he says with a laugh. Turning serious, he adds, "I like being on the sidelines. I like being that quiet person who doesn't get the acclaim but who knows he had a part in it. If in the history books of gay journalism, if I am even half a footnote, then maybe the twenty years I've spent in journalism so far are worthwhile."

J. Ford Huffman has demonstrated the power of one person to foster understanding between gay and straight people. Through the strength of his own character, he turned himself into a re-markable person, the kind of backstage hero he needed as a role model when he was a despairing teenager. Largely thanks to Huffman, Deb is able to bring other everyday heroes onto center stage, where millions of newspaper readers can see them. These heroes have one thing in common. No, they're not all gay. But they are all making the world a more pleasant place to be gay. And one of them is just wild about rodeo.

Chapter

4

COLUMNS

OCTOBER 9, 1992–

FEBRUARY 12, 1993

> ## NO BULL—THIS GAY RODEO
> ## IS EASY ON ANIMALS,
> ## ROUGH ON RIDERS

OCTOBER 9, 1992

Life turned into a rough-and-tumble affair for Mike Lentz when he lost his heart to gay rodeo. But to hear him tell it, the thrills more than make up for the spills, even the one that broke his collarbone.

"If you like roller coasters, you'll love steer riding," the lanky federal accountant insists with the enthusiasm of an evangelist.

Strangers think that what Lentz has really lost is his mind, he says, when they see him roping parking meters for practice.

Lentz is still hazy about the time he was competing in an appropriately named "rough stock" event and landed on his head. "I was definitely funny for a couple of days." But, he says, "You never forget your first gay rodeo."

His was in Denver two years ago. And this month thousands of us living near Washington, D.C., experienced a gay rodeo—the first east of the Mississippi—thanks to the one-year-old Atlantic States Gay Rodeo Association, which Lentz helped form. (True cowboys always wear long sleeves, but rodeo spirit was best captured by the T-shirt that read: "I've fallen and can't giddyup.")

"Atlantic Stampede" was the last of twelve charity fund-raisers sponsored this year by the eight-thousand-member International Gay Rodeo Association. Once the roping and riding began, a few competitors quickly showed they were not rent-a-horse cowhands.

One Dallas cowgirl sporting a prize buckle turned out to be a twelve-year veteran of the "straight rodeo." She prefers the gay circuit because the crowds are more receptive and women compete in all events, not just the cloverleaf-shaped horse race around three barrels.

The gay prize money is better for women, too. She's won $35,000 this year but notes that she's barely covered entry fees and the cost of traveling with her horse.

She seemed a bit dismayed by the knot of gays protesting outside the Stampede arena. "There's none of this animal-rights stuff in Texas," she says.

Despite the demonstrators' "cruelty-for-a-buck" charges, the gay rodeo breaks with tradition by being unusually gentle with animals. Calves running at top speed don't risk broken necks because gay cowpokes' ropes aren't tied to saddles, for example.

It's true that one goat repeatedly forced into jockey shorts during one campy event did get quite upset and should have been allowed to leave the game. But generally the animals seemed less at risk than the humans.

Lentz downplays the danger. The worst that happens during the bizarre event known as steer decorating—in which one person holds a thousand-pound creature by the horns and another ties a ribbon on its tail—is that you might get some "guacamole" on your hands, he says.

He even tried to sweet-talk Joyce into bull riding, saying her "low center of gravity" makes her a natural. But then he made the mistake of explaining to me that the difference between a steer—

the animal that put his right arm out of commission—and a bull is "a half ton and two testicles."

The Stampede bulls resembled giant, angry, double-wide refrigerators. Bull riding was definitely the most exciting contest. But, on the afternoon we were watching, it should have been called Revenge of the Hamburgers.

Again and again, riders crashed into the ground long before the six-second horn sounded. One Houston lawyer caught his hand in the rope as he fell and was turned into a Raggedy Andy doll for several heart-stopping moments as he dangled helplessly from a raging titan.

The only successful bull rider that day would have been barred from the event except at an equal-opportunity gay rodeo. But even that rider didn't escape unscathed: She broke a fingernail.

For details on gay rodeo, call (303) 832-IGRA.

A TRULY DANGEROUS FLIRTATION WITH FANATICISM ISN'T FOREIGN TO AMERICA

OCTOBER 16, 1992

Subhuman. A blight on society. An irritant to be removed by any means. That's how the Nazis thought of Gypsies. Shipped to concentration camps, 500,000 Gypsies paid with their lives for the "crime" of being different.

Killed along with them as part of the Third Reich's Final Solution were Jews, anti-fascists, Jehovah's Witnesses, homosexuals, the mute, the epileptic: more than 11 million people who did not fit Hitler's vision of a perfect world.

My heart knows the truth of the Gypsy saying "Our ashes were mingled in the ovens." But my mind finds the horror too great to truly grasp. How could it have happened? How did a nation slip into hell?

Holocaust historian Raul Hilberg writes in *Perpetrators Victims Bystanders* that among people not directly targeted by the Nazis there prevailed "a sense of indifference, even apathy."

Fanatical haters can perpetrate tremendous human suffering. But bystanders—those who look the other way—play a key role by allowing events later viewed with outrage and dismay.

Richard Plant notes in *The Pink Triangle: The Nazi War Against Homosexuals* that the specter of the Third Reich comes to life when fanatics "take over a nation and call for a holy war against its most vulnerable and vilified minorities."

Warning sirens are sounding today. They are eerily similar to ones largely ignored in the late 1930s.

"Germany to Deport Gypsies," a recent *Washington Post* headline declared. I reassured myself history doesn't really repeat itself but then wondered, with a shudder: Why can't it? What's to stop hate groups in Germany and our own country?

Racked with anti-foreigner violence since reunification, Germany has chosen to appease its lunatic fringe. Instead of reining in the neo-Nazi gangs responsible for thousands of attacks, the German government is ridding the country of its most widely despised foreigners: Gypsies seeking asylum from persecution.

Beginning November 1, Romania will be paid to take them back.

But Germany's club-wielding thugs are no more frightening than its law-abiding citizens who have failed their history lesson.

"I'm against the violence, of course, but isn't it pretty here without the Gypsies?" a mechanic asked a *Post* reporter after a firebombing forced Gypsies to flee.

Germany is not alone in flirting with right-wing fanaticism. At the Republican National Convention, Pat Buchanan rabidly denounced gays to wild cheers. "There is a religious war going on in this country," he declared. "It is a cultural war . . . for the soul of America."

That war is being waged in Oregon and Colorado, where voters are being asked to outlaw any legal protection for gays. The Oregon amendment would require the state to work actively against gays, proclaiming them virtually subhuman—"abnormal, wrong, unnatural and perverse."

Proponents of the outrageous referendums—who vow to take this war to every state—decry "special rights for homosexuals."

Yet the U.S. Constitution promises all Americans equal protection under the law. And that is all we as gay people want: not to be fired from a job, kicked out of an apartment or denied the honor of serving our country simply because of whom we love.

Oregon Governor Barbara Roberts knows her state is toying with disaster. Calling the anti-gay referendum "malignant," she warns: "If anyone's rights are at risk, then each of us is at risk."

Those who sow hatred reap violence. Already Oregon reports an alarming rise in anti-gay assaults.

Before dawn on September 26, a Molotov cocktail was thrown into the Salem, Oregon, home of a lesbian and a retarded gay man. Both were killed. Police have arrested a pair of skinheads and a neo-Nazi.

What today's hate-mongering will ultimately lead to no one can predict. But its victims—whether Gypsies or gays—don't have the power to stop it alone. Bystanders do.

BUSH TO LEARN JUST HOW MUCH GAY VOTERS COUNT

OCTOBER 23, 1992

Playground bullies are rarely the most studious boys in the class, so it's not surprising that George Bush and Dan Quayle didn't do their homework before deciding to pick on gays.

To a pair of Republicans wanting to win right-wing friends by kicking sand in a few faces, we must have seemed the perfect ninety-eight-pound weakling: a small, despised group of Democrats.

On November 3, millions of gay and gay-friendly voters will teach Bush/Quayle just how thoroughly they miscalculated.

The error is big enough to turn a narrow Bush victory into a narrow Clinton victory or transform a narrow Clinton victory into a Clinton landslide. Either way, the anti-gay attacks authorized by the "kinder, gentler" president will have cost him the White House.

Just before August's hate-filled GOP National Convention, political analyst and lawyer Linda Hirshman correctly predicted in the *Los Angeles Times* that the Bush team would try to turn gays into the Willie Horton of 1992—and that the tactic would backfire.

Because they had "played the race card effectively in every election since 1968," the Republican strategists "thought that you can demonize anyone," she now says.

Hirshman, whose best friend is lesbian, says Bush failed to realize how many straight voters care about someone gay. A Harris poll this month found Democrat Bill Clinton holding a thirty-five-point lead among folks with a close friend who is gay. More than one in four voters put themselves in that gay-friendly category.

But George Bush's political radar is a little old-fashioned. It failed to detect that stunts like having Quayle campaign at an anti-gay Cracker Barrel restaurant were forging a powerful single-issue group: 17 million gay voters (Overlooked Opinions, a Chicago-based gay polling firm).

In 1988, as in all past presidential campaigns, the candidates did not offer gay voters a meaningful choice. Both Michael Dukakis and George Bush took moderately anti-gay stances. And Bush won about 32 percent of the gay vote, according to Voter Research & Surveys, the networks' exit pollster. That translates into 5.4 million votes.

Jeff Vitale of Overlooked Opinions says that in attacking people who had supported him in large numbers Bush "didn't understand what he was doing, not for one minute. . . . His advisers were off the mark. They assumed that these folks weren't out there."

Most of us wear no buttons, carry no signs. Call us the Stealth

Voters. Our clout is visible inside the voting booth, and we vote at rates almost double the rest of the population. This year the impact of a united gay electorate will be felt for the first time in the history of presidential politics.

Bush will get only 3 percent of the gay vote, Vitale's polling indicates. That would shift 4.9 million votes—enough to have decided nine of the twelve White House races in the last fifty years.

Bush became the candidate of hate after right-wing extremists blasted him for inviting gay rights activists to the signing of bills to track hate crimes and ban discrimination against people with AIDS. Instead, he could have said, as Ross Perot did recently: "If you hate people, I don't want your vote." But he did not. And, as Perot pointed out, Bush could have yanked Pat Buchanan off the GOP convention podium when he began his hateful diatribe. But he did not.

The gay Log Cabin Republicans wanted a reason to support their party's nominee. But he gave them none. They won respect in the gay community by refusing to endorse him.

Bush blames gay people with AIDS for their illness, derides what he calls the gay "lifestyle" and upholds the military ban.

In contrast, Clinton promises a Manhattan-style project to combat AIDS, civil rights protections and an end to the military ban.

Meeting with gays in Los Angeles earlier this year, Clinton said, "I have a vision, and you are part of it." Now gay voters and our allies have a vision. And Bill Clinton is part of it.

GAY PHILANTHROPISTS BRING GOOD FORTUNE TO A COMMUNITY THAT GETS SHORTCHANGED

OCTOBER 30, 1992

Indulge for a moment in the ultimate American fantasy: being handed a fortune. Think of the freedom, the opportunities. Or listen to David Becker of Portland, Maine, and think of the guilt. For him the fantasy is reality. His dough is Pillsbury. His social conscience is strong.

Philanthropy, he says, "always starts off with a sense of guilt. It's just disgusting that we have all this money."

One of a new breed of gay philanthropists—open about their inherited wealth and sexual orientation—Becker shares his money with the gay community in hopes of sharing the power it brings. Since the mid-Seventies he's contributed $750,000, including funds for an Academy Award–winning documentary, *The Times of Harvey Milk*.

Now, Becker says, "The AIDS crisis has gotten many gay men with resources to realize their money can make a difference."

But for former Michigan state legislator Mike Dively, channeling a portion of his family fortune into our fledgling movement is part of the "coming-out process, of letting people know it's okay to be gay, and I'm very proud and happy to be a gay man."

Dively, who represented the Traverse City area as a Republican from 1968 to 1974, calls himself a "late bloomer." He had a sexual encounter at age eleven with a boy at camp but didn't come to terms with his sexual orientation until he was forty-two, near the end of a brief marriage. The intervening decades might have been less of a struggle, he believes, if Williams College had helped him sort through his feelings.

Now he has become the role model he never had. The Class of '61 grad has donated $75,000 to his Massachusetts alma mater for the Michael Dively Fund for Human Sexuality and Diversity.

Dively, who lives in Key West, says he's usually not inclined to emblazon his name on gifts. But Becker convinced him "it's important for people to see that other people are willing to be out."

His fund's first event was a sold-out performance this fall of *Fierce Love: Stories from Black Gay Life,* by a San Francisco troupe known as Pomo (for postmodern) Afro Homos.

It's vital that wealthy gay men and lesbians be generous with their gay family, because traditional philanthropic foundations have slammed their vault doors in our faces. In 1989 only 2.6 cents out of every $100 distributed by major foundations went to projects explicitly supporting gays, according to the Foundation Center.

The 1992 Foundation Directory indicates only 5 out of 8,729 foundations give to gay causes. And only two non-gay endowed foundations list our civil rights movement as a funding priority.

One of the biggest gay-rights donations in history was made by James Hormel of the chili and meat-packing family. Gay history is important to Hormel—so important that he gave $500,000 to San Francisco's new main library to preserve and mainstream it. Hormel, who gets "enormous psychic rewards out of being a philanthropist," calls bankrolling the gay archives "the opportunity of a lifetime."

Meanwhile, Joan Drury of Minneapolis works to redistribute the millions her parents earned by transforming a mom-and-pop garbage company into Browning-Ferris Industries. She sees her wealth as a blessing and tries to "pay back the universe" by nurturing lesbian authors.

She notes many lesbians keep their riches secret, fearing pressure or envy. "If I wasn't in the closet about being a lesbian," she says, "I sure as hell wasn't going to be in the closet about having money. Being in the closet about anything means . . . lying about yourself."

These new gay philanthropists are trying to make it easier for gay people to know the truth about themselves—and to tell it. As Mike Dively puts it: "What I'm promoting is for everybody to be able to be who they are."

AFTER THE ELECTION,
FRIENDS OF DOROTHY
AWAKE IN LAND OF PROMISE

NOVEMBER 6, 1992

The electoral tornado transformed Washington overnight into a dazzling emerald city of hope. I find myself wonderfully disoriented, living in a land where dreams we dared to dream really do come true.

After Bill Clinton survived a nasty campaign in which anti-gay rhetoric helped melt away his rivals, the gay community is equipped with ruby slippers and an invitation to see the new wizard.

Tim McFeeley of the Human Rights Campaign Fund wasn't exaggerating when he called November 3 the most significant day in the struggle for gay civil rights since the Stonewall riots of 1969.

Gay voters lined up behind the first gay-rights presidential nominee: CNN reported 71 percent of gays backed Clinton while George Bush got a paltry 17 percent—half his '88 percentage. Chicago's Overlooked Opinions found 89 percent of gays voted for Clinton and only 2 percent for Bush.

"If Bush had taken as positive a stand on our issues as Clinton has done," McFeeley says, "he would have been re-elected president."

Instead, Bush reaped the whirlwind.

As president, Clinton promises to lift the ban on gays in the military, prohibit anti-gay bias in the federal government, and sign legislation outlawing similar discrimination in the private workplace.

Our president-elect undoubtedly will have the chance to shift the balance of the Supreme Court toward recognition of the constitutional rights of gay men and lesbians. His lower court appointments also are likely to have a profound impact. "When we lose cases, it's normally Reagan and Bush appointees who write the decisions," notes Arthur Leonard, an expert on gay legal issues.

The wind of change that powered Clinton's candidacy brought a record number of open gays into office. Victories in races for posts from state legislature to school board boosted the total to seventy-five.

Both openly gay members of Congress—Massachusetts Representatives Barney Frank and Gerry Studds—won re-election by wide margins. And a record number of gay-friendly candidates won seats in Congress. The expected result: 21 senators (including all 4 newly elected women) and 119 House members will co-sponsor the gay civil rights bill.

Meanwhile, Representative William Dannemeyer, Republican of California, who stirred the caldron of anti-gay fervor long before Pat Buchanan brought it to a boil, will not be returning to Congress.

On anti-gay initiatives, the election results were mixed.

Portland, Maine, refused by a vote of 57 percent to 43 percent to overturn its gay-rights law. And the dangerous effort in Oregon to declare homosexuality "abnormal, wrong, unnatural and perverse" was rejected resoundingly.

Governor Barbara Roberts told the press that the outcome in Oregon "shows a commitment . . . to look for ways to work together to solve our problems instead of looking for ways to divide us."

But Tampa, Florida, voted to repeal its gay-rights law. And Colorado voted to ban a state gay-rights law and to erase protections already passed in several towns.

Three steps forward, two back: That's long been the gay struggle.

But Clinton wants the United States to leap ahead. His victory, he says, was "a clarion call . . . to bring our people together as never before so that our diversity can be a source of strength in a world . . . where everyone counts and everyone is part of America's family."

Many gays, now proud to be a "Friend of Bill," have long

called ourselves "Friends of Dorothy" because we identify with her yearning in *The Wizard of Oz* for a better world somewhere over the rainbow.

Oz's wizard showed the scarecrow, tin man, and lion that they already had what they desperately sought: a brain, a heart, and courage.

If Clinton's wizardry helps our nation find those things within itself, then we gays will know the happiness Dorothy found by clicking her heels:

We'll feel at home.

GAY TALENT READY TO TAKE PLACES AT CLINTON'S TABLE

NOVEMBER 13, 1992

Even before getting the keys to the front door, Bill Clinton is telegraphing a historic message about his White House to the best and the brightest of the gay community:

UNDER NEW
MANAGEMENT.
NOW HIRING.

David Mixner, serving as First Gay Pal, is spreading the word that a cornerstone of Clinton's administration will be his belief that this country doesn't have a person to waste. Openly gay talent is being scouted.

Gays who receive Clinton's call will have to adjust quickly to having a place at the table after decades of shivering—and shouting—out in the cold.

"We've all been taught . . . to think in an atmosphere of repression and outright government-sponsored discrimination," says Mixner, a senior Clinton adviser and longtime friend. "Now we have a person who is not perfect but willing to work with us and listen to our ideas."

Our community overflows with advanced degrees and first-rate credentials, making it easy to find a qualified gay person for almost any of the three thousand executive branch jobs and one hundred judgeships now open. Imagine Massachusetts Representative Barney Frank as attorney general.

Many wanna-be appointees are lawyers or political scientists, economists or educators, physicians or psychologists with traditional skills. Other gay Americans possess special talents, forged in a hostile or indifferent environment, that could help Clinton address the most pressing needs of gay adults and teenagers.

◆ A presidential order lifting the military ban on gays won't automatically make it easy to be "out" in uniform. Jay Lucas of the Philadelphia-based Kaplan, Lucas and Associates, a consulting firm helping companies make the most of their gay employees, notes that "just changing [anti-gay] policies doesn't change the attitudes." He's one of the experts who could help teach troops to see diversity as a strength.

◆ Who better to help reshape anti-gay policies and laws than their most stouthearted foes? Clinton could turn to gay-rights attorneys such as Paula Ettelbrick of Lambda Legal Defense and Education Fund and San Francisco Supervisor Roberta Achtenberg, who wrote the book on *Sexual Orientation and the Law*.

Achtenberg, a national co-chair of Clinton's campaign, says the president-elect knows "he has helped bring us in from the wilderness."

◆ Clinton properly credits our community with leading the fight against AIDS. He promises that an AIDS czar will coordinate and oversee all federal efforts. "The person who takes this job has got to be able to take on Jesse Helms and Pat Buchanan," warns Larry Kessler of the AIDS Action Committee of Massachusetts.

Kessler, appointed to the National Commission on AIDS by the U.S. Senate, is the kind of warrior Clinton needs. Others include Frank Lilly, a geneticist at Albert Einstein College of Medicine and a former member of the national AIDS commission; Timothy Sweeney of the Gay Men's Health Crisis in New York; Daniel Bross of the Washington-based AIDS Action Council; and Scott Hitt, a Los Angeles physician specializing in HIV care.

♦ Gay teenagers desperately need a friend in the White House. Minnesota pediatrician Gary Remafedi could tell Clinton about research showing that growing up in a society that values only heterosexuality puts gay youths at extreme risk for suicide and unsafe sex. And Los Angeles school counselor Virginia Uribe could describe how her Project 10 helps gay students survive adolescence.

A master of the art of the possible, Clinton has been careful not to promise to rid our government of all the anti-gay bias accumulated over the past 216 years. But he has promised "a White House staff, a Cabinet and appointments that look like America." To my gay ears, that sounds like progress.

RESEARCHER RESCUED GAYS AND LESBIANS FROM THE TORTURE OF MEDICINE'S DARK AGES

NOVEMBER 20, 1992

They put him on the table in his pajamas. That much the young gay man could remember.

And later, though he couldn't move, couldn't remember what had been done to him, he could hear the others scream.

"There's one loud scream—'Ahhhhh!!!'—very loud, each time they give you a shock. . . . They always did it in the morning, it went on all morning, three hours of those loud, single screams, one person at a time."

That was 1964. The young man, a beginning art teacher, was

forced to undergo seventeen electroshock treatments in a mental hospital after his parents had him involuntarily committed to "cure" his homosexuality.

Ten years later, as he told Jonathan Katz in *Gay American History,* he was still gay—and still suffering horrible bouts of memory loss because of the electroshock.

Changing our minds.

Electroshock. Lobotomy. Castration. Hysterectomy. Aversion therapy with nausea-inducing drugs. Hormone injections. In the psychiatric dark ages, these medical procedures were used to try to change gay and lesbian minds.

But one woman—psychologist Evelyn Hooker—labored to change the minds of the mental health professionals.

"Hooker did the first breakthrough research that asked a new question—not how to change gays but are gays really sick?" explains James Harrison, a New York clinical psychologist. "And she found no, not as a group. That opened a floodgate."

The story of how Hooker successfully challenged the idea that homosexuality is a mental illness is told in a superb new documentary, *Changing Our Minds,* which Harrison produced.

The movie—which is showing at film festivals and will premiere in art houses in January—intertwines archival footage of horrifying medical treatments with glimpses of smiling gay men and lesbians meeting to dance and party in the early Fifties. The juxtaposition is mind-boggling. Hooker, interviewed in the documentary at her vintage age of eighty-five, comes across plenty gutsy and intelligent enough to have taken on the establishment in her day.

Director Richard Schmiechen, who produced *The Times of Harvey Milk,* says Hooker "innately has no prejudices. She just responds to people as individuals."

Hooker stumbled into her life's work while teaching at the University of California at Los Angeles in the 1940s. She had become friends with former student Sam From. Through him she was quickly accepted into an "intellectually lively" circle of gay men—poets, engineers, philosophers.

She wasn't gay, just—in the slang of the day—"in the know."

Eventually, From told her, "It is your scientific duty to study people like us. We have let you see us as we are. And people don't know what we are, really."

No one had ever studied the mental health of homosexuals outside of a prison or mental ward. She asked the National Institute for Mental Health for a grant to try. When the grant officer asked to meet her, she remembers thinking: "He clearly wants to see what kind of kook this is who wants to study the 'normal homosexual' and who has access to 'any number of them.' " Yet he must have been impressed—she got federal funding.

Hooker's research involved giving thirty gay men psychological tests, then pairing each man's results with those of a heterosexual from a similar background. She challenged three internationally renowned experts to study the results and pick out the gay men.

None could do better than chance. All concluded that the mental health of gay men, as a group, was no different from that of heterosexuals.

Hooker presented those findings in 1956. Seventeen years later the American Psychiatric Association finally stopped calling homosexuality an illness because, as Hooker points out, "there's nothing to cure."

"She's a hero for all of us," Schmiechen says.

By changing her colleagues' minds, Hooker helped stop the torture. Some victims of that torture cannot remember. The rest of us must.

WHAT'S UP, DOC?
GAY STUDIES LAYS CLAIM TO THAT WASCALLY WABBIT

NOVEMBER 27, 1992

Faster than you can say "wabbit," that wascal Bugs Bunny dresses Elmer Fudd in a slinky green gown, matching heels and Joan Crawford wig.

A dazed Elmer—now a knockout with an hourglass figure and fire-engine-red lipstick—finds himself pounced on by a pack of sex-starved wolves.

"Gwa-cious!" Elmer cries as he hikes up his dress and runs for his life, pausing only long enough to ask the audience, "Have you giwls ever had an ex-pewience like this?"

The classic Warner Bros. cartoon *The Big Snooze* invited the moviegoers of 1946 into a sexual fantasy of men chasing men, of men feeling desirable to men, of men being allowed to dress up and act out. The story of Bugs' desperate attempts to keep Elmer from leaving him, *Snooze* ends with the lovable sparring partners reunited and Bugs declaring: "I love that man!"

Bugs Bunny toyed with gay themes in ways that were off limits for regular movies after the industry's Production Code banned "sexual perversion" in 1934. Yet most of us who munched popcorn as Bugs imitated Carmen Miranda or played Elmer's fiancée were in the dark about his significance.

That was before Gay Studies, which, like all the best educational endeavors, shows us previously unseen dimensions of our world. Bugs became a Gay Studies star at the University of Chicago recently when his campy cartoons opened each night of a ten-week film festival exploring the depiction of homosexuality in the movies.

At top universities across the nation, scholars are applying their academic skills to explorations of homosexuality. Most everything eventually finds itself under a gay-filtered microscope—novels, law, politics, newspapers, medical research.

"It's phenomenal," says George Chauncey, the history professor who organized the Chicago film festival. "Courses have started being taught all over the place."

Classics professor David Halperin, who teaches an introductory Gay Studies course at MIT, says the emerging field is "where a lot of the best minds are doing their best work."

Carolyn Dinslaw, a Chaucer scholar at Berkeley, is even designing a program that will allow students to minor in Gay Studies.

And a research institute—the Center for Lesbian and Gay Studies—is now an official part of the City University of New York.

Still in its infancy, Gay Studies is toddling along the interdisciplinary path broken by Women's Studies and Black Studies. Gay Studies delves into fields as diverse as anthropology, literary criticism, law, social history and biology.

Serious Gay Studies courses were impossible before the boom in scholarly gay books that began in 1976 with *Gay American History.* Jonathan Katz's astounding collection of historical documents proved that it is possible to chart an invisible minority's evolution.

Then came such important works as John Boswell's *Christianity, Social Tolerance, and Homosexuality,* a look at Europe before the fifteenth century (1980); World War II historian Allan Berube's *Coming Out Under Fire* (1990); Eve Kosofsky Sedgwick's *Epistemology of the Closet* (1990), and Judith Butler's *Gender Trouble* (1990).

Courses built on such scholarship expose the narrowness of most education. Turn-of-the-century English schoolboys in E. M. Forster's *Maurice* are warned while translating to "Omit: a reference to the unspeakable vice of the Greeks." Yet in most classrooms homosexuality never rises to the level of the forbidden—it is nonexistent.

But is Gay Studies academically legitimate? Sedgwick frames that question this way: "Has there ever been a gay Socrates . . . a gay Shakespeare . . . a gay Proust?" Yes, she answers, "their names are Socrates, Shakespeare, Proust."

And one of their hares—I mean heirs—is Bugs Bunny.

PLASTIC SKIRTS AND COCONUT BRAS BELIE THE HISTORICAL SWAY OF THE HULA DANCE

DECEMBER 4, 1992

The swaying arms of hotel hula dancers teach only commercialism. To learn about Hawaii's true past and culture, look instead at the arms of Pele, goddess of fire, as she reaches into the sea.

"Pele is unpredictable and tempestuous, as only a proud and jealous female can be. She does not ask for love. She demands respect," declares the official map of Hawaii Volcanoes National Park.

Standing on a jagged cliff just a pineapple's throw away from the latest eruption of the Big Island's Kilauea volcano, Joyce and I watched in awestruck silence as molten orange lava illuminated the night and poured into the onrushing waves to create new land.

Seeing, hearing, smelling the slithering inferno battle the tides for territory, we realized that a thousand volcano facts could not adequately convey its hypnotic power. At once we understood the endurance of volcano fictions, the majestic Hawaiian legends passed down through chants and solemn hulas.

In a society with no written language, the intricate tales kept Hawaii's history, beliefs and dreams alive: Pele is driven from island to island by her cruel older sister, goddess of the sea. Pele falls in love with a chief, who is more interested in another man.

The Pele stories are the inspiration for most hula dances, says Robert Morris, a Honolulu real estate lawyer devoted to reclaiming Hawaii's gay past. He gets a faraway look in his eyes as he describes the sensuousness of an art never meant to be practiced by men and women together—a dance nothing like the performance of the women in orange plastic skirts and coconut bras who flirtatiously show male tourists how to wiggle their hips.

"Many of the chants are by Pele's [younger] sister to her girlfriends. And they're love songs," Morris says.

The homosexual romances woven into the hula chants reflected Hawaiian society as Captain James Cook and his crew found it in 1778. Love between men or between women carried no stigma for the Hawaiians. They made no attempt to hide it.

Ship's surgeon David Samwell shyly reported: "We have great reason to think that that Unnatural Crime which ought never to be mentioned is not unknown amongst them."

In fact, Morris' award-winning anthropological research indicates that every chief of importance had *aikane,* the Hawaiian word—pronounced *I-connie*—for a gay lover.

The missionaries began arriving in 1820. Their position, of course, was that homosexuality was an abomination.

"The *aikane* of the chiefs were also their lieutenants, their messengers, their go-betweens. And foreigners dealt with the king through the *aikane,* which just rankled the missionaries. They couldn't stand that," Morris reports.

The missionaries were the first to convert the Hawaiian language to a written form. But this gift to the native people turned out to be a whale-boned corset capable of constricting island thoughts to conform with New England ideas of propriety.

Through their ownership of the first printing presses, the missionaries laid claim not only to the Hawaiians' future but also to their heritage. Words critical to the understanding of Hawaiian culture had their meanings twisted. Legends fell prey to pronoun swapping to heterosexualize them.

By 1883 a printer was prosecuted on obscenity charges simply for publishing the hula chants to be used at the coronation of the king. And by 1922 the word *aikane* had been stripped of its sexuality. Its dictionary definition had become "friend."

Long before then, "homosexuality went underground except for the chiefs," Morris says. "It went into the hula schools. Hula is the great center of Hawaiian culture and art. The dance, the music, the chants. That is where the center of gay life is today on Hawaii."

And just as the tireless sea has never been able to extinguish the spirit of Pele, the dance of homosexuality survives in Hawaii.

HAWAII COULD BECOME
AN ISLAND OF FREEDOM
IN A SEA OF INTOLERANCE

DECEMBER 11, 1992

Sleeping here, sleeping there. That was an accepted custom of Hawaiian life before the missionaries.

Relationships were defined by the people in them, not by outside institutions. Some lasted a lifetime. Others faded as quickly as footprints erased by the morning tides. And love between people of the same sex was as common as the white sand beaches and coconut palms fluttering in the warm island breezes.

Immediately after they began arriving in 1820, the missionaries imposed their view of life on the Hawaiians. All but heterosexual marriage became *kapu*—forbidden—requiring all other romantic love to be hidden.

Sexual freedom—the right of adults to love whom they choose—was also the essence of the modern gay-rights movement. Sleeping here, sleeping there—decisions to be made by individuals, not outside institutions.

But Ninia Baehr and Genora Dancel are fighting to have the Aloha State ratify their commitment through marriage.

"Since I was a kid, I always wanted to take care of someone," says Dancel. "And when I found Ninia, she was like the combination to the lock—it just opened."

Gay and lesbian couples in other states have searched in vain for the combination to heterosexuals' lock on marriage rights. But in Hawaii—known for its fruit salad of ethnic and racial groups and its privacy guarantees—gay couples are feeling lucky.

A lawsuit filed by Baehr and Dancel and two other gay couples is awaiting action by the Hawaiian Supreme Court. If they lose there, they'll turn to the gay-friendly legislature.

"Hawaii is really a checkerboard, and I think that's our great strength," says lawyer Robert Morris, who has coached the couples' attorney on Hawaii's tradition of same-sex love. "If we have a chance anywhere, it is here."

It was chance that brought Baehr and Dancel together. Baehr, a take-charge lesbian feminist, was at her mother's office in Honolulu one day two years ago when Dancel happened by.

"That's my wonderful friend Genora," Baehr recalls her mother whispering. "I've heard she's a lesbian. Why don't you go and meet her?"

Dancel was taken aback when Baehr introduced herself. "She just had that look in her eye," recalls Dancel, whose curiosity quickly conquered her fear. She called Baehr that night.

The thirty-year-olds immediately began dating. Two months later, they moved in together and applied for a marriage license.

Baehr was the catalyst. She incorporates life's complexities. Taught by her anti-war, liberal parents that conscience outweighs comfort, she's now protesting for the right to be a traditional wife.

A smitten Dancel eagerly agreed on their legal course.

"All through my life I thought I'd marry a guy 'cause that's what society told you to do," explains Dancel, the couple's bread-winner. "To me, that was second best. But here I met a woman who . . . gave me the chance to have everything I really wanted."

Nervously hoping for anonymity, Dancel wore sunglasses to the courthouse. "We saw you on the news," her co-workers later teased. "Why were you wearing the sunglasses?"

That laid-back reaction might be expected in a state where highway construction signs encourage motorists to "hang loose." But the rest of the nation isn't far behind: One-third of adults endorse gay marriage, a Wirthlin Group poll found last March.

Our civil rights movement, born from the desire to get government out of our bedrooms, has been slow to reflect that the rite many of us desire most is legally recognized marriage.

Hawaii might give us that chance. And in the process, Hawaii's native and missionary heritages—so seemingly contradictory—would be woven together to make the state an easier place in which to love.

Dutch Military Works at Making Gays Feel at Home

DECEMBER 18, 1992

One woman practices violin. Another entertains guests. A young man changes his shirt. An evening stroll through Amsterdam offers an American traveler disconcertingly personal glimpses of home life in the Netherlands: The Dutch don't close their curtains.

Yet what seems odd to Evert Ketting, deputy director of the Netherlands Institute of Social-Sexological Research, is the American habit of snapping the front curtains shut at sundown. "My feeling is that the United States is a hostile society where you need a small secure island that you can protect, defend, and where you feel comfortable, where you can withdraw."

The Dutch don't feel so fearful inside their homes, he says. "And that opens up the possibilities. You don't have anything to hide."

Because the Dutch equate living openly with feeling at home, their top military officials have been disturbed to find that most gay men and lesbians in uniform hide their personal lives. Eighteen years after homosexuality stopped being a reason for dismissal, only about 50 people in the 120,000-member Dutch armed forces are openly gay.

"Straight people are out, so I think the best thing for us is for all gays to be out." That's the opinion of a Dutch Air Force lieutenant colonel, Abel van Weerd.

His viewpoint is not surprising since he's the gay founder of the government-funded Foundation of Homosexuality and the Armed Forces. Yet as an American more accustomed to hearing military leaders voice fears about openly gay soldiers, I was delightfully amazed that his views are shared by the Defense Ministry.

The ministry's responsibility is to ensure that everyone feels "at home and safe and happy," says military personnel chief A. P.

den Butter. That means, he says, military leaders must conquer the unfounded biases of heterosexuals and "enable gay people to come out without any problems."

Interviewed in his boxy government-issue office in The Hague, den Butter bragged that his boss, Defense Minister Relus ter Beek, is getting an award from Holland's gay group. "Our policy is a good one," den Butter said. "We are quite successful in arranging conditions that will benefit the emancipation of homosexuals within our organization."

The Defense Ministry is trying to obliterate misguided stereotypes. Its chief weapon is education. And its goal is to make heterosexuals better colleagues to gays.

The ministry views the issue of gay soldiers largely from a gay perspective because the fear common among heterosexual troops has proved groundless.

Sexual attacks on straight soldiers? "No, it hasn't been a problem, but we wouldn't accept that, of course. That is forbidden in a comparable way to heterosexuals doing such things," den Butter reports.

Nevertheless, Major Frans van Dorp, a gay infantryman, says, "The straight guys think they are going to be raped by gays. What they say is straights have self-control and gays do not. It is just a fear that is based on nothing."

The real problem in the Dutch military, researchers found, is that many straight men are wary of sharing a tent or going drinking with anyone known to be gay. (Military women were far less concerned about lesbianism.)

So only "moderately pugnacious" gays with successful careers feel free to be themselves, the report concluded.

But with the defense minister telling a Dutch gay paper that his military needs a "complete change of culture," that awkward situation is likely to end soon.

Sociologist Ketting, who polled soldiers' attitudes toward gays, says the message the Dutch military must spread is simple: "You can feel at home as a homosexual in this house."

If the U.S. military wants to guard freedoms rather than fears, it will broadcast that message once Bill Clinton takes office.

Although forced to live behind a curtain, gays proudly serve our country. Now we need to follow Holland's example and proudly support those soldiers.

GAYS' BADGE OF OPPRESSION BECOMES MONUMENT OF PRIDE

DECEMBER 25, 1992

Amsterdam made room in its heart for the artistry of Karin Daan. Her gift in return was a monumental, pink granite triangle that points simultaneously to the past, present and future:

The Homomonument.

Built in a public plaza just around the corner from the Anne Frank house, the five-year-old work of art commemorates the horrors homosexuals suffered under the Nazis. And it pays tribute to the struggles and aspirations of today's gay men and lesbians.

The monument's name sounds odd when you've never heard "homo" used as anything except a slur. But in the Netherlands, "the word 'homo' is not aggressive. It is friendly," Daan says, calling herself "lesbo."

There is nothing comparable to the Homomonument anywhere. Now gay people "come from all parts of the world and photograph themselves there. To have one point in the world that is especially for you, that is beautiful," Daan says with justifiable pride.

According to Pieter Koenders's history of the monument, the idea of a permanent tribute to "the unknown homosexual" originated with poet Jef Last in 1961, who wrote: "No one knows how many there were. There are simply no statistics, nor are there figures for how many were tortured or starved to death or killed in other ways in the [Nazi] camps."

Each year the Netherlands, which was occupied by the Nazis,

honors the victims of World War II. In 1970, when members of a gay group tried to include a wreath honoring homosexuals, they were arrested. In later years, such wreaths were sometimes allowed, sometimes not.

But in 1979, spurred by dedication of a Gypsy monument, gays persuaded Amsterdam to set aside land for a Homomonument. Soon a call for design proposals went out. A panel reviewed 137 ideas and unanimously endorsed Daan's pink triangle, a symbol of oppression now worn as a sign of gay pride.

Koenders speculates that the Nazis forced homosexual men to wear pink badges to ridicule them as unmanly. In Germany, "pink was even taboo for boys and expressly intended for women, girls and babies." (Lesbians, classified as "anti-social" along with prostitutes and the longtime unemployed, were marked with a black triangle.)

Daan's elaborate project—actually three separate triangles that form the points of a thirty-nine-yard equilateral triangle—cost $200,000. Fund-raising proved difficult. Just when it seemed the monument might never be built, Parliament matched the city's $50,000 gift.

One of the smaller triangles of the monument unveiled in 1987 points, Daan says, to the house where Anne Frank hid before being sent to a death camp for being Jewish. The "past" triangle is level with the pavement, as if a gravestone for the victims of fascism.

The "present" triangle juts into a canal and points to Dam Square, the site of all sorts of political demonstrations.

The triangle of the future, a two-foot-high platform for gay rallies, points toward the home of Holland's chief gay group. Mayor E. van Thijn hopes it also points toward "a society where homosexuality is an integrated part of life."

Daan lives and works nearby in a double loft studio carved out of a seventeenth-century grain warehouse. Just as her home and office blend seamlessly, her Homomonument is woven into the city's life.

Taxis line up on a road that cuts through the monument. People picnic and fish from the canalside triangle. And bouquets are left in memory of those who've died of AIDS.

Now forty-eight and designing the Dutch embassy grounds in Tokyo, Daan sees the "living" Homomonument as her finest work. "I can't imagine I can do something more important."

The Homomonument, built with considerable government help, is an especially powerful symbol in this season of hope and remembrance. The fight for gay rights is no longer just a gay fight. As the official marker puts it: The monument "demonstrates that we are not alone."

Men Often Wear
Their Sex Roles
Like Black-Tie Straitjackets

JANUARY 2, 1993

There's a secret in everyone's closet: Mine is a blue-spangled evening gown that cost half a week's pay.

Joyce and I had gone in search of a simple black dress, something nondescript that I could wear to my first Washington power dinner despite a lifelong aversion to skirts. The "black tie" on the invitation irked me—life was always so easy for men, I thought.

But as I tried on a half dozen boring black shifts, Joyce gazed over at a rack of wild, sequined gowns and remarked, "You know, a lot of gay guys would kill to wear one of those."

It was almost a dare: Could I be as playful as the fellas who see life as a costume party? Or would my entire self-image be undermined by spending a single evening dressed as a femme fatale?

Well, I ended up buying three-inch spike heels, dangling earrings and a sky-blue dress, slit up to here. And, after Joyce dropped me off and locked the car door behind me so I couldn't lose my resolve, I went to the dinner party and had a fabulous time.

I found myself pitying the gentlemen, uniformly roosting in

their black-tie pigeonhole. Women could have worn most anything dressy, even a tuxedo. The men were locked in a gender
straitjacket. Too bad if one of them didn't want to look like a
penguin.

Who wears the pants in your family? The answer is supposed
to tell us something about power and freedom. Perhaps the question should be: Who feels free to wear a skirt—even a kimono or
kilt, even on Halloween?

Our society has begun talking about the fact that women are
stunted by glass ceilings on the job. We've yet to address the huge
problems caused by the way men's lives are confined by glass walls.

Don't cry. Don't play with dolls. Don't play with Mommy's
makeup. The rules and walls go up early for little boys. Little-girl
limits, which chafed some of us as much as the crinolines Joyce
demanded be cut out of her Sunday dresses, tended to be much
less strict.

Boys raised to believe in a very rigid definition of manhood
grow up to be frightened of their "feminine instincts," fearful
they will jeopardize their manliness by stepping outside a very
narrow role, according to clinical psychologist Lois Shawver of
Oakland, California.

These men, who "feel men should be breadwinners and
women should mind the kitchen," are more apt than other men—
or women in general—to dislike homosexuals, Shawver found
while studying heterosexual attitudes toward gays for the Canadian
government. Most of their antipathy is directed toward gay men,
especially feminine ones.

These heterosexual men see being attracted to another man as
the ultimate violation of the male role. So, they despise gay men
and are terrified by their own homosexual impulses. "The men
who have tremendous homophobic prejudice," Shawver says,
"are men who don't understand that occasional homosexual feelings are normal [for heterosexuals] and that other men have them,
too."

It is as if they feared catching a Frisbee with their left hand
would make them left-handed or wearing a bracelet would make
them female. They have a "brittle hold" on their masculine identity, Shawver notes.

Straight men with a more secure hold on their identity feel no need to believe little girls are made of "sugar and spice and everything nice" and that a completely different recipe is used for little boys. They know most ingredients are the same for everyone.

Because such a man doesn't live in fear of gay or feminine feelings, he can be comfortable having women or gay men as friends. "He can do things that are less clearly male-defined. He can cook, for example. . . . He can violate the male 'role' in small ways without feeling threatened by that," Shawver says. "He can wear a pink shirt."

Perhaps if we can learn to tailor our wardrobes to fit the diversity within ourselves, we'll be better suited to accept the diversity of others.

THAT ELUSIVE RECIPE FOR HOMOSEXUALITY IS LEANING MORE TOWARD GENETICS

JANUARY 8, 1993

Eve Adams' twin sister, Ann, gave her a bear hug at the door and whispered, "Mom knows about you, too."

The secret that the identical twins had discovered while at different colleges was out.

Ann had broken the news of her own lesbianism to their mother after getting upset at an anti-gay remark over dinner. The swift reply was a blunt question: "Is Eve, too?"

Their mother knew instinctively what researchers in the Nineties have made great strides toward proving: If one identical twin is gay, the other probably is, too.

Now thirty-one-year-old professionals in long-term relationships, Eve and Ann were among more than one hundred sisters who participated in a recent study that produced some of the strongest evidence so far of a link between genes and sexual orientation.

Psychologist Michael Bailey of Northwestern University and psychiatrist Richard C. Pillard of Boston concluded that the closer sisters are genetically, the more likely they are to have the same sexual orientation.

If a lesbian has an identical twin, they found, there is about a 50 percent chance her genetically identical sister is gay, too. (That's far greater, of course, than the odds a woman chosen at random is gay.)

But if a lesbian has a female fraternal twin—no closer to her genetically than any other sibling—the chances that her sister is gay are considerably below 50 percent. An adoptive (genetically unrelated) sister of a lesbian is even less likely to be gay.

"We found evidence for a fairly substantial genetic contribution" to sexual orientation, Bailey says of the work, details of which will soon be published in *Archives of General Psychiatry.*

However, Bailey adds, some non-genetic elements must play a role as well or else all the lesbians' identical twins would also be lesbian. Hormones, he believes, are most likely a key contributing factor.

Before turning their attention to lesbians, Bailey and Pillard, in research published in 1991, found a similar pattern among gay men: 52 percent of their identical twins were also gay, compared with only 22 percent of their male fraternal twins and 11 percent of their adoptive brothers.

Other researchers have found indications of physical differences between the brains of heterosexuals and gays.

What makes someone heterosexual instead of gay—or vice versa? All these findings tip the scale toward "nature" and away from "nurture."

But genetic research worries some gays because it raises the prospect of a fetal sexual orientation test. How many women would choose to bear a gay child?

Some lesbians in the Bailey-Pillard twins study insist that the origin of their sexual orientation is irrelevant. "We really shouldn't be looking for excuses," says Phoenix real estate broker Jan Dahl. "There is nothing to apologize for."

Her identical twin sister, Judy, now a minister in Ventura, California, came out to her more than twenty years ago. "I remember being upset about it and wondering what that meant about me," says Jan, now forty-four.

Most of us who are gay think—indeed, deeply feel—that sexual orientation is innate. We have no indisputable proof.

In the absence of such proof, theories built on anti-gay myths linger. The idea that a teacher or Scout leader could "turn" a child gay would be laughable if it weren't so dangerous. And if having a dominant mother and a weak or absent father were truly a recipe for homosexuality, wouldn't most Americans be gay?

Despite the growing number of clues, the riddle of sexual orientation remains unsolved. Science often advances slowly: The theory that the Earth is round was proposed about 500 B.C., but we didn't have snapshots to show Flat Earthers for nearly 2,500 years.

Yet I think someday, perhaps long after we're gone, scientists will know exactly what combination of genes, hormones and magic gave the Adams and Dahl households lesbian twins.

A STORYBOOK ENDING FOR CHILDREN WHO LOVE SOMEONE GAY

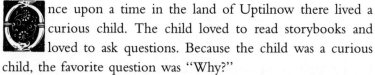

JANUARY 15, 1993

Once upon a time in the land of Uptilnow there lived a curious child. The child loved to read storybooks and loved to ask questions. Because the child was a curious child, the favorite question was "Why?"

The curious child had a cat, a puppy and a favorite toy, a teddy bear named Wondering. Because the curious child was very special and very ordinary in the way most children are, the child had a very special and very ordinary family. One person, or maybe two, was gay. The number was no secret to the curious child, but fairy-tale records were smudged by a misplaced piece of fudge.

Every night and twice on Saturdays the curious child read a stack of storybooks. In the storybooks, the curious child saw cats that looked quite familiar, puppies that looked quite familiar, teddy bears that looked quite familiar and even hiding-under-the-bed monsters that looked quite familiar.

But the more the curious child read, the more curious the child became. Finally, the child—being ever so curious, as children tend to be—started asking questions.

First the child asked the parent who wore jeans and worked in the basement: "Why don't the people in my books ever look like our family?"

"I don't know," replied the parent who wore jeans and worked in the basement.

Then the parent who wore suits and worked downtown came home. The curious child ran to the front door to get a big hug and ask: "Why don't the people in my books ever look like our family?"

"I don't know," replied the parent who wore suits and worked downtown.

On the next school day, the curious child went to the teacher with short hair and a long name and asked: "Why don't the people in my books ever look like my family?"

"I don't know," said the teacher with short hair and a long name.

On Saturday the curious child was still curious and went to the library. "Mister Librarian, why don't the people in my books ever look like my family?"

"I don't know," said Mister Librarian, who used a different name around grown-ups.

Finally, the curious child turned to the teddy, who was always sitting around just waiting to be asked curious questions. "Why don't the people in my books ever look like our family?"

The trusted teddy bear gave the answer it could always be trusted to give: "I'm wondering."

And then the curious child and Wondering, the teddy bear, did what they did every time the world seemed curious in a way that made them sad. They held each other tight and whispered: "I bet things will be different when we're big!"

The curious child grew big and moved along with the rest of us into the land of Now. And here the child, who is no longer a child at all, found something wonderful: Thanks to Alyson Publications of Boston there is a series of storybooks and coloring books especially for curious children with lesbian mommies or a gay uncle or a friend who has gay parents.

Some books help kids understand that "being gay is just one more kind of love," as a boy is told by his mom in *Daddy's Roommate*, by Michael Willhoite.

Heather Has Two Mommies, by Leslea Newman, explains how a loving couple can grow into a family of three even when there are obstacles. And *The Daddy Machine,* a funny rhyming tale by Johnny Valentine, says it's okay to daydream about what we don't have.

Valentine's story collections, *The Duke Who Outlawed Jellybeans* and *The Day They Put a Tax on Rainbows,* put gay parents just where all parents belong in storybooks: far, far in the background.

Provided adults close to them aren't lost in the land of make-believe, curious children who love someone gay no longer need to search in vain for family portraits: The world is different now.

———

If your wish is for a catalog of Alyson Wonderland children's books, call (617) 542-5679.

| COLORADO VOTERS SHOT DOWN |
| GAY RIGHTS, BUT THE ASSAULT |
| COULD VERY WELL BACKFIRE |

JANUARY 22, 1993

T hirty years ago, our national conscience was jolted out of a deep slumber: Millions of decent but normally apolitical folks watched TV newscasts in horror as police dogs and fire hoses were turned on black children peacefully protesting segregation in Birmingham, Alabama.

Many whites who had believed they had no personal stake in the civil rights struggle suddenly felt compelled to side with freedom. They joined black Americans in pushing for federal intervention. Within fourteen months the Civil Rights Act of 1964 was signed, outlawing racial bias in housing, employment, and public accommodations.

The fight for racial equality was far from over, of course, but it no longer had to be waged from lunch counter to lunch counter, town to town. The moral weight of the nation was finally behind integration.

Birmingham's racist police commissioner, Bull Connor, earned a footnote in history for inadvertently speeding up desegregation. Colorado, the first state in U.S. history to vote to strip gay men and lesbians of all protection against discrimination, will deserve a similar footnote if that effort backfires.

When 53 percent of Colorado voters declared in November that it's fine with them for us gays to be fired or thrown out of restaurants because of our sexual orientation, the reaction of national gay-rights groups was swift and blunt: Boycott Colorado.

The Reverend Martin Luther King, Jr., who led the children hosed in Birmingham, advocated boycotts. "Basic to the philosophy of nonviolence," he said, "is the refusal to cooperate with evil. There is nothing quite so effective as a refusal to cooperate economically with the forces and institutions which perpetuate evil in our communities."

"Boycott"—a word that sends a simple, unsettling message: Choose sides.

Many mainstream groups and entertainers are siding with personal freedom. Already Colorado has lost more than $25 million in business because organizations as diverse as the National Conference of Mayors and the American Association of Law Librarians have moved their conventions.

Austin, Atlanta, Boston, Chicago, Los Angeles, New York, Philadelphia, and Seattle also have closed their wallets to Colorado, forbidding city employees to go there on business. Meanwhile, a Denver judge, citing a "reasonable probability" that the law will be found unconstitutional, has kept it from taking effect.*

Just as the events of 1963 Birmingham helped turn racism into a matter of national conscience, current Colorado events are helping the nation's leaders realize that the rights of gay Americans should not hinge on the whims of individual towns or states.

Eighteen years ago, Congresswoman Bella Abzug (D-N.Y.), the mother of a lesbian, introduced the first federal gay-rights bill. Despite hearings in 1980 and 1982 and a growing number of co-sponsors, such legislation has never made it out of subcommittee.

Testifying at the first congressional hearing, Art Agnos, now a former San Francisco mayor, said the question is not whether a gay-rights bill will pass Congress, "but when . . . [and] how many people will needlessly suffer before the law passes."

When? Maybe this year, thanks to Colorado and a pro-gay president. Representative Don Edwards (D-Calif.) says he will hold hearings that coincide with the April 25 gay march on Washington. And powerful Edward Kennedy (D-Mass.) will be the Senate sponsor.

Kennedy recently declared: "For too long the denial of gay and lesbian rights has been an accepted form of discrimination based on ignorance, misunderstanding, and false morality."

After twelve long years in a Reagan-Bush coma, our national

conscience is awakening to face the problems and promises of a diverse nation. We are on the brink of understanding that none of us is free until all of us are free.

---

* On October 11, 1994, the Colorado Supreme Court declared the state's anti-gay initiative unconstitutional. The state promptly said it would appeal to the U.S. Supreme Court.

> # THE MILITARY HAS CREATED
> # A MONSTER IT MUST NOW
> # SEEK AND DESTROY

JANUARY 29, 1993

For fifty years, a monster created by power-hungry scientists has stalked the vast halls of the Pentagon, ruining careers, hounding patriots into suicide, and forcing decorated warriors into hiding.

The out-of-control monster is the U.S. military's ban on gay men and lesbians.

In the early 1940s, psychiatrists—seeking to prove their profession's value to the war effort—patched together the monster out of their ambition and ignorance. The mind doctors wooed the military brass: Hire us to test your recruits, they said, and we will use our special powers to weed out the homosexuals.

The brass had long regulated sexual conduct, without regard to the sexual orientation of those involved. But the psychiatrists persuaded the brass that the more "enlightened" approach was to see all homosexuals as mentally disturbed and unfit for military service, historian Allan Berube explains in *Coming Out Under Fire: The History of Gay Men and Women in World War Two.*

Today's villainous anti-gay policy was born.

Yet despite conducting such ludicrous research as whether gay men fail to gag when a tongue depressor is shoved down their throats, military doctors never found a way to detect what they called "homosexual tendencies."

Gay men and lesbians served in the military in large numbers in World War II and continue to do so today. The number currently in uniform might be as high as 200,000, according to the General Accounting Office (GAO), an investigative arm of Congress.

As Senator Edward Kennedy (D-Mass.) pointed out in denouncing the monstrous ban, "It isn't a question of whether there will be gays in the military. There already are. The question is whether they have to lie about it."

The question is also whether we want our tax dollars paying for anti-gay witch-hunts that cost us some of our most dedicated and highly trained officers and enlisted personnel. About twelve hundred people a year are expelled for being gay. The GAO estimates it costs $27 million a year to replace them. The price of ferreting them out has never been calculated—neither has the emotional cost.

Air Force Sergeant Leonard Matlovich, who earned a Bronze Star in Vietnam, was one of those hounded out. On his tombstone are these words: "When I was in the military they gave me a medal for killing two men and a discharge for loving one."

By 1973 the American Psychiatric Association realized its latter-day Dr. Frankensteins had created a beast that it was powerless to stop. Having determined that being gay isn't an illness, the APA declared to no avail that there is no basis for the ban.

The Pentagon commissioned—and then ignored—its own studies. The first, in 1957, found: "No factual data exist to support the contention that homosexuals are a greater [security] risk than heterosexuals." Then a 1991 report concluded that gay people tend to be as suited—or even better suited—for military service as the average heterosexual.

Left to defend a monster disowned by its psychiatrist parents, the military has fallen back on the morale rationale it used to justify racial segregation. But, as the 1991 report noted, "The [1948] order to integrate blacks was first met with stout resistance by traditionalists in the military establishment. Dire consequences were predicted. . . . None of these predictions of doom has come true."

President Clinton is moving to destroy the anti-gay monster. Gays now forced to lie are jubilant. One gay Air Force officer exclaimed to me: "This is my emancipation. This is my July Fourth, my Independence Day!"

But Independence Day was only the beginning of a long war. And so it will be in this battle. President Clinton needs our help to dismantle the monster, stereotype by stereotype, myth by myth. We must not stop until we've stilled the monster's heart—which is raw prejudice.

―――――

Call the White House at (202) 456-1111.

―――――――――――――――――――――――――――――

SILENCE ISN'T GOLDEN WHEN BATTLING THE MILITARY'S BRASS

FEBRUARY 5, 1993

The Joint Chiefs of Staff, always pushovers for clever names, are embarked on what's likely to be the most memorable U.S. military engagement of the Nineties: Operation Phantom of the Opera.

It's a losing battle with a winning tune: *Masquerade. Paper faces on parade. Masquerade. Hide your face so the world will never find you.*

Having been forced to concede that many homosexuals have had outstanding careers in the armed forces, the defenders of the military ban now say that those gays would not have served our country well if they hadn't been camouflaged as heterosexuals. Unmasked gays, the ban's backers say, would destroy morale.

The argument, which usually mentions group showers, is all wet, especially since the Pentagon has dragged more gay people out of the closet than any other American institution.

Masquerade. You can fool any friend who ever knew you.

Regardless of whether the ban is lifted as President Clinton has promised, the military uniform of most gay men and lesbians is likely to continue to include a disguise: The last thing most of us gays want to do is come out in a hostile workplace.

It may be generations before most of the country learns, as General Dwight Eisenhower did with a jolt in World War II, that much of our military's might has a lavender tinge.

Eisenhower had ordered Sergeant Johnnie Phelps to root lesbians out of her battalion, according to Lillian Faderman's *Odd Girls and Twilight Lovers: A History of Lesbian Life in Twentieth-Century America.*

Phelps replied, "Sir, it would be unfair of me not to tell you, my name is going to head the list. . . . You should also be aware that you're going to have to replace all the file clerks, the section heads, most of the commanders and the motor pool. . . ."

Eisenhower: "Forget the order."

Unfortunately, the words "forget the ban" aren't yet being uttered by General Colin Powell and his braid-covered buddies.

But a counter-offensive is under way: Operation Broken Silence.

The most powerful weapon in the arsenal of those who consider gay people second-class citizens has always been silence. Labeling homosexuality "unspeakable" has kept lies from being scrutinized and gay people hidden. In such silence, injustice thrives.

For fifty years the Pentagon quietly expelled homosexuals and went to great lengths to avoid discussing that policy. As ban-supporting Senator Phil Gramm (R-Tex.), said, "I can assure you that the Joint Chiefs of Staff could have gone for an eternity without ever considering this problem."

The uproar during Clinton's first week in office was the sound of silence being shattered. It signaled the beginning of what amounts to a six-month diversity training workshop for the entire nation.

Such workshops often begin with participants being forced to list vile stereotypes, to say things almost no one wants to hear. The idea is that we can't rid ourselves of ingrained prejudices until we bring them to the surface and confront them.

So, now that the news media have broadcasted all the outrageous myths, those of us who are gay have an unprecedented opportunity to teach the truth. We can do that by breaking the silence about our own lives.

"Coming out to heterosexuals is perhaps the most powerful strategy lesbians and gay men have for attacking prejudice," says Gregory Herek, a researcher who studies attitudes toward gays.

A January 12–14 *New York Times* poll indicates attitudes can change profoundly once we drop our masks. Overall, 42 percent of the people surveyed wanted the gay ban lifted. That number leaped to 69 percent among folks with a gay relative or close friend.

While the military forces our brothers and sisters to wear a mask or face swift punishment, most of us in civilian life volunteer for closet duty.

Each of us holds a key to the freedom of all of us. Unlock the truth. Come out.

IGNORANCE IS THE GREATEST THREAT TO OPENING UP THE MILITARY TO GAYS

FEBRUARY 12, 1993

Shoot from the lip and ask questions later. That's standard operating procedure for much of Washington. It stopped surprising me long ago. But the loose talk the nation's missile-minders are trying to pass off as smarts these days makes me want to echo detective Philip Marlowe:

"My, my, my. Such a lot of guns around town and so few brains."

If the detective in the moody 1946 thriller *The Big Sleep* were pounding the pavement of the capital now, he'd be tripping over a lot of red herrings. The smelliest was tossed at President Clinton by General Colin Powell, the man who lately makes "military leadership" seem like an oxymoron.

Powell claims that lifting the ban on gays in the military would increase straight soldiers' risk of AIDS. His battle cry is now coming from Capitol Hill as well: "Since soldiers must be available to provide life-saving transfusions in combat, the military's walking blood bank would be endangered," said Senator Bob Smith (R-N.H.).

Gay = AIDS. It's a bogus equation long used to justify discrimination against people with AIDS as well as those of us who are gay.

As any good detective could discover, this is not the first time that Stalwarts of the Status Quo have tried to slow the progress of minorities by painting them as disease carriers.

Listen to the second-ranking Democrat on the Senate Armed Services Committee in 1948, Richard Russell of Georgia, argue against racially integrating the military:

"I submit that it is unfair to vote to compel a [white] boy . . . to serve against his will in an unsegregated unit where the chances for his innocently acquiring this dread disease of syphilis is nineteen times greater than it would be if he were permitted to serve only with members of his own race."

Unfortunately, such ignorance about sexually transmitted diseases continues to abound.

Can AIDS be spread by coughing or sneezing? "Yes," said 23 percent of active-duty military personnel in a poll the Pentagon released last September. Can it be spread by sharing eating utensils? "Yes," said 26 percent. By using public toilets? "Yes," said 12 percent. By mosquitoes? "Yes," said 28 percent.

Even though our troops have failed to learn the basics about AIDS, the disease and the virus that causes it have had "little impact on military operations," the General Accounting Office (GAO) found in 1990. The Department of Defense agreed, noting that less than one-tenth of 1 percent of its active-duty people are HIV-infected.

All this is despite the fact that as many as 200,000 gay people are now serving in the military, according to the GAO.

Unlike most of its civilian counterparts, the U.S. military reacted fairly quickly to the threat posed by AIDS. In 1985 it began rejecting recruits who tested positive for HIV.

The military then looked inward, testing everyone in its ranks. Those found to be infected may remain on active duty as long as their health permits. However, they must practice safer sex and inform sex partners of their condition. Otherwise, they can be prosecuted.

To safeguard the blood supply in battlefield situations, the military also requires all those about to be deployed overseas to have been tested recently and found HIV negative.

Despite these elaborate precautions, we hear warnings that openly gay soldiers would somehow jeopardize "buddy" transfusions. The number of times this emergency procedure was used in the Persian Gulf war? Zero.

AIDS isn't a gay disease. It isn't spread by sharing a fork or a latrine. The biggest threat to sexually active straight soldiers is ignorance. Yet Powell wants to rely on exclusion more than education to fight AIDS. Clearly, he hasn't done his detective work.

There's only one group in our society not known to have transmitted AIDS sexually. If Powell doesn't wise up, he might end up commanding the world's first all-lesbian army.

Chapter

5

———

SAVING DEB PRICE

"THE SOONER YOU CALL, THE BETTER CHANCE WE HAVE OF SAVING Deb Price."

What? Was a nutsy newsletter for misguided missionaries trying to rescue the gay columnist from the devilish delights of lesbianism? No, that wouldn't have been so surprising. The alarm actually was being sounded in a flyer distributed in northwestern New York State in an urgent campaign to keep Deb in the *Niagara Gazette*. (For a discussion of written warnings that Deb will toast, roast or fry in Hell, see Chapter 7.)

The Niagara Falls paper was running the Deb Price column as a one-month experiment in June of 1992. A month earlier, features editor Terry Murphy had spotted the column's debut on the Gannett News Service wire. She thought Deb's column was "terrific," "everything a gay column should be." And she had wanted to find a way to get it into her paper, if only for a short while. In an inspired moment, Murphy had persuaded her top editor to run the column in honor of Gay Pride Month, which marks the anniversary of the 1969 Stonewall rebellion.

Now June was drawing to a close and, as at most other papers, the initial reaction reaching the ears of the managing editor wasn't encouraging. "Our gay community is so closeted he wasn't getting any positive feedback," Murphy recalls. She and features reporter Judy Kay, who occasionally writes about gay topics, were getting positive calls about Deb's column from gay people afraid to call managing editor Rick Jensen even anonymously. They worried that he might recognize their voices.

Murphy's own homosexuality was a closely guarded secret. The thirty-three-year-old editor had told no one in her newsroom, except Kay. Deb's column had quickly become very important to Terry Murphy. "It just felt so good to read something I could relate to for a change," she says. "And I thought, 'If I feel like this, there are people out there who are just starving for this stuff.' I was also hoping that maybe straight people could read it and it would help them, that it would educate people. . . . There's nothing in the column that I wouldn't want my grandmother to read." Murphy was forced to have a heartfelt talk with herself: "It was, 'Okay, I want to keep this column. How far do I push it?' " Looking back, Murphy sees that while she was worrying about pushing the Deb Price column, the Deb Price column was pushing her. "Deb pushed me out of the closet," Murphy says of the columnist she had never actually met.

Murphy and Kay knew that it simply wasn't enough for gay readers to tell them that they wanted the column to run beyond June. The message had to go directly to Jensen. Frustrated, Murphy brainstormed with Kay about how to let gay men and lesbians know the importance of seizing the moment, if they wanted to keep a gay voice in their paper. Somehow they had to help readers understand that they could have a real impact on the direction of their paper. Together, Murphy and Kay hit upon the idea of creating and distributing a flyer. **"Support Deb Price—Our first gay columnist,"** it declared in large type. A copy of the first column that had appeared in the *Gazette* was reproduced on the front of the flyer. The back explained that Deb's column was running in June and described how to call the *Gazette* to voice support. "You will be calling an answering machine. You do not have to give your full name, although leaving a first name and the city or town you live in is helpful. . . . Her last column will appear June 28 if you don't let your opinion be known."

After paying a printshop to make hundreds of copies, Murphy handed them out at a gay-pride candlelight vigil in nearby Buffalo, where Niagara Falls folks usually must go to find gay activities. Soon, she says, her flyers were showing up all over northwestern New York. Murphy's backdoor, activist approach to tapping reader sentiment undoubtedly is enough to make more traditional editors shriek in pious horror. A creature of conventional journalism myself, I was floored when Murphy told me she directed the **"Save Gay Column"** flyer campaign. How unorthodox, how risky—and how brave. One more "how" springs to mind: How many people would put their careers on the line to push for something that they truly believe would help their town? Murphy contends she was just doing her job. "I just think I've got a responsibility to educate people about how a newspaper works," she says. "Our role was education, not persuasion. We didn't put a pen in anybody's hand."

While trying to educate gay people about her paper, Murphy was also trying to educate her paper's chief editor about gay people, especially his own gay readers. She recalls Jensen wondering aloud why, if gay people are so proud, they are afraid to have the *Gazette* publish their names on letters to the editor. The Niagara Falls paper, like most dailies, refuses to print letters without including the author's name. (Signed anti-gay letters were running in the *Gazette* fairly often.) To explain why something as mundane as signing a letter to the editor can be a high-risk venture for a gay person, Murphy came out, telling Jensen the price she's paid for honesty. "I said, 'I told my mother I was gay two years ago—and I haven't laid eyes on her since.' "

Murphy wishes her mother could accept her, but she knows it's more important that she's finally come to accept herself. Her childhood was nowhere near as traumatic as J. Ford Huffman's; the road didn't get rocky until she reached adulthood. Murphy started tripping over her sexuality. She dutifully dated men yet awkwardly kept falling for unavailable women. She refused to admit the implications of her feelings. Miserable, she took an overdose of tranquilizers in 1984. Even that flirtation with death at twenty-six failed to make her see her life clearly. Then, six years later, she happened to talk to the mother of a lesbian while vacationing in Florida. That conversation nudged Murphy into admitting to herself that she's gay. "When I finally came to terms with it, I felt like a weight had been lifted off my shoulders. As soon as I got back from vacation I got on the hot line, and within two days I was meeting lesbians," she says. Her life completed its turnaround when she met college professor Sally Weidler. "When I used to sleep with guys," Murphy says, "the next day I couldn't wait to leave their apartment. I would have gnawed my arm off to get out. But with her I wanted to stay."

Murphy certainly knows why colleagues and friends keep their closet doors locked from the inside. She just refuses to live that way any longer. Deb's column helped her stop taking paranoia to work. "She personally made me feel more proud of who I am," says Murphy, who posted Deb's publicity photo on her computer terminal at the *Gazette*. Feeling proud made Murphy dedicated to finding a way to keep sharing Deb's upbeat column with the extremely timid gay community of Niagara Falls, where even the town's handful of gay-rights activists are too closeted to use their last names in their own newsletter.

Every time I think about Murphy's campaign to reach beyond that community's defenses, I think of a *New Yorker* cover by cartoonist Charles Addams. A man in pajamas stands inside an apartment whose entrance is bolted and barred in half a dozen ways. Yet someone has managed to slip a valentine under his door.

All of Niagara Falls is in need of some loving attention. The falls themselves are as photogenic as ever. But visiting the economically depressed, blue-collar town long known as the (heterosexual) Honeymoon Capital of the World is like paying a call on Tennessee Williams' Blanche DuBois: All the glory is faded, out of style, sagging. "In a lot of ways, Niagara Falls lives in the past," notes Jensen, who pointed out how much more hush-hush being gay is in Niagara Falls than in progressive Rochester, New York. Very little about Niagara Falls encourages townsfolk—straight or gay—to let go of the stifling conservatism that makes every change seem frightening.

One of the town's few instruments of social change calls himself an "undercover activist." A physician in his late forties, he fears he'd lose his job, since he's not in private practice, if his homosexuality were not cloaked in secrecy. While Murphy was trying to instruct gay readers on how they could maintain their anonymity yet register support for a gay column, unbeknownst to her, Dr. Anonymous was launching his own flyer campaign to save Deb Price. He says that when he spotted Deb's column in the *Gazette,* he thought, "Oh, this is fantastic!" He was especially happy that her column was landing on Niagara Falls doorsteps along with the rest of the *Gazette.* That way, he says, people afraid to be seen buying a gay publication finally had access to information on gay issues.

A man of many words and even more action, Dr. Anonymous immediately assigned himself to the case when he heard Deb's column was in danger of being dropped by the *Gazette.* He produced a flyer and handed it out at a performance by the gay singing duo of Romanovsky & Phillips. Everywhere he went he told gay people to write to the *Gazette.* He feared they would procrastinate or forget.

How could he ensure that letters really got written? Murphy stopped short of putting pens in people's hands. Dr. Anonymous had no such qualms about giving himself over completely to saving Deb Price. So he shifted strategies. Swinging by a stationery store, he bought several kinds of paper and various colors of pens. He didn't simply want the *Gazette* to get an armload of letters. He wanted the newspaper to get an armload of different-looking letters, which wouldn't appear to be part of a concerted effort. He gathered up his supplies and headed first to a gay picnic. *Gazette* readers wrote eighteen letters on the spot, and Dr. Anonymous pasted on the stamps.

Later, outside a Buffalo bookstore that carries the *Gazette,* the good doctor approached two lesbians about showing their support for the column. Dr. Anonymous loves to talk, so I'll just let him describe his successful operation: "And one of the women was a little more frightened. And her friend was like, 'No, no, we can do this.' And I kind of demonstrated how she could be an activist without being awkward. And we talked about things she could say. And she writes it out, and her friend is encouraging her to do this. And then she says, 'But I can't sign my name.' And I say, 'Right. You don't have to. You write 'A Friend in Buffalo' or 'A Lesbian Reader of Your Paper.' And she did it. And when she was finished—I would love to have a movie of this because her body language was completely different, just like 'I've done something!' " Indeed she had. As for his own energetic efforts, Dr. Anonymous says, "I just wanted to make a difference."

Soon the emergency attempts to save Deb Price were felt inside the *Gazette* newsroom. The response "really educated Rick [Jensen]," Murphy believes. "He would come in on Monday morning and the answering machine would be full of messages about the column," she recalls. A P-FLAG mom telephoned a local radio station to praise the column when Jensen appeared on a call-in show. And while Jensen received what he terms "a trickle" of letters damning the column, dozens of letters of praise poured in. A typical one, signed "Rich & Jerry," told Jensen: "We were not readers of the *Gazette,* being from Buffalo, until you began running Miss Price's column on Sundays. We wish to thank you for being open to new things and seeing our need to be represented in the local mainline media. The column gives our community a source of accurate, helpful, and sometimes lifesaving information that is not otherwise available."

Rick Jensen, a straight white male who probably cringes at being described that way, was in his late thirties when he authorized the column's trial run. Looking back, he says, "I was agreeable to run the column for a month to see what sort of reaction we got—not so much the negative, because I was prepared for that. I wanted to see what sort of positive: Is this something that people, especially the gay community, were looking for? And, frankly, I was surprised by the number of letters I got saying, 'I'm interested.' My guess is that probably word got around and people said, 'Well, gee, if you want to keep it, you better send a letter.' So there might have been a little bit of a letter campaign, but in my mind that was fine. . . . After the response, I said, 'What the heck. We'll just do it on a weekly basis.' And the rest is history." Niagara Falls did save Deb Price.

"Her column filled a void, a huge void," Jensen adds. "If you ask me how many people are gay in Niagara Falls, I don't have the foggiest idea. But, just based on letters, there are some people out there. And whether we're talking one hundred or five thousand, there's a constituency that this paper needs to serve."

Jensen kept running Deb's column to please gay readers, but he's personally been changed by getting a chance to see life from a gay perspective. "It's opened my eyes," he says. The senior prom column especially touched him. He now wonders who in his high school class was gay.

TO "SAVE DEB PRICE," THE QUIET, CAUTIOUS GAY COMMUNITY OF Niagara Falls managed to speak up and make its existence known as never before to its hometown newspaper. What happened in Niagara Falls was extraordinary. But, in city after city, gay people of all ages have rushed to embrace Deb's column. They integrate the column and its messages into their lives in a myriad of ways: They clip it, mail it, read it over long-distance, hitch computer rides for it on the information highway, take it to class, lobby newspaper editors to begin running it, rally behind it, come out in reaction to it and let it point them toward living more openly. Hungry for the column's positive approach, gay readers also cherish it as tangible evidence that we are part of the mainstream and are progressing toward full equality. Neither Deb nor I has ever been good about keeping up with personal correspondence. Unanswered letters from dear friends gather dust. So we've been awed by the many people who diligently send the column to their out-of-town pals. At a party in Rochester, New York, a member of the Eastman Kodak gay employees' group confided to me that he had a special reason for being pleased that more papers are picking up Deb's column. He could cut back on the size of his weekly mailings.

Gay readers' hearty, often deeply emotional possessiveness toward the column is especially gratifying to Deb because she wants gay men and lesbians all across the nation to see her column as theirs. (Before her own *San Jose Mercury News* started using the column, a transplanted New Yorker wrote, "My friend Amy has sent me all your columns to date. I am thrilled that the Rochester paper is running this column about us and our lives. Gee, we don't seem so scary after all, do we?") Deb tries to help gay people feel a bit more proud, a bit more powerful and substantially more connected to their daily papers. "The design of the column," Deb says, "was always to empower gay people and to give them the ammunition and information they need to protect themselves and affirm their lives." There are many wonderful things about being gay, but in this stridently heterosexual society it's easy to feel disenfranchised, alienated, estranged. Through her column, Deb wants to help gay people feel a greater sense of belonging, of ownership, of having someone on their side. And by showing that courage and action are just as much everyday commodities as fear and passivity, her column helps others find their own voices.

Deb and I have been astounded by the number of gay people who've told us with almost a religious fervor that they save her column every week and never go on vacation without arranging to have the column put aside for them. Clearly, for a great many readers, the column satisfies a psychological craving, not just a need for gay information. While Deb's words matter, of course, the fact that they come to gay readers in mainstream publications that have long been a source of pain is, perhaps, just as important. Quite a few gay people have told us that reading the same words in a gay publication would not strike such an emotional chord.

For many gay readers, Deb's column offers validation and encouragement not easily found elsewhere. If all a gay person ever hears is that "if you come out, you'll lose your job, you'll lose your friends, you'll lose your family," why risk trying to enjoy the freedom of speech that most Americans take for granted? Deb shows readers the joy of leaving secretiveness behind. And while never flinching from describing the distance between today's gay reality and truly fair treatment, she also tries to help her gay readers see the leaps that have already been made and how each of us can work to close the gap. In letter after letter, fiercely loyal gay readers tell Deb her positive, yet un-Pollyannaish approach is "refreshing." It's an approach that often inspires a desire to cling to copies of Deb's column as a talisman.

Affection for Deb's column inspired Russ Perry of La Quinta, California, to become a virtual one-man publicity department for it. Russ, a semi-retired public relations consultant, discovered Deb's column after moving to the Palm Springs area. He immediately took it upon himself to widen the column's reach by mailing it to friends scattered around the country and by talking it up locally. Thanks to Perry, the column gained a tiny foothold in Europe: He regularly sends it to a gay friend in Louisville, Kentucky, who forwards it to a mutual friend in England. Closer to home, Perry makes sure his gay acquaintances are aware a gay column runs in *The Desert Sun*. "I think I've increased the weekly readership," he says with considerable pride, "because I say, 'Wasn't Price's column excellent this week?' And they'll give me a blank stare. And I'll say, 'Well, you're missing out. Every Tuesday. Look for it.' "

One Tuesday, Perry was horrified not to find Deb's column anywhere in *The Desert Sun*. "That was like the shot heard 'round the world—when the column wasn't there!" he says. When Perry and other readers called to protest, the *Sun*'s editors suddenly got a real sense of how many people take a very personal interest in the column running every week. "I said, 'What have you done—given in to the pressure of those goddamned bigots?' " Perry recalls. "And they said, 'No, no, no, no, no. There wasn't room today. It'll be in tomorrow.' "

The meticulous Perry, now in his early seventies, treats the column like a beloved grandchild. He was outraged to discover the *Sun* was running the wrong mailing address for Deb. "You are misprinting the ZIP!! The correct one is 22209-1000," he scolded the editors. "We all make mistakes, but I really find this to be one which is gross!"

When the inevitable hostile letters about Deb's column started cropping up on *The Desert Sun*'s editorial page, Perry began a counteroffensive. Together with his friend Dal Turner, he wrote three letters to the *Sun* under a pseudonym. (Neither of them, Perry explains, wants kooks calling on the phone.) Then Perry drafted four more letters to the editor and had a woman a little older than himself sign them. My favorite of those declares, "It would appear that if ever there was to be a candidate for martyrdom in the publishing world, Deb Price is the nominee. I am happy to note, however, that in spite of tying her to numerous stakes surrounded by wooden faggots, her clothing refuses to ignite! Thank you, *Desert Sun,* for taking the heat and saving her."

Perry was taking the heat for being gay years before Deb was born. During World War II, he was a Navy hospital corpsman. He was called back to active duty when hostilities began in Korea. In 1953 he was stationed in Corona, California, and having an affair with another serviceman. They discreetly rendezvoused at a Los Angeles hotel. One morning they were awakened at 6:30 by a knock on their door. Navy investigators had uncovered two more homosexuals. Perry's naval career was over. He received an undesirable discharge.

Perry, who says he enjoys reading about gay history in Deb's column, shares his own military history with no trace of bitterness. Although he was drawn to the Palm Springs area partly because so many year-round residents are gay—30 percent, he estimates—and fairly visible, Perry looks back to a more clandestine era with some nostalgia. "I often ponder the total benefits we have gained with closet doors removed and a gay lifestyle being such a generally accepted fact," he once wrote Deb, adding that "the mystique of the late Thirties and Forties, etc., was fun and in many ways a lot more interesting and provocative. It kept you on your toes without ballet classes!"

These days Perry stays on his toes by trying to keep Deb's column safe from harm. From the very beginning, the column has brought out protective feelings in gay people delighted to have a gay voice in their paper and fearful that opposition might silence it. Soon after the column debuted in *The Detroit News,* Deb told Michael Hodges she was upset about the volume of hate mail the *News* was receiving. Hodges, the gay reporter who had prodded Bob Giles into adding sexual orientation to the paper's anti-bias policy, swung into action: "I just called up every queer I knew in the state of Michigan and told them about the column—most of them weren't aware of it yet—and tried to explain that newspaper editors and publishers will be looking at it all around the country and that if it fails, it'll kill the idea that there might be a legitimate place for a gay voice."

Hodges then typed up a handbill asking people to contact the

News in support of the column. He distributed copies in book-stores and gay bars in Detroit and nearby Ann Arbor. Because Hodges knew that his publisher had staked his reputation on mainstream America's first gay column, he wasn't taking the kind of professional risks that Terry Murphy did a month later in Niagara Falls with her secret flyer campaign. But that doesn't make Hodges' rescue mission any less terrific. "What I did was small," he claims, "but it was fun—I'll tell you that. It gave me this real wonderful sense of, goddamnit, being a lot more out than other people are willing to be and pushing for something."

The column's success at the *News* has turned out to be important not just for the message it sends to newspapers outside Detroit but for the way it has changed journalism in Detroit. "The column," Hodges reports, "has helped other gay journalists in town be more aggressive in pushing gay stories and arguing about their importance and, in some cases, coming all the way out."

After reading the sagas of Michael Hodges, Terry Murphy, Russ Perry and Dr. Anonymous, some people might think that letters of support for Deb's column are somehow less sincere, less authentic, than the column's hate mail. In fact, none of their efforts would have been necessary if gay and gay-friendly people were anywhere near as practiced as anti-gay people at orchestrating responses. For decades right-wingers have been schooled in the importance of acting swiftly and in concert whenever they feel threatened. When a character in the popular national cartoon strip *For Better or for Worse* announced that he was gay, eighty Oklahoma readers responded by canceling their subscriptions to the *Muskogee Daily Phoenix,* according to editorial page editor Shirley Ragsdale. Twenty-five subscribers soon returned to the paper on their own. When the paper began calling the rest to ask whether they were ready to renew, Ragsdale says the answer was: "We don't know because our pastor hasn't told us if it's okay to subscribe to your paper." The feisty Ragsdale adds, "That kind of thinking is behind the [negative] reaction to the column."

Speaking out publicly in favor of something gay remains more difficult in this society than speaking out against it. Seeing gay readers care enough about having a gay column in their family paper to find the courage to defend it or push it or save it has been quite an emotional experience for both Deb and me. Deb was feeling quite embattled in mid-1992 when, mixed in with the burn-in-Hell letters, she found a copy of the **"Save Gay Column"** flyer. She didn't know who had created the handout. She just knew that it gave her a much-needed bear hug, one that would sustain her on days when her own fortitude waned.

THROUGH THE COLUMN, DEB DISPENSES QUITE A FEW BEAR HUGS herself. She tries to encourage gay readers to feel more comfortable with themselves. Despite their non-confrontational tone, what her weekly columns don't encourage is complacency. "There's a call to action in every one of them," notes Jeffrey Montgomery, president of Detroit's gay-rights Triangle Foundation. One of Deb's most successful rallying cries was a one-sentence aside tucked into her saga about the day-long adventure she and I had searching for signs of gay reality in Perry, Georgia, hometown of Sam Nunn, then chairman of the Senate Armed Services Committee. We explored Perry in the summer of 1993, just after Nunn thwarted President Clinton's less than half-hearted attempt to lift the gay ban.

When an established order—such as the military ban—is built on lies, distortions, and false stereotypes, simply sharing factual information becomes a subversive act. Every time another person learns the truth about homosexuality a sledgehammer slams into the foundation of anti-gay discrimination. After Deb and I discovered that Nunn's hometown contained almost nothing that could help fair-minded heterosexuals understand gay people, Deb targeted the Perry public library on August 6, 1993. Send a book, she urged.

Gay readers, sometimes fretful about the potential hazards a high-profile gay columnist faces, embraced that suggestion as a constructive way to stand in solidarity alongside Deb and me in unfriendly territory. Sending a book was, in part, a symbolic way for them to journey to Perry with us.

Columnists rarely cause a stir that spills over onto news pages. Yet two months after Deb's shelf-filling proposition, a headline at the top of the Sunday paper in Macon, Georgia, declared: "Perry library getting plenty of books on homosexuality." (Macon is thirty miles north of Perry and happens to be my hometown.) The article in *The Macon Telegraph* began, "PERRY—The public library here has received a steady stream of books related to homosexuality after a columnist on gay issues wrote that U.S. Senator Sam Nunn's hometown is blissfully out of touch with the reality of gay lifestyles."

Library director Judith Golden was quoted as saying, "We have received material from various parts of the United States—California, Minnesota, New Orleans, Detroit, Alabama, Atlanta. . . . Everywhere her column has appeared. . . .' "

In targeting the Perry library, Deb had twin goals: making it easier for fair-minded heterosexuals in one small town to understand gay people and helping gay people see that each of us can have a positive impact on the institutions that now misrepresent our lives. The very institutions that should be educating people about our changing world—schools, libraries, churches, newspapers, courts, legislatures—are letting down everyone, straight or gay. Deb's message is that we don't have to accept this, that we can encourage change. Instead of simply getting angry and frustrated over something like support for Clinton's "don't ask, don't tell" military policy, we can try to bring about change through education. And just as Dr. Anonymous nudged a nervous lesbian toward activism, Deb helped her readers see themselves not as victims of an anti-gay society, but as people who have the power to make our world a bit more gay-friendly. We can claim that power through an act as simple as donating a library book.

Having grown up in middle Georgia, I was dubious that gay books generated by a columnist for a Yankee newspaper would be welcomed by the Perry library. Visions of garbage dumpsters danced in my head. Turns out, I seriously underestimated Judith Golden, director of all three public libraries in Houston County. She says she first learned of Deb's send-a-book column through a letter from a Michigan woman, who "thanked us for not having any gay material—which wasn't true."

Then scores of books began to arrive. Golden kept at least thirty-five gay books, adding them to the collections in Perry, Centerville, and Warner Robins. On the shelves went enough good books to give anyone a solid grounding in what it really means to be gay: *One Teenager in Ten; Culture of Desire; Pink Triangle;* Congressman Barney Frank's *Speaking Frankly; Your Questions Answered About Homosexuality; Homophobia; Now That You Know; Consenting Adults; On Being Gay;* several AIDS books, including *You Can Do Something About AIDS;* three works on lesbian poet Emily Dickinson (her collected poems, *Comic Power in Emily Dickinson* and *Rowing in Eden: Re-reading Emily Dickinson),* and assorted paperbacks by gay authors. (Before Deb's library column, the two thousand people of Centerville, Georgia, had only one AIDS book in their public library.) Deb's readers sent the Perry library subscriptions to *Southern Voice,* Atlanta's gay newspaper, and *The Advocate,* a national gay magazine. Golden welcomed those as well.

"I've gotten some real nice things," she says, adding that her library already had quite a few gay novels. "I always loved it when somebody sent something [gay] that we already had and I can write back to say, 'Thank you very much, but I already have this.' " There were important gaps, though. "Where we didn't have any material, when we went back and looked, was for a young person. And we did get a couple of good things, one of which disappeared the second day we put it out. *One Teenager in Ten* was the name of that one," Golden recalls. The Perry library has since bought two books on human sexuality, including homosexuality, that are geared toward teenagers, she adds.

Donated gay books that were duplicates or in bad shape were turned over to the Friends of the Library to be sold. That still got them into the hands of Houston County residents with too few sources of gay-friendly material. The Friends of the Library also received the bulk of the books that Deb's detractors sent to Perry. Most of those were conservative political works; none dealt solely with homosexuality. One reader horrified by the notion of the Perry library getting more up-to-date on gay issues contributed fifty Bibles. Golden kept three.

Golden, who describes herself as "a pretty liberal person," believes her libraries are better stocked because readers responded to Deb's call to action. "We certainly did get some books that we would not otherwise have purchased. We have a real small book budget." When people are not asking for something, her libraries don't buy it. (Of course, many of the people most in need of gay facts—whether gay teenagers, gay elders, or the parents of someone who has just come out—are probably the ones least likely to tell a librarian what they're looking for. That's why those of us no longer afraid to be associated with homosexuality need to get acquainted with our local libraries and our local librarians. We need to ask the library to purchase specific books—or contribute them ourselves.)

Golden didn't mind that the Perry library was briefly in the spotlight. What did upset her were the virulently anti-gay letters she received from people who called themselves religious. "I'm a very religious person," she says. "And maybe it's the New Testament versus the Old Testament, but I don't think He would approve of some of the way they write." Golden adds, "Sometimes you know why the religious wars were the bloodiest in history—because of what people will do in the name of religion."

When Deb and I had visited Perry, we couldn't find anyone who admitted knowing gay people. The resulting column would have been different if we'd met Golden then. "I have been friends with lots of people and then found out later they were gay," she says. "And it's never personally made a difference to me."

After Deb's educate-Nunn's-hometown column generated so much publicity, Golden ran into the senator. "I saw him at Kiwanis [Club] one day. And he told me he was glad he was helping put books in the library," she says with a chuckle.

Golden, who is definitely a good sport, wants to add at least one more gay book to Perry's collection. After graciously drawing up a list for me of the contributions she's kept, she enclosed them in a letter that ended: "Good luck with your book. Remember our autographed copy."

We'll remember to send that copy, just as we'll remember the Southern hospitality Golden showed to gay books from out of town. And we'll not soon forget the readers who responded to Deb's call by sharing a favorite gay book or two with the people of Perry.

AGAIN AND AGAIN, DEB HAS ENCOURAGED GAY READERS TO WORK to close the gap of misunderstanding that so often separates gay

and straight Americans. Some responded by becoming book do-
nors; others by incorporating Deb's work into college courses.

Wiggsy Sivertsen keeps the nickname left over from her wig-
gly childhood because her staid Norwegian first name just doesn't
fit. Now in her late fifties, Sivertsen teaches an upper-division
sociology course on homosexuality at San Jose State University.
Every semester four dozen students—90 percent of them straight;
80 percent of them female—take Alternative Lifestyles. "What I
learn from them, which just hurts my heart tremendously, is that
they know *nothing* about discrimination. Their basic core level of
understanding of prejudice is so incredibly limited that it's amazing to me," Sivertsen says.

That's one reason she saves Deb's columns and escorts them
into her classroom. "This is a very multi-cultural campus, so I try
to show the similarities of discrimination in all the communities.
Deb's articles oftentimes allow me to do that," she explains. "It's
kind of like having a second teacher in the classroom."

Sivertsen can quite literally see her students become more
comfortable with the subject of homosexuality by watching what
they do with their textbook: *Looking at Gay and Lesbian Life,* edited by Warren Blumenfeld and Diane Raymond. At first, some
students try to keep the book out of sight or cover it with brown
paper. But by the end of the semester, many casually read it on the
bus without caring who sees the title. "They are always really
proud of themselves when they are able to do that," Sivertsen
reports.

She and Deb partly teach by example. By appearing week
after week in the students' *San Jose Mercury News,* Deb's column
"really jars the stereotype that you can't be successful and be out. I
think that stereotype is maintained by straight people as well as gay
and lesbian people," Sivertsen says. For the gay students in the
class, she adds, Deb becomes "a mentor." Sivertsen herself is quite
a role model: a full professor who has been openly gay for twenty-
five years.

She learned through firsthand experience that closets protect
clothes, not people. She tried to keep her sexual orientation completely private while working, immediately after graduate school,
at a day-care treatment center for schizophrenic children. When

the center's administrators discovered Sivertsen's lesbianism, they fired her. "They thought I was going to molest the children," she says with fury. A quarter century later her outrage that homosexuality can be mindlessly equated with pedophilia remains undimmed. "I told them, 'Man, you've got perverted ideas about children. And they certainly aren't mine. It would never have occurred to me.'" Sivertsen was determined not to repeat that horrible job experience. "So when I came to the university [in San Jose], I insisted that they hire me as an out lesbian. I'd lived in the closet and thought I was protected and I realized, 'This is nonsense. I'm not!'" She now has tenure, a word that really does mean protection.

GAY PEOPLE LIKE WIGGSY SIVERTSEN HAVE TAUGHT DEB AND ME THAT courage grows when shared. We're gratified that some readers have learned the same lesson from us.

As executive director of the city's gay community center, Jan Stevenson couldn't be much more openly gay than she is in Detroit. She isn't from Detroit, though. She's from Bedford, a small Ohio town just outside Cleveland. And in the summer of '93 Stevenson, then thirty-eight, was torn over whether to go back for her twentieth high school reunion and take her partner of seven years. Two years before, Stevenson recalls, "My lover had gone to her high school reunion—gone closeted and had a horrible time. It was really traumatic." Her lover, cardiologist Cathy McGowan, was quite nervous about the idea of accompanying Stevenson to Bedford. But the two of them had read about how Deb and I went—with some trepidation—to my twentieth high school reunion in Macon and had a wonderful time. That column "had a big impact on me. Having that article there was just a nice push," Stevenson recalls. She told her partner, "This will be okay," that they should go to the reunion together. "And we did. And our experience was very similar to yours. . . . It was great!"

Courage is an excellent navigator. And letting courage choose the road to take becomes easier with practice. Deb finds that writing a gay column constantly challenges her to confront her fears—both personal and professional—and then try to move beyond them. During the first nine months of her column, the too-hot potato for Deb was religion. She was afraid to touch it. She knew that the hostility directed at her as a gay columnist reflected prejudice, misunderstanding and, yes, fear, but she also knew that it came to her gift-wrapped in Bible verses. When foes of the column wrote about saving Deb Price, sometimes their words were gentle, but far more often they were venomous. (If we had ten dollars for every time someone mentioned Deb's name and Leviticus in the same sentence . . .) Yet Deb gradually realized that she could no longer in good conscience yield the entire subject of religion and homosexuality to the Jerry Falwells of the world.

Deb and I both grew up in the Christian church: Deb's father was an Episcopal priest; I was in a Presbyterian choir for a dozen years. We'd been raised to sing the praises of a God of love. That certainly wasn't the kind of God that we heard about in Deb's hate mail. We knew that the real message of the Bible was being distorted beyond recognition. Deb resolved to overcome her anxiety, really study the Bible, learn about the great spiritual revival among gay people and write about what she found.

Everywhere Deb's column appears, gay and gay-friendly people rise to its defense. Helping those readers better arm themselves against religious attacks was, in part, a way of saying thanks. Without the support and encouragement that she receives in letters from around the country, Deb would never have had the courage to challenge the deepest beliefs of her angriest critics.

One of the most difficult columns Deb has written—certainly the one that generated the most mail, pro and con—examined head-on how the Bible has been misused over the centuries to try to justify prejudice. Once a particular prejudice recedes, the verses that had been quoted to support it tend to be reinterpreted or ignored. Deb's Bible column was published on August 20, 1993. Six months earlier, she had written about religion for the first time, describing a sanctuary we found on a trip to Dallas. For us, that journey marked the beginning of a spiritual awakening.

Chapter

6

COLUMNS

FEBRUARY 19–JUNE 25, 1993

GAY SOULS FIND
A TRUE SANCTUARY IN THE BUCKLE
OF THE BIBLE BELT

FEBRUARY 19, 1993

I believe in traveling light. To Joyce that means she'd better do the packing.

She reluctantly let me pack for our recent weekend in Texas because she was running late. But to make sure that whatever I left behind wasn't essential, she zipped her cowboy boots into our suitcase before heading to work.

We're talking about a woman whose response to being in the doghouse with me is to play Hank Williams: *My hair's still curly and my eyes are still blue. Why don't you love me like you used to do?* So, her response to the prospect of a stopover in Dallas was to extract a promise that we could go country-and-western dancing.

We did find a terrific women's bar, which even had a boot

polisher who made Joyce's battered boots shine and her feet feel like they'd had a massage. And we discovered some spirit-lifting music, but it didn't come out of a Saturday night jukebox.

It came Sunday morning from the choir, orchestra and energized congregation of Dallas' thousand-member Metropolitan Community Church (MCC): *When morning gilds the skies, my heart awaking cries, may Jesus Christ be praised!*

There, in a beautiful light-filled room in a six-week-old building in the Buckle of the Bible Belt, we found a true sanctuary. And we felt something neither of us expected to ever feel—separately or as a couple—in a house of organized religion: welcome.

The Dallas church that began twenty-three years ago when twelve people gathered to worship in a private home is now the largest congregation in the predominantly gay Metropolitan Community Church, which has 235 churches worldwide.

That congregation, which proudly dedicates its $3 million church building this month, was forced to meet for years in what senior minister Michael Piazza called "a glow-in-the-dark pink office building with nine-foot ceilings, a flat floor and folding chairs with whoopee cushions. . . . The space was designed for 280 people, but 650 people came to church each week to listen to a service they couldn't hear and watch worship they couldn't see."

They were drawn, no doubt, by the way the church lives up to the vision expressed in its hymnal: "a community of hope proclaiming God's inclusive love; removing barriers to faith; and empowering all people to grow in grace toward wholeness."

Even in its stained-glass symbols, the Dallas MCC reaches out to women and men, people of all races, gays and straights, the disabled, the Spanish-speaking. And although the church has lost five hundred members to AIDS, the voices that lift up toward the new, vaulted ceiling make a really joyful noise.

"Every time I leave the place I'm walking on air," said founding member Phil Johnson.

Joyce and I felt the same way after hearing a sermon on commitment. Jesus tells us, the Reverend Piazza said, to "take the vows and promises you make to one another seriously." Even if you can't legally marry, he continued, "mutual, mature and authentic love takes root and grows in the soil of commitment."

The minister then asked every committed couple to stand together and hold hands. "Bless these couples with genuine love," he prayed as his own partner stood with him.

Never before in our seven years together had Joyce and I received such support for our relationship. Our souls felt massaged, our hearts awakened, our burdens shared.

Jesus never condemned same-sex love. Yet most Christian denominations do. That has forced countless religious gay men and lesbians to travel too light, to leave behind their church homes simply to be true to themselves.

But now there are a thousand tongues to sing praise in Dallas for the chance to worship together without masking our glorious diversity. Out of common brick and mortar a people of remarkable faith have built a Cathedral of Hope.

———

For information on MCC, call (213) 464-5100.

GAY RADIO GIVES A SIGNAL THAT IT'S OKAY TO BE A BIRD OF A DIFFERENT FEATHER

FEBRUARY 26, 1993

For failing to fit society's expectations, the youngster was judged defective, ridiculed, assaulted. "Leave him alone!" said the mother. "He's not bothering anyone."

"Yes, but he's too big and queer! . . . So he has to be pushed around."

After being pushed around for quite a few pages, Hans Christian Andersen's "Ugly Duckling" has an intellectual breakthrough: Not only does he not look like a duck or quack like a duck, he's not a duck.

Most of us who are gay have relived the young swan's story: We know the loneliness of feeling as if we were born in the wrong nest. And we know it can take a while to realize you're a swan when all your friends and neighbors are birds of a different feather.

But instead of freeing us, the realization at fourteen or forty that we're simply gay—not defective heterosexuals—often at first deepens our sense of isolation. After all, how do you find other swans in downtown Detroit or the oil fields of Oklahoma?

Los Angeles radio show producer Greg Gordon recalls feeling fearful and alone before he came to appreciate his homosexuality.

"I was convinced that everybody knew about me by some physical trait they could see," he says. "I thought I was the only one."

When we feel we're the only one, we can't connect with people who've already gone through the process of accepting themselves. Fear keeps us from picking up a gay newspaper, calling a gay hot line or even checking out a helpful library book. We want a gay friend but haven't the slightest idea of where to find one. We feel cooped up in a world where we don't fit in, but we don't know how to take flight.

Nearly five years ago, Gordon found a way to reach into the closets and countrysides where gays are painfully isolated: gay radio.

He started *This Way Out,* a weekly half-hour show of news and commentary that now airs on seventy radio stations in six countries.

"The consistent tone of the program is a message in itself," says Gordon, the show's co-host. "Anybody who tunes in to the show is going to get a positive portrait of gay and lesbian life in all its diversity."

Those who tune in are often older gays in rural areas or young people who feel they can't talk to their parents or teachers about being gay.

One seventeen-year-old in rural Missouri, for example, wrote that the program is "like finding an oasis in the middle of the desert, the desert being a tiny Midwest town. . . . The only thing for gays here is the highway to leave this hellhole and *This Way Out.*"

Another youth from Pomona, California, who signed his letter "a gay fan," told of being teased at school. "I listen to your program every Sunday with my earphones so nobody will hear me listening," he wrote.

Openly gay voices are seldom aired by the nation's privately owned stations. But thanks to public radio, there are about forty local gay programs around the country. If your car radio can't pick up one of their signals, an inexpensive shortwave can.

And now KGAY—it's "all gay, all day"—is available to anyone with a C-band home satellite dish. The twenty-four-hour-a-day, Denver-based station airs music by gay and gay-friendly artists. It also has live call-in segments and interviews with entertainers.

"We get a lot of calls from military people who are glad we're on the airwaves," says programming director Vickie Dee. "And a lot from people from small towns . . . who have no way to talk to gay people, to be part of the community."

No matter how shy, gay people no longer need to feel alone. Now gay radio enables its flock of listeners to share the ultimate exhilaration of the young swan by discovering we're not such rare birds after all.

———

For information on This Way Out, write P.O. Box 38327, Los Angeles, CA 90038.

BABY STEPS CAN LEAD
TO GIANT GAINS WHEN TEACHERS
COME OUT AT THEIR SCHOOLS

MARCH 5, 1993

I s she in the closet? The question makes being gay sound like a high-stakes game of Sardines—either you're crammed into an overcrowded hiding place or you're visible to the world. But for most of us, the coming-out process is more like playing Mother May I: a lot of hesitant baby steps a few giant steps and a couple of playmates equally unsure of their footing.

For gay teachers, the scariest step often is the one that bridges the chasm they've dug to separate their professional and personal lives. Most fear losing their credibility or careers. "People wouldn't be able to see beyond my lesbian identity to see me as a good teacher," a closeted teacher told researcher Pat Griffin.

Special education teacher Mary Lorenz of Northampton, Massachusetts, recalls years of clamming up whenever conversation in the faculty lounge turned to life beyond the schoolhouse walls. "I was always very, very careful," she says. "I never made up stories or changed pronouns, but I was reticent. I definitely felt isolated."

Lorenz and a dozen other Massachusetts educators found the courage to integrate the two halves of their lives during a fifteen-month research project designed by Griffin, a University of Massachusetts education professor.

When Griffin first met them, many of the thirteen were trying to be Superteacher. "They just knocked themselves out to create a reputation that was above reproach," Griffin said. Yet their hard work failed to banish the terror "that they'll be accused either of molestation or recruitment just by being gay or lesbian," she found.

Such fears had long kept them quiet about anti-gay remarks and AIDS, even though they instinctively felt a duty to educate their students and fellow teachers.

"The conflict between concealing and revealing their lesbian and gay identities was as much a part of every school day as were lesson plans and faculty meetings," Griffin writes in *Coming Out of the Classroom Closet,* a collection of essays edited by Karen M. Harbeck.

Griffin's own life changed when she realized that "I'm never not going to be scared and I'm just going to have to do stuff in spite of being scared." Now she believes "gay people have a responsibility to always be on their boundary of comfort. Maybe you don't feel you can go over it, but you ought to be on the edge of it."

The thirteen educators in her project included a principal, a librarian, and a guidance counselor, as well as classroom teachers. In the beginning, none was publicly out at school or completely closeted elsewhere. By the end, through positive reinforcement, all of them had taken steps—whether giant or baby-sized—toward openness at school, all felt more effective professionally and none had suffered job repercussions.

At first, nine of the thirteen said being gay had nothing to do with being an educator. "I don't think of myself as a gay teacher," one said. "I'm just a teacher who happens to be gay."

But as the met together month after month, they realized how much energy they devoted to compartmentalizing their lives. And they began to see ways that being gay was an asset to them as educators by, for example, helping them identify with students who feel "different."

Gradually, "I'm out at school" stopped seeming like a true/false question. Instead, they saw multiple choices, which they expressed at a gay-pride parade. Marching inside a yellow cloth school bus marked "Gay and Lesbian Educators," some members of the group partially hid their faces while others were completely out.

Nancy Hoff, a high school shop teacher, recalls that the group's bravery helped her "to go to the next steps—little steps of being bolder at school and hiding less, starting to use my partner's name, and talking about my life."

Thanks to the strides she made while in Griffin's group, Hoff felt free to take her partner to the prom that she chaperoned as senior adviser. Then, taking one more step in a round of Truth or Consequences, they danced.

In the game of life, example can be the best teacher: Homosexuality is nothing to hide.

THE MARCH OF TIME
KEEPS ADVANCING HARVEY MILK'S
MESSAGE OF FREEDOM

MARCH 12, 1993

Dinnertime has become the coming-out hour in our house. The telephone rings, a dating service pitch begins and Joyce interrupts with "No, thank you. I'm gay."

Ignoring my shouts of gratuitous advice, like: "Tell them you're in a long-term, committed, monogamous relationship and don't want to be called about a lesbian dating service either!" Joyce politely hangs up and comes back to the table knowing Harvey Milk would be proud.

San Francisco Supervisor Milk, who managed to have both a sense of history and a sense of humor, strongly believed that gay people need to come out not only to Mother and Dad but to the butcher, baker and candlestick maker, to every colleague and acquaintance.

In the late Seventies, when gay teachers were under siege in California and Anita Bryant was crusading against gay civil rights in Dade County, Florida, Milk banged his fist on millions of closet doors:

Come out. It's a civic duty, he lectured. Come out. It's a political necessity, not just a personal decision, he declared.

"We must destroy the myths once and for all, shatter them, continue to speak out," Milk said at a San Francisco rally in June 1978. "And most importantly, every gay person must come out. As difficult as it is, you must tell your immediate family . . . You must tell your friends . . . You must tell the people you work with."

Come out and tell the truth about gay lives, Milk pleaded. Freedom is too enormous to be slipped under a closet door.

Part of Milk's message, his friend Pat Norman remembers, was that "movement and change do not come without pain. So what if it hurts? . . . If you don't move, you're going to be in pain much longer than if you're part of solving the misconceptions."

At the June rally, Milk called on gay men and lesbians everywhere to get moving, to march on Washington in 1979. Milk never made it to that march. He was assassinated on November 27, 1978.

"His legacy is that he gave us hope that the [gay] community could have a say in the way we were treated, that we had control over our own destinies," says Scott Smith, Milk's longtime lover and business partner.

After the Supreme Court ruled that the constitutional right to privacy doesn't extend to gay people, hundreds of thousands of us marched on Washington in 1987.

"Eighty-seven was about digging in our heels and saying, 'No more,'" says Nadine Smith; co-chair of the next Washington march, set for April 25. "The '93 march is about building momentum and moving forward again."

"Harvey would be absolutely giddy with excitement," says Norman, an '87 march co-chair.

And when the day of the march rolls around, "I think he'd be right there in front," adds Scott Smith.

Milk seemed so young when he was taken from us at forty-eight. But so many of those who marched shoulder-to-shoulder, heart-to-heart with us in '87 were cut down decades younger.

None of us is really here for long. But busy and brief as our lives are, we all—whether gay or gay-friendly—do have the time to lend liberty a hand. Choose to take it.

Exercise the constitutional right of every American: Come to Washington and petition the government we fund with our tax dollars to outlaw discrimination against gay people. Demand that the military's ban be lifted. And push for more AIDS funding.

Milk taught that each of us can be instruments of change—whether with a dating service or the U.S. military service. Even Milk's memorial was almost a political rally, Randy Shilts notes in *The Mayor of Castro Street*.

The Reverend Bill Barcus joked with thousands of fellow mourners, "Tradition would expect me to tell you Harvey's gone to Heaven. Harvey was much more interested in going to Washington."

Share Harvey Milk's vision. Join him in spirit on April 25. Make this a time to remember.

THE PINK TRIANGLE TELLS ANOTHER SIDE OF THE HOLOCAUST

MARCH 19, 1993

The pink triangle is sported around the world on T-shirts and jewelry as a sign of gay pride. History professor Klaus Mueller is gay and proud but cannot bring himself to wear it: The pink triangle can never be just an abstract symbol to him. It remains the very real way Nazis marked the clothing of homosexuals.

"The more you know about personal victims' stories, it is not so easy to wear it," says Mueller, a German who teaches in Amsterdam.

Who were the men forced to wear the pink triangle? We have no hope of fulfilling the admonition "Never forget" if they remain a nameless, faceless symbol of oppression.

A few of their names and faces have been rescued from oblivion by the United States Holocaust Memorial Museum, set to open April 26 in Washington, D.C.

The remarkable museum will attempt to help each visitor identify with someone who, at a similar age, was marked for persecution for deviating from the Nazis' twisted vision of a perfect world. Each visitor will receive a passport-like ID card with the name, photo and background of a Holocaust victim. Descending through the museum, visitors will gradually learn more, including the fate of their "silent companion."

Thanks to museum consultant Mueller, the silent companions include nine men of the pink triangle and a lesbian, probably branded "asocial."

The museum's artifacts include cloth pink triangles worn in concentration camps, photos of homosexual men sent to the camps and a taped interview with a homosexual survivor.

The heart-wrenching museum explains the similarities and differences of the horrors faced by Jews, the severely disabled, Gypsies, Jehovah's Witnesses, political dissidents and homosexuals. The tragedy of the Jews—singled out by Hitler for annihilation—naturally dominates the museum.

"There were a variety of people victimized. . . . What the museum has successfully done is to include everybody respectfully and do so truthfully, fully and accurately," says theology professor Michael Berenbaum, author of the museum's historical guide, *The World Must Know.*

Nearly five decades after Hitler's defeat, little is known about the men who wore the pink triangle. The reason is simple: Homosexuals freed from the hellish camps were viewed as criminals, not victims. They feared that speaking out would mean new persecution.

"For homosexuals, the Third Reich did not fully end with its defeat," explains Richard Plant in his groundbreaking *The Pink Triangle: The Nazi War Against Homosexuals.* Some homosexuals found that being "liberated" by the Allies meant a transfer back to prison, not freedom. Time in a concentration camp did not even count as time served.

"None of the lucky few who came out alive was granted any compensation. . . . Families frequently refused to take back a homosexual ex-inmate. And former gay friends were usually displaced or dead. Although they were no longer compelled to wear the stigmatic pink triangle, they felt marked for life," he writes.

Their tragedy began with arrest under Germany's Paragraph 175, an 1871 law toughened by the Nazis, which until 1969 outlawed sex between men. Homosexuals had no place in the Nazi dream of a master race. They were "as useless as hens which don't lay eggs," Nazi SS chief Heinrich Himmler said.

Up to fifteen thousand men are believed to have worn the pink triangle in Nazi camps. Most did not survive.

They routinely were assigned the most deadly jobs, ostracized by other inmates and used as lab animals in hideous medical experiments. "Theirs was an insoluble predicament and virtually all of them perished," survivor Eugen Kogon writes in *The Theory and Practice of Hell*.

The museum guide is dedicated to all those consumed by the Holocaust: "May their memory serve as a blessing—and a warning." And may it help us cherish the freedom to choose whether to wear a pink triangle.

MOTHER STANDS BY SON AFTER HE ENCOUNTERS A FEW NOT-SO-GOOD MEN

MARCH 26, 1993

Something inside the fine-looking young man who was her son was broken, Marie Pridgen decided. With the same determination she had brought to putting her two children through college by working as a hairdresser and real estate agent, she set out to make things right.

"There wasn't anything I didn't do to try to fix it. Anything I suggested for him to do, he did. Anyone I asked him to talk to, he talked with. . . . Psychiatrists, everybody," she says.

Gradually, Marie Pridgen, a Wilmington, North Carolina, woman who has built her life around her faith and her family, came to see that what needed to change was her way of thinking: Her twenty-four-year-old son, Crae, knew his own heart. He really was gay. And that was as normal for him as being heterosexual was for her.

"I loved my son. And I would never have pushed him out the

door and said, 'I won't deal with this.' But at first it was hard for me," she admits.

Marie Pridgen lost both her own parents by the time she was a year old. Only with the birth of her own children had she felt that she had a family she couldn't lose.

Crae and Marie Pridgen have always been very close, but she never suspected he was gay because "girls have always worshiped Crae. He's had thousands of girlfriends."

But when Crae broke off an engagement sixty days before he was to have married and began spending time with new friends, his mother realized it was time for them to talk. "I just looked at him one morning and I said, 'Son, I want to know what's going on with you.' And he shared with me. He said, 'I'm gay, Mom.' "

"We went through some difficult times," Crae recalls, "but my mother came to the understanding that this is my only son and I love him so I'm going to have to learn to accept and approve of him."

It was a lesson she learned at church with the help of a group especially for parents of gay people. "They basically have shown me how to look at Crae and not see any sin in him," she explains.

Having realized there was nothing about Crae's sexual orientation that needed to be fixed, Marie Pridgen was able to stay close to him. It was she whom Crae turned to the morning after his body was broken by men he says were marines. "I remember them saying, 'Clinton will pay, and you faggots will die!' while they were kicking my head into the pavement," Crae Pridgen says.

In a fight at a Wilmington gay bar just hours after President Clinton announced his intention to lift the ban on gays in the military, Crae Pridgen says he was left with a fractured skull, an injured leg, a missing tooth and a mouthful of loose ones.

Two other men and a woman were hurt in what Crae Pridgen calls a brutal, unprovoked attack. Only he has spoken out against it. "They said, 'Crae, you're doing something we wish we could do, but we can't for fear of losing our jobs or our families rejecting us,' " he says. "I knew I was standing up for my dignity, but at the same time I was standing up for theirs."

When Crae Pridgen—whose past gay-rights activism had

consisted of writing an occasional check—came to Washington, D.C., to denounce the attack, his mother was at his side. At first, she says, she was there just to awaken him every two hours throughout the night, for fear that he would lapse into a coma as a result of the head injury.

But she quickly found that standing by her gay son meant standing in the spotlight. And fifty-three-year-old Marie Pridgen told the world that three marines had kicked her just as surely as they kicked her son. "I feel every pain that they struck him with. They don't realize how many lives they affect when they do this to a person."

The marines from Camp Lejeune charged with beating Crae Pridgen are scheduled to go on trial April 5.* His mother is praying for them.

---

*On April 13, 1993, the three marines, who argued self-defense, were acquitted of assault charges. In 1994 they settled a related civil suit in which they did not admit fault but agreed to donate $100 to AIDS research.

PASTEL DREAMS RISE FROM STARK DAYS OF BLACK AND WHITE IN SOUTH MIAMI BEACH

APRIL 2, 1993

Coconut palms, dark against the night sky, sway to the sounds of a smoky, just-forgotten melody. In the distance an ocean liner, gleaming in its suit of white lights, slips toward the horizon. Another, just as beautiful, twinkles close behind. Then a third and a fourth and a fifth pull out to sea, forming a hypnotic conga line.

It seems like a moment out of a lost era, a time when Americans dreamed in black and white: For the price of a movie ticket you could leave the Depression, travel with Fred and Ginger to a land of sophistication and whimsy.

South Miami Beach came to life back then. Its boxy hotels and apartment buildings were fairly spartan inside because most of their tenants were of modest means. But their exteriors were a delight, shouting, "I belong in southern Florida and nowhere else!"

Flat roofs proclaimed that it never snowed. "Eyebrows"—flat and narrow concrete awnings over windows—said the rain and heat of summer were nothing to wink at when air conditioning was just a glimmer in some inventor's eye.

And building after Art Deco building—"skyscraperettes" as the stocky structures are affectionately called—expressed illusions of grandeur, often nautical ones. They flattered the cruise ships that called the nearby port home by mimicking their features—curved edges, clean lines, porthole windows, pseudo smokestacks and metal-railing balconies.

The outside walls were stark white then, decorated with a streak or two of color—perhaps even neon. But as the beach town lost its luster, so did its buildings. By the Seventies they tended to be painted tired tan or bilge beige. The resort turned into a dowdy nursing home, then into a crime capital.

Under layers of crud, the small semi-precious jewels of Art Deco architecture waited to be rediscovered. Eventually a group of disgruntled designers formed a preservation league. They were looking for a native architectural style to counter the rise of glass monoliths that could have been plunked down in any U.S. city.

They found it in South Beach, now called SoBe.

Though the charms of many buildings are still obscured by boarded-up windows, an infusion of money and energy—much of it gay—has given a new shine to scores of rescued-from-the-wrecking-ball Art Deco gems.

"We developed from a ghost town," says Wayne Whynot, who helped start the local gay business guild that has 155 members.

"What is happening here is really the American dream," says longtime businesswoman Barbara Shack. "We have a billion little mom-and-mom and pop-and-pop stores."

On a springtime Saturday night in revitalized SoBe, Joyce and I found ourselves in the ocean-liner-send-off scene, which seemed straight out of a late Thirties romantic comedy. We were safely seated in what was a crime zone as recently as 1983, according to *Deco Delights,* by Barbara Baer Capitman. The ships were an intoxicating sight, one of the few SoBe still offers in black and white.

The gay spirit of South Miami Beach is expressed in—and attracted to—its wonderful new coloration. The hotels and apartment buildings are now flamingo pink, light blue, seafoam green, lavender—pastels aptly dubbed "cotton candy" colors by *Vogue.*

Like the movies of the era that gave birth to SoBe, the beach town loves sophistication. Joyce and I found that the computerized telephone in our fairly spare hotel room could dim the lights, wake us, turn on the TV or CD player and even control the room temperature by degree. If only it could have turned down our neighbor's radio . . .

For the price of a plane ticket, the best of the Thirties comes alive with the colorfulness of the Nineties along SoBe's Ocean Drive. Rolls-Royces mingle with Rollerblades. And the stylish couple at the next cafe table just might resemble Nick and Nora Charles. Then again, they might look more like Nick and Charles.

DRIVING INTO THE LAND OF SEMI-RECOGNIZED RELATIONSHIPS

APRIL 9, 1993

Foolishly, I imagined the relationship could last forever. I invested time, energy and an unreasonable amount of money. The object of my affection remained thrilling yet unreliable.

Now, with Joyce's help, I've made it through a painful crossroads. After seventeen years, the romance is over: I've bought a new car.

Soon after we met, Joyce realized that getting involved with me meant getting involved with my little red sports car. At first, that was not a problem. The car actually ran.

I taught Joyce how to downshift in heavy traffic. And every year she gave the little car a Christmas present—a wooden steering wheel, seat covers, a new dashboard.

But the car began spending more and more time in the shop. Once, after an especially extended and expensive stay, I tried to celebrate the car's triumphant return by taking Joyce out for dinner. We rode home in a tow truck.

Joyce began getting jaded, an attitude that only worsened when she found out the repair shop made videotapes to show spouses of sports car owners where all the money was going.

But I think the real break between Joyce and my car came when we were trying to get to a Gay Pride Day celebration and the right rear wheel fell off. That's when I became all too familiar with the obnoxious little ditty Joyce learned at her grandmother's knee:

Wheels are broken, axle's draggin'. You can't ride in my red wagon.

Since loving me has meant coming along for the ride, so to speak, in the sports car I'd been given as a teenager, Joyce was quite interested in helping me choose its successor.

I wanted adventure, which means a rag top, stick shift and every bell and whistle that can be added to a vehicle that I can honestly describe as larger than a bread box. She wanted to quibble over silly things like why a convertible needs air conditioning and whether the glove compartment could actually hold a pair.

One thing Joyce won't dispute is that we found adventure even before driving my new car off the lot: We entered the land of semi-recognized relationships.

The salesman quickly threw us off guard by being respectful. The dreaded "G" word—"girls"—never passed his lips. Then, to further confuse us, he treated us like a couple, rather than as friends who just happen to bicker like an old married couple.

"I see you've brought along your better half," he said with a grin when I returned to pick up my new little car. Joyce'll take a corny compliment over invisibility any day.

Then my longtime insurance agent wouldn't change my coverage until Joyce filled out a driving record. He assumed—cor-

rectly—that since we live together we use each other's car. Joyce's
form also asked "Nature of relationship?"

"Domestic partner" satisfied my agent but bothered us. Although we're proud to be partners and happy to be open, we're
disturbed when businesses or government officials pry into private
lives without offering anything in return.

My insurance company wanted to know whether we're more
than housemates. We said "yes" but still bombed out on the nuclear family discount.

The Census Bureau also wanted to know whether we're a
couple. Our enthusiastic nod didn't make us count in the eyes of
any other federal agency.

We'd love to drag Uncle Sam into the modern world, but
celebrate his backwardness at tax season—such a happy time for
gay working couples. Our taxes are lower—yes, lower—than if we
could file jointly.

More than anything else, we want equality. Yet the IRS insists
that we pay $1,431 less than if we were married.

Joyce probably will do something frivolous with her half. I, on
the other hand, made a sound investment: a CD player for my
new little car. I crank it up so loud that Joyce couldn't hear a
wheel drop off.

INTOLERANCE IS THE PRICE WE PAY FOR SLAMMING THE DOOR ON OUR PAST

APRIL 16, 1993

Gregory Peck frantically searches his mind but finds no
trace of his past. He's *Spellbound.*

And Ingrid Bergman is his serene psychiatrist/lover
in Hitchcock's 1945 Freudian mystery. She tries to reassure Peck
that she can break the spell: "Loss of memory is not a difficult
problem."

"Yes, I know," he replies, sounding as dubious as the audience feels. "Amnesia, a trick of the mind . . . You remain sane by forgetting something too horrible to remember. You put the horrible thing behind a closed door."

America has cultural amnesia. We can't remember who we were. We only know who we are.

Forbid blacks to use the same drinking fountains as whites? Deny married women the right to own property? Lock the disabled away in attics? Post "No Jews Allowed" signs at beaches?

"That's not the America we know," says much of the nation, slamming the door on the past. "We'd never let such things happen today. We believe in equal treatment, except for gays, of course. But they're not like those other groups. Gays are, well, different."

The most prominent symptom of America's cultural amnesia is the debate over gays in the military. And the prime example of our capacity to forget what we no longer find either pleasant or convenient to remember is South Carolina Senator Strom Thurmond.

A reporter asked Thurmond, ranking Republican on the Senate Armed Services Committee, to explain the differences between his current opposition to lifting the ban on gays in the military and his opposition in 1948 to racially integrating the armed forces.

"No comparison," Thurmond snapped.

Pressed for more, he said, "General Powell has already stated them. I don't care to reiterate them."

Then the same senator who, according to *Truman* biographer David McCullough, labeled desegregating the armed forces "un-American" added: "There's no opposition to blacks in the military. That's all settled years ago."

Thurmond broke with the Democratic Party in 1948 over President Truman's support of civil rights. He ran for president as a renegade Dixiecrat, whose "states' rights" battle cry meant states were within their rights in discriminating against blacks.

". . . There's not enough troops in the army to force the Southern people to break down segregation and admit the Negro race into our theaters, into our swimming pools, into our homes and into our churches," Thurmond declared back then.

Decades later, asked about those words, he initially refused to believe he'd ever uttered them.

Thurmond says he now shares the attitudes of the first black chairman of the Joint Chiefs of Staff, Colin Powell. Skin color, Powell declares, is a "benign" characteristic while being gay is not.

Thurmond is a political barometer showing how much calmer the racial climate is now than it was forty-five years ago. He has come to see blacks as constituents, not servants, says Nadine Cohodas, author of *Strom Thurmond & the Politics of Southern Change*.

That doesn't necessarily mean Thurmond was more educable than his old race-baiting pals. It just means that, at ninety, he's outlived them.

But, surely, he recalls how adamantly he opposed black soldiers bunking next to whites?

Perhaps not. Memory is not chiseled in stone. Instead, the mind pieces together threads from the past to fit whatever opinions we hold today. When opinions shift, recollections tend to shift as well.

"You don't retrieve memory. You reconstruct it," explains University of Georgia psychologist Leonard Martin.

Harvard psychologist Ellen Langer predicts that a year after the military ban is lifted many foes of that policy change will truly believe that they always favored allowing gays to serve.

Perhaps if Thurmond and the rest of us last long enough, we'll forget that we ever hated anyone.

GAYS AND JUSTICE:
REJECTING THE CLOSET

USA TODAY
APRIL 21, 1993

One of the great American myths is that the closet is an uncomfortable but safe place. In reality, it is an exceedingly dangerous place that can feel comfortable simply because it is familiar.

The hundreds of thousands of gay men and lesbians who will march on Washington Sunday to demand fair treatment will undoubtedly be described as risk-takers, people willing to jeopardize their jobs, their ties to their parents and their futures to fight for personal freedom. Yet many of us know the truth is quite different: The biggest risk for each of us individually and for all of us together is to remain hidden, silent, isolated.

For far too long we naively believed that if we kept our sexual orientation secret—if we didn't "flaunt" it by putting a personal photo up at work, for example—we'd be safe from harm.

But being closeted didn't keep gay soldiers from being hounded out of the service or keep gay parents from losing custody of their children or keep gay couples from being separated by "family only" rules during serious hospital stays. And being closeted didn't keep gay people from being beaten or even killed by teenage gangs cruising gay neighborhoods for kicks.

We cannot effectively fight the attitudes and laws that put us at constant risk without leaving the closet behind. We are coming out in record numbers not simply to breathe the air of honesty and openness but also to ask for the support of our relatives, friends, colleagues, religious leaders and lawmakers.

As a community, we are finally learning that the simple facts of our lives are the most effective counter to the stereotypes and lies that persist about being gay.

Everyone in America knows someone gay. But survey after survey finds that people who realize they do are far more likely to understand that we deserve the same right to fair housing and jobs that they do.

In the late 1970s, when gay teachers were under siege in California and Anita Bryant was crusading against gay civil rights in Dade County, Florida, San Francisco Supervisor Harvey Milk banged his fist on millions of closet doors.

Harvey Milk was assassinated in 1978, long before most of us understood his political message: The straight people who love us will hurt us at the voting booth if they don't know who we are. Only by risking rejection and identifying ourselves as gay can we forge the alliances necessary for our protection.

As the AIDS epidemic magnified the dangers posed to our community by secrecy, millions of us have flooded out of the closet. Our personal declarations of existence are already having a tremendous impact on the direction of the nation.

President Clinton has acknowledged that he would not be in the White House today if it were not for the gay vote—which includes countless moms and dads, sisters and brothers, who have made our fight their fight.

This Sunday we march—gay and straight together—for justice. It is a demand we make openly and loudly. The days of silence are over.

ONE NIGHT AT THE BAR, GAYS LEARNED TO SAY: "NO MORE!"

APRIL 23, 1993

Nobody knows why it started. Nobody knows who was first to fight back.

But what the New York City police had intended as just another raid on just another gay bar quickly turned, on the night of June 27, 1969, into a remarkable rebellion: Gay people

long accustomed to passively submitting to arrest or fleeing to
keep their names out of the papers instead said, "No more!"

The Stonewall rebellion.

Few of us know much about that battle for freedom, except
that it involved a bar and some drag queens. Despite its reputation,
it wasn't really the start of the gay-rights movement, historian
Martin Duberman reminds us in his new book, *Stonewall*. Hand-
fuls of gay people had demonstrated, quietly in business clothes,
here and there over the years.

Yet the raucous Stonewall rebellion deserves its honored place
in gay history. It was the first time that large numbers of gay
people stood their ground and resisted mistreatment. Even today it
has much to tell us: Rather than being a haven from an abusive
world, the closet is dangerous, making those who live inside it
easy to victimize.

The 1969 rebellion gets its name from the police raid's target,
the Stonewall Inn, which was the most popular gay bar in Greenwich Village despite its lack of running water. "Many saw it as an
oasis . . . that drew a magical mix of patrons ranging from
tweedy East Siders to street queens," Duberman says.

That view was far from universal, Duberman admits, quoting
one gay man as calling the bar "a real dive, an awful, sleazy place
set up . . . for hustlers."

Customers frequented the bar because it was one of the few
places in the city where gay people could feel free to be themselves and it was the only men's bar that allowed dancing.

When eight police detectives arrived at the Stonewall on June
27, they immediately began harassing patrons. A forty-five-year-
old, who "looked sixty," was arrested for not being able to prove
he was of legal drinking age—eighteen. Another man was arrested
for talking back.

Drag queens were collared for violating the ordinance requiring everyone to wear at least three items of clothing "appropriate"
to their gender.

The insults, the arrests, were routine. The police were used to
"two or three cops being able to handle with ease any number of
cowering gays," Duberman says.

But when the officers began loading their prey into a police van, something extraordinary happened. The cowering stopped. A flash of anger swept through the patrons and the crowd that had gathered outside. Years of pent-up rage at being treated like scum simply for being gay could be held in no longer.

The uproar continued over five nights and eventually involved thousands of people. Coins, bottles and epithets were hurled at police, who responded with nightsticks.

A transvestite who calls himself Sylvia remembers setting garbage cans afire. "I wanted to do every destructive thing I could think of to get back at those who had hurt us over the years," Sylvia says. "Letting loose, fighting back, was the only way to get across to straight society and the cops that we weren't going to take their [abuse] anymore."

The rebellious spirit of Stonewall didn't fade with the uprising. Gay people—hidden, victimized, cowering for so long—had begun to be transformed. One police officer recalls, "For those of us in public morals, things were completely changed . . . suddenly they were not submissive anymore."

Stonewall did not teach gay people to embrace violence; our movement is blessedly peaceful. Yet we learned not to cooperate with injustice. And we learned a powerful word: Resist.

THE BATTLE CRY: "THE RIGHTS OF EVERY HUMAN BEING ARE THE SAME"

APRIL 25, 1993

There's never been room for secrets between my mom and me. She knew the contours of my heart long before I found the courage to speak of them. Finally, as a college junior, I sat her down at the kitchen table and told her what she already understood:

"I am gay."

Those three simple words can topple a wall between family members or open up a chasm. Rarely uttered lightly, they carry an unspoken question: Can you love me for who I am?

Fear of the answer once kept most gay people thoroughly hidden, too timid to speak out against unfair treatment. We watched enviously as other minority groups, with struggles so similar to our own, drew on the strength of their biological families. Being different was one thing that united, not divided, them.

But now, all across the land, the words "I am gay" have been spoken between mother and daughter, brother and sister, grand-mother and grandson. And, increasingly, the reply is the support-ive one I received at twenty: "I know that. I accepted that a long time ago. Whatever makes you happy in your life makes me happy."

The power of love to overcome prejudice and misunderstand-ing has made the struggle for gay civil rights into a shared struggle. Straight relatives and friends and neighbors are among the hun-dreds of thousands of Americans marching in Washington today in one of the greatest civil rights demonstrations in U.S. history.

The goal is justice—equal treatment under the law. Nothing less is acceptable. Nothing more is wanted.

We draw our strength, in part, from the rich river of freedom fighters who demanded their rightful share of the American dem-ocratic dream. We march, as they did, for human rights, not spe-cial rights. We are nowhere near the beginning of our journey; we are likely nowhere near the end.

"Freedom is never voluntarily given by the oppressor," the Reverend Martin Luther King, Jr., taught us. "It must be de-manded by the oppressed."

Our forefathers had a narrow vision of freedom, but they blessed us with a blueprint for a democracy flexible enough to respond to the persistent cries of the downtrodden. In 1863 Afri-can Americans finally secured their emancipation. In 1920 women finally won the vote. In 1990 disabled people finally knocked down legal barriers to mainstream life.

Our message today as we march near the White House, Capitol and Supreme Court is the same one that suffragist Elizabeth Cady Stanton gave the all-male New York Legislature in 1854:

"We ask for no better laws than those you have made for yourselves. We need no other protection than that which your present laws secure for you. . . . The rights of every human being are the same and identical."

The rights that gay Americans should share with their fellow citizens are routinely violated:

♦ Gays have fought and died in every American war. The right to serve our country without lying is not a special right.

♦ We can be fired, refused housing or denied public accommodations in most of the country because of whom we love. Equal protection under the law is not a special right.

♦ We build strong and lasting relationships but are denied any government recognition or benefits. The right to marry is not a special right.

♦ We are the targets of hate crimes, including murder. But the children educated with our tax dollars are not taught to respect diversity. Life is not a special right.

We gays often call ourselves "a gentle, angry people." Our anger at the trampling of our rights has spread to people like my mother, a secretary who has never been political. Today, she marches.

"I'm telling the politicians who make the laws in this country that I'm one of the people they'd better watch if they want me to vote for them because I'm supporting the gay movement," she says.

All too often, love sets gay people apart. But love also builds bridges. Today, families like mine cross those bridges to march for freedom.

THE MARCH'S REAL MEANING
IS WHAT WE BRING HOME

APRIL 26, 1993

The silence was broken and our message delivered: No more second-class citizenship.

But the true measure of the success of Sunday's historic march won't be what each of us took to Washington, but instead what each of us brought back home.

Home to our parents and friends. Home to our jobs and places of worship. Home to our elected officials and the shops and restaurants where we spend our money.

We return home buoyed by the strength gained from a weekend of experiences in which we felt free to be out:

When a flight attendant asked passengers on a plane headed into Washington whether anyone had lost a makeup kit, rows upon rows of playful gay men waved their hands to claim it.

Gay-packed subway cars burst into song between stations: *"If you're gay and you know it, clap your hands. . . ."*

A trio of yuppie gay men, dashing in front of a TV camera filming a kid with a purple Mohawk, dared the media to show the less flamboyant side of gay life.

Signs and T-shirts reflected our humor as we marched: "Honey, God Shrank My Hypothalamus"; "Homos Are Sapiens Too"; "Fundamentalists Believe in the Power of Preyers."

And our standing ovation to Colorado gays, who marched behind a black banner, showed our determination to help each other fight ballot-box terrorism.

In each instance, we knew that every other gay face represented a singular victory—over fear, over denial, over secrecy.

We knew we counted—to ourselves and to each other. And further, that each of us could be counted on to take that pride and power back home to work for change.

Because our first challenge isn't whether straight America takes us seriously, but whether we ourselves do. And if we do, it will be reflected in every vote we cast, every company we work for, every person we call "friend" and every dollar we spend. Each of our acts will demonstrate our determination to secure the equality guaranteed to us by the Constitution.

We will work in our hometowns to help lift the military ban and work to ensure that gay couples receive equal benefits. We will conquer hatred that turns into anti-gay violence. We will help those with AIDS. And we will tell our members of Congress that we want federal legislation to protect us from discrimination.

"Everyone in our community needs to find a way to be a Rosa Parks in their hometowns," said marcher Kasey Reese, a gay man from Chicago.

It's far riskier to sit at the back of our buses, he has found, than to challenge the forces that order us back there.

"I feel responsibility goes with freedom," said Carol Chaney, an openly lesbian marcher and Army veteran from Flint, Michigan. "If you don't exercise that right, you lose your freedom."

That responsibility, she believes, means seizing each triumph, being out at your job, for example, when your company bans anti-gay bias. "We must exercise that freedom once we get it," she stressed.

Too many of us have kept our closet doors locked tight with endless excuses: Our parents might reject us. Our bosses might fire us. Our neighbors might stop speaking to us.

But the truth is, they can't begin to accept us until we open up our lives.

"So many gays and lesbians are so far back in the closet they've got the TV and bathtub in there with them," said Nina Deadwyler, a lesbian marcher from Atlanta. "It hurts the rest of us when people won't accept who they are and the responsibility for changing where we are."

Marcher Judith Ulseth of Webster, Minnesota, who has a gay son, said gay people must come out to their parents: "Give us a chance and some credit. . . . It's not fair to assume how we'll react."

Hiding the truth only keeps our "families from starting the journey toward acceptance," added Mitzi Henderson, president of Parents, Families and Friends of Lesbians and Gays.

And from there, they also can come out as parents with gay kids and help us break down the myths.

"You hold the key that can unlock your family's closet," Henderson said.

And America's closet, too.

Because almost everyone already knows and cares for somebody gay, but we just haven't let most of them know it. Now—bolstered by the memory of our forceful voice—we must.

THE "SHRINKING" GAY COMMUNITY WON'T LET THE CANDLE OF ITS FERVOR BE SNUFFED

APRIL 30, 1993

Reflected in the looking glass of sex surveys lately, we appear so small. There's hardly any of us to count at all.

One day our incredible shrinking community was 10 percent of the population, then 3 percent, then just 1. It's as if we drank the same strange potion Alice did in Wonderland.

"Being so many sizes in a day is very confusing," Alice declared.

Very confusing, indeed.

Anytime now I'm expecting to hear that a new study has found that the entire lesbian world really can be divided into two softball teams.

But implausible as many of us find these new low figures to be, the researchers responsible for them aren't budging. "As long as people told the truth, it would yield accurate numbers," says Koray Tanfer, who helped conduct the National Survey of Men.

That poll of men in their twenties and thirties found that 1 percent said they had been exclusively homosexual for the last ten years and 2.3 percent reported sexual experiences with both men and women during that time.

Let's not pause here to wonder why one-third of the men asked to participate refused. And let's not get bogged down in little matters like the fact that some gay men have been celibate for a decade because of the AIDS crisis and others have been engaging only in no-risk activities. Neither group would have been counted as homosexual in the survey of men.

Instead, let's get to the truth about lying: Pollsters hear a lot of it.

There aren't enough bars of soap sold for all the baths people claim to take. Ditto toothpaste.

People tend to overreport behavior that their society endorses, explains Humphrey Taylor, president of Louis Harris and Associates. For example, he says, 30 percent of people in a British survey said that, yes, they attended church the previous week. But when asked to list everything they did on Sunday, only 3 percent mentioned going to church.

"There are some things that are very, very difficult to measure," says Taylor, who has just released a survey in which 4.4 percent of men reported same-sex activity. "There are things people don't want to tell us about or are uncomfortable telling us about because it's awkward."

The distortions of the polled aren't confined to behavior. Many folks balk at being seen as part of a minority group, even one much less stigmatized than gay people.

Yet a boost in social acceptability can translate into a surge in official numbers. Between 1980 and 1990, the number of Native Americans jumped 38 percent, in part because of a new willingness to embrace that identity.

Surely, there are a great many gay people today who feel as hesitant about being honest with pollsters as large numbers of Native Americans did thirteen years ago. The unfortunate result: undercounts.

Are we 10 percent? Perhaps not. There's no way to really know. Yet these sex surveys do tell us something.

"The reality is that the number of people in this country who are willing to admit to a complete stranger that they are having gay sex is roughly 2 or 3 percent," says Jeff Vitale of Overlooked Opinions, a gay polling firm. "That's not surprising."

It's also not surprising that those numbers made many gay people as nervous as Alice was when she feared she would continue shrinking: "For it might end, you know, in my going out altogether, like a candle."

But whether gay men and lesbians turn out to be just 2.5 percent—like the politically powerful Jewish community—or four times that size, we count in this democracy.

As we showed when we marched on Washington in record numbers, the flame of our desire for equal rights burns brighter than ever before. It shall not go out.

GAYS' LOVE OF FLOWERS DOESN'T MEAN THAT THEY'RE SHRINKING VIOLETS

MAY 7, 1993

A box of violets arrives for a young woman. She opens it, crushes the flowers to her bosom and rushes offstage to the arms of her beloved.

Lesbian love had finally arrived—and triumphed—on Broadway and in Europe. "They Say It with Violets," proclaimed one 1926 review of *The Captive*.

People with more mundane messages in mind for their bouquets immediately stopped sending violets. Sales plunged, according to Kaier Curtin in *We Can Always Call Them Bulgarians,* a history of homosexuality and the theater.

Before the curtain rose on *The Captive,* feminists had often exchanged violets to show affection. Eleanor Roosevelt biographer Blanche Wiesen Cook notes, for example, that the future first lady arrived at a 1922 luncheon with a bouquet of violets for the "boyish" Nancy Cook. "Their relationship was marked by an element of romance," the author writes.

But *Captive* playwright Edouard Bourdet said he seized on violets as a symbol of romantic love between women because one of Sappho's poems mentioned that she and her lover wore "violet tiaras," Curtin writes.

Beautiful, delicate, fragrant, cultivated. Flowers have been closely associated across cultures and times with homosexuals, most often with gay men.

Perhaps because flowers' traits are ones commonly called feminine, straight men tend to fence themselves off from flowery delights. How many feel comfortable buying themselves flowered sheets or receiving a bouquet?

Gently going where many of their straight brethren fear to tread, countless gay men have openly appreciated flowers, arranged them, signaled with them. Even today they risk being mocked as "pansies."

That put-down dates from a 1907 Scottish humor collection, *The Daft Days*. But Joyce, my resident gardener, argues that we in the gay community should embrace the hardy pansy—a relative of the violet—as a symbol that tough needn't mean rough.

Despite Joyce's botanical boosterism, I doubt pansies will soon replace pink triangles or rainbow flags as signs of gay pride. Yet a century ago blossoms became a way for gay men to spot each other.

Oscar Wilde loved to stroll through London carrying a tall lily —traditionally a symbol of virginity—or a giant sunflower in honor of His Royal Gayness Louis XIV. Wilde's favorite floral companion was a green carnation, a natural beauty rendered exotic.

"Wilde became so identified with the green carnation that it actually became a symbol in Victorian London for gay men. And they would wear it to discover one another," says Michael Bronski, author of *Culture Clash: The Making of Gay Sensibility*.

(Imagine how loudly cultural symbols would clash if Wilde's green carnation crowd could return and spend St. Patrick's Day in an Irish-American bar.)

By wearing a green carnation, a gay man in Wilde's time was no longer isolated and defined by an occasional sexual encounter.

His boutonniere transformed him into a member of a gay community.

Wilde used flowers to signal those in the know that, not only was he gay, so were many characters in his books and plays, such as Dorian Gray, explains Neil Bartlett in *Who Was That Man?*, his personal reflections on the Irish writer.

Decades earlier, Walt Whitman had named his most homoerotic poems *Calamus,* after the aromatic, pale pink reed also known as sweet flag.

As gay people and gay ideas have found ways to express themselves more openly, flower codes have faded into history. Yet Robert Mapplethorpe's sensuous flower photographs illustrate that blooms can still be used to make our world more gay. Few things flower in a hostile environment. But the sons and daughters of Whitman and Wilde blossom more beautifully every spring.

HOW ONTARIO'S TWO MICHAELS SCORED A SINGULAR VICTORY FOR GAY CIVIL RIGHTS

MAY 14, 1993

Prosecutor Michael Leshner put his own life on trial—and won. Front-page articles on the sweetest victory of his career line a wall of his row house in the gentrified Cabbagetown section of Toronto. Along with the news stories, papers ran photos of a handsome, curly-haired couple: Leshner and the man he's built his life around, Michael Stark.

The Michaels, as their neighbors call them, proceed with caution: They dated for two years before moving in together a decade ago. And even though they have good jobs, they are intent on quickly paying off the mortgage on the home they share with Mikey—teasingly called "the Jackie Kennedy of schnauzers" because of his prim posture.

Leshner, who at forty-five earns more than twice as much as his younger mate, wanted to ensure Stark's financial future. That's where his ardent belief in equal treatment collided with the rules of his boss, the government of Ontario.

When Leshner first asked in 1988, Ontario refused to give Stark the family benefits automatically provided straight couples. Less than three years later the government largely relented, making Stark eligible for health benefits and everything else but a survivor's pension.

No U.S. state has gone nearly as far toward recognizing the equality of gay couples.

Yet to Leshner, often kidded by Stark for being gloomy, the glass was still half empty. "As naive as this sounds, it was just wrong," he says.

Together, the Michaels filed a legal challenge. Nine months ago they won, making all same-sex partners of Ontario's public employees eligible for the pension benefits long restricted to married couples. The Ontario Human Rights Commission followed up with a warning to private employers: Voluntarily erase benefit distinctions based on sexual orientation or prepare to lose when gay employees complain.

Oh, Canada, can it be that when your constitution says "every individual is equal before and under the law" it really means it? In ruling after ruling, judges are answering with a resounding and astounding "yes."

Within the last year our civilized neighbor to the north has surged to the forefront of the world's most pro-gay nations. Despite some setbacks, Canadian lesbians and gay men now stand on the brink of full equality.

"There's been a tremendous change, a really profound change," says Max Yalden, Canadian Human Rights Commission chairman. Yalden credits that change to the fact that Canada, after being forced to live under a British-made constitution, finally is playing by its own rules. Since 1985 those rules have been headed by a Charter of Rights and Freedoms.

"The government's own lawyers tell it that it is against the charter to discriminate based on sexual orientation. You can't carry on very long in the face of that," Yalden, an ex-foreign service officer, says with undiplomatic directness.

Apparently, Canada's defense department agrees. Last October, in response to a challenge by Air Force Lieutenant Michelle Douglas, it was ordered to produce evidence justifying its gay ban. With refreshing honesty, the department admitted there is none—and immediately retreated.

Even the oh-so-proper Mounties are sharing their reins with openly gay people.

But what can Canada teach a neighbor nation that is tying itself into knots over gay civil rights? "One thing to learn," Yalden says, is that equality "doesn't turn out to be the problem you think it is." His nation greeted the gay integration of the armed forces with a collective yawn.

Positively hopeful for once, Leshner declares: "We're a nation of laws. And the law's on our side."

The country twenty miles from Leshner's Toronto is also a nation of laws. Gradually, those laws are being read as requiring equal treatment for gay Americans. Time is on our side.

CLINTON NEEDS TO USE HIS PULL TO WIN THE TUG-OF-WAR OVER GAYS IN THE MILITARY

MAY 21, 1993

President Clinton declared a six-month-long national tug-of-war over gays in the military, then dropped his end of the rope and walked away. No wonder the struggle has seemed one-sided.

Just when the millions of fair-minded Americans who don't know much about gay people should be grappling with a reasonable explanation of why our new commander in chief believes the ban should be lifted, Clinton is instead bragging that he's only spent two and a half hours on the issue since taking office.

Presidential wanna-be Sam Nunn has no such qualms about devoting attention to the issue. Proving himself a master of propaganda, the Georgia senator has stacked his hearings, manipulated the press, inflamed unfounded fears of gays as sexual predators and downplayed the fact that the Pentagon's own studies have found nothing to support the ban.

While Nunn is busily twisting the tug-of-war rope into a noose to strangle the dreams of patriotic gay Americans, Clinton has tied himself in knots with legalistic mumbo jumbo about "status" vs. "conduct."

Some opponents of the ban are ready to declare defeat, but this struggle is far from over. Our new young commander still has time to prove that he is not gun-shy, that he can lead our nation—and our military—in the direction that he knows we must go.

To do that, he must take the time to explain to the nation why the gay ban is both unwise and unjust. Here's the speech that everyone who waited in line more than two and a half hours to vote for Bill Clinton is waiting to hear:

"My fellow Americans, I address you tonight as your commander in chief on a matter of great importance: the fifty-year-old prohibition on allowing gay men and lesbians to serve in our nation's armed forces. I intend to lift that ban because it is morally wrong, militarily unnecessary and financially unsound.

"For far too long we have wasted taxpayers' hard-earned money—more than $27 million a year—harassing, intimidating, spying on and expelling fine gay and lesbian soldiers.

"Despite what some who fear progress have said, I am not lifting the gay ban to appease a so-called special interest group. I am doing it because the ban has never been justifiable.

"As U.S. District Judge Terry Hatter, Jr., noted in his order reinstating Navy airborne sonar instructor Keith Meinhold, 'The Department of Defense's justifications for its policy banning gays and lesbians from military service are based on cultural myths and false stereotypes.'

"The Pentagon's first rationale was that homosexuals were supposedly emotionally unfit to serve. When that did not withstand scrutiny, homosexuals were accused of being security risks. When forced by the facts to abandon that justification as well, the Pentagon asserted—again, with no justification—that gay men and lesbians undermine 'unit cohesion.'

"Doomsayers similarly predicted decades ago that, first, racial integration and then women in non-traditional jobs would undermine military morale. History, of course, has proven them wrong.

"Gay Americans, by and large, are people who pay taxes, work hard and play by the rules. But ending the ban isn't really about gay people. It is about civil rights. As the Kentucky Supreme Court recently wrote, 'We need not sympathize, agree with or even understand the sexual preference of homosexuals in order to recognize their right to equal treatment.'

"Other Western nations, including Canada and Australia, have abolished their gay bans. Ours, too, will end. If Congress attempts to reinstate it, I will veto that legislation. If such a veto were to be overridden, the U.S. Supreme Court ultimately would rule the ban unconstitutional.

"I was elected to lead a diverse nation. And I shall. Justice knows no race, gender or sexual orientation. It is the birthright of every American."

IT'S CONFIRMED:
SENATE'S VOTE FOR "ROBERTA!"
DEFEATS PREJUDICE

MAY 28, 1993

Avowed, admitted, acknowledged. Even in polite company, we gay people tend to attract quite a few unnecessary adjectives when we lead our lives in a straightforward—or perhaps I should say forthright—manner.

But the U.S. Senate has added a welcome and long-overdue gay modifier: confirmed.

The word is most upsetting to Senator Jesse Helms (R-N.C.)

when used twice in one sentence, as his colleagues did: Confirmed lesbian Roberta Achtenberg confirmed.

Yes, it's true.

Just twenty-three years after America put a man on the moon, it has put an openly gay person in a federal office requiring Senate confirmation. That's one small step for a lesbian; one giant leap for civil rights.

Achtenberg—or *Roberta!* as she is called on campaign posters—is a former San Francisco supervisor. Helms accused her of also being "the showpiece of the homosexual movement." That's a label she can wear with pride.

Because Bill Clinton is the first president with the courage to nominate an uncloseted gay person, Achtenberg is now assistant secretary for fair housing.

But as everyone who read *Advise and Consent* and shuddered when the homosexual senator shot himself recalls, the president only proposes. The Senate disposes.

And the Senate, with all its Old Boys Club decorum and moth-eaten Southern charm, has never been kindly disposed toward homosexuality—at least not the avowed, admitted, acknowledged variety.

Year after year, Helms turned legislation even slightly gay-related into a punching bag as most of his colleagues turned their heads and did their best not to get involved. Too bad if something they believed in got mugged.

But that was before the election last November of four women dedicated to throwing open the Senate's windows and letting in some fresh perspectives.

Democrats Barbara Boxer of California, Dianne Feinstein of California, Carol Moseley-Braun of Illinois and Patty Murray of Washington won with the help of quite a few gay votes and quite a few gay dollars.

They all know what it feels like to be judged by the shape of their bodies or the color of their skin rather than by the content of their minds or the shape of their characters.

These were not senators who could sit silently as Helms tried to turn Achtenberg into another notch in his anti-gay belt.

Helms chose the low road, of course, but found little there.

The most the Helms Dirt Squad could get on Achtenberg was that she "embraced and kissed" Judge Mary Morgan—her long-time lovemate and the other mother of their seven-year-old son—at a gay-pride parade. (If only all our politicians were guilty of honest affection toward their spouses . . .)

The Senate's freshwomen responded to every Helms charge but never became defensive. Achtenberg should be confirmed, they argued, for one reason: She is supremely qualified.

And, appropriately, the Senate's first black woman, Moseley-Braun, signaled the chamber will no longer cower before Helms. Opposing Achtenberg because she is gay makes Helms a "bigot," she declared.

Helms was reduced to whining, "All they want to talk about is her résumé."

The final 58–31 roll call showed that while sexism, racism and homophobia are not the same, people subject to one brand of bias are often more sensitive to other forms. Our *Roberta!* won the unanimous support of the nine minority and/or female senators.

But as Murray reminds us: "The country is tired of those who would view America in terms of us vs. them." Most white male senators supported Achtenberg. Senator Don Riegle (D-Mich.) did so eloquently.

The only loser was prejudice.

IF YOU FIND THE PERFECT PARTNER,
NOTHING CAN STEP
IN THE WAY OF LOVE

JUNE 4, 1993

With Cupid's help, I leaped over the locked gate to deliver roses by moonlight. A life of excitement was what I offered. And Joyce, who offered me stability, accepted.

She quickly discovered excitement isn't always a bed of roses. Take, for example, my recent business trip to New York:

We arrive at Union Station just minutes before my train is scheduled to leave. I don't yet have a ticket. I don't have any cash. My credit card is maxed out. And I've left my bank machine card at home by mistake.

Joyce comes to my rescue, of course, but not without a stern reminder that dancing on the edge of chaos is not what she had in mind when she signed up for the only lifetime membership to my heart.

I try to feel properly contrite—or at least look properly contrite—until I see Joyce break into a grin. She knows she'll never quite tame me. And every now and then we'll do what couples do: drive each other nuts.

Don't tell Ms. Advance Planning, but I'll be driving her somewhere a bit more pleasant this week for our "bronze" anniversary, number eight.

We're going for the gold. But we're running decades behind a Rochester, New York, couple who met when John was twenty-one and Dick was nineteen. This month they celebrate thirty years together. "I just cannot imagine me without him or him without me," John says.

Strong as their relationship is, the two devout gardeners do battle—over turf. "I'm flowers and bushes," Dick explains. "John is vegetables.

"We curse when we trip over the other's pots, tools, etc. In early March, we compete for the grow lights for our indoor seedlings. Outdoors, in summer, I become furious when his zucchini vines start strangling my pansy bed, and he becomes likewise when I cut them back.

"What he grows is rambling, naughty and in need of constant spanking. What I grow is beautiful and well behaved."

Together they cultivate a perennial love.

But even they aren't as close to the golden fifty-year mark as James Egan and Jack Nesbit of British Columbia. They met in a Toronto bar when Jack, who was twenty-one and "kind of tipsy," beckoned the twenty-six-year-old James over to the table where he was sitting with several other men.

"He said, 'I've asked all these guys if they want to go steady with me, and they've all turned me down. How about you? Would you like to go steady?' " James recalls.

"And I said, 'Well, that's a big decision to make. Why don't we meet tomorrow night and go to a show and have a beer and we'll talk about it?' And that's how it all began." The year was 1948.

Forty years later, 125 of their closest friends—all but a dozen of them straight—rented the local community hall and threw them a magnificent anniversary party.

"It was the most electrifying evening of our lives," James says.

Like the Rochester fellows, James and Jack bicker as they garden. And, like all of us, they sometimes drive each other crazy. Yet, James says, "In all the disagreements we've ever had, we've never had a disagreement over a third party, if you know what I mean."

Nevertheless, he adds, "A lot of people say, 'You and Jack are so totally different; I don't know how you've managed to survive as long as you have.' "

They've also managed to become the elders of Canada's gay civil rights movement, taking their demand for equal treatment on old-age spousal benefits to their Supreme Court.

On August 23 they will mark forty-five years together.

"It's my belief," James declares, "that if you get two men or two women together who are determined that they will maintain a relationship, there's no power on earth that can separate them."

Love can thrive even in a harsh environment. All around are gay couples so strong that if they were plants they could sprout through concrete. The secret is being crazy—about each other.

TORIE OSBORN'S PLAN TO GROW THE GAY MOVEMENT

JUNE 11, 1993

The national climate is changing. Long frozen out of mainstream American politics, gay issues are finally being discussed. Yet most gay men and lesbians aren't yet outfitted to take advantage of the warming trend.

For generations we wrapped our personal lives in layers of secrecy as a survival tactic. Now it's time to come in from the cold and realize that the gear that seemed so protective is weighing us down, stifling not only our political progress but our emotional lives.

"It takes a lot of energy to live a lie," says Torie Osborn, the vibrant new executive director of the National Gay and Lesbian Task Force. She's determined to rechannel gay energy to fight for full equality.

"The point isn't to be permanent victims or outsiders or powerless," says the forty-two-year-old Osborn. "The point is to transform society. And you need a lot of money and power to do that."

Just three months ago Osborn took over the leadership of the task force, the gay movement's oldest national political organization. What she found was an underfinanced, overextended SWAT team: a staff of fifteen attempting to do the job of a small army.

Combating the likes of Jesse Helms, Pat Buchanan and Dan

Quayle consumed so many resources that NGLTF had little left for building itself up. By the end of 1992, after twenty years in existence, it had only 26,000 members and a $1.7 million budget.

What does Osborn, who came to Washington armed with an MBA, plan to do to the task force? "Grow it."

She is intent on commanding a small army, fifty staffers in two to three years. Membership already is up to 34,000, and she is aiming for 60,000 by the end of 1994. She's signaled her seriousness about expansion by boosting the budget for 1993 to $3.3 million.

"I plan to continue to expand the membership base as fast as possible," Osborn says. "We need to be imaginative in reaching gays and lesbians, whether at the softball game or the bar."

Osborn proved she has a green thumb when it comes to growing gay groups during her five years as head of the Los Angeles Gay and Lesbian Community Services Center. She boosted its staff from 60 to 160. She simultaneously showed her commitment to diversity, increasing the people of color on the staff from 17 percent to 45 percent and women from 22 percent to 50 percent.

Besides expansion, her task force priorities are fighting the right wing, lifting the military ban, formulating a national lesbian health policy and encouraging the spread of gay employee groups.

Osborn offers a "wonderful combination of vision and pragmatism," says task force board member Deborah Johnson.

Osborn knows, for example, that she must fight the closet as well as the right wing. "You cannot organize people who are in the closet," she says. "People need help breaking through to that level where they can find their own courage and act on it."

She found her own courage slowly.

At fifteen she invited a friend over for the night. "I woke up in the morning and we were holding each other. . . . Waves of shame rolled across her eyes and mine, too. I will never forget what that felt like."

By college she was living a double life, romantically involved with women but taking a boyfriend home to meet mom and dad. Only after graduating did she admit to herself that she is gay. A year later she told her folks.

Although it took six painful years for her mother to accept her, Osborn never regretted stripping away the deception.

"What made me an activist were the baby steps I took to fight back my own shame and self-hatred," Osborn says. "There's a big difference between being a survivor and taking control of your life and fighting back."

Taking charge as the gay debate heats up, Osborn is a commanding presence. She needs foot soldiers who realize survival is not enough.*

* Osborn stepped down as head of NGLTF in November 1993.

MILLIONAIRE'S LEGACY PROVES REWARDING TO "REAL-LIFE HEROES" OF THE GAY COMMUNITY

JUNE 18, 1993

Paul Anderson had a sure sense of when to risk bucking the crowd. His instincts paid off handsomely.

At the Chicago Board of Trade, his mastery of esoterica about anything that could affect the future price of plywood, platinum or pork bellies transformed him from the "ordinary kid" his mother remembers to a multimillionaire with a private plane, an estate in Michigan and a vacation home in San Francisco.

But at the height of his career, fate sold short on Anderson: He was diagnosed with the AIDS virus.

"AIDS really radicalized him" as a gay man, recalls Martin Delaney, executive director of an AIDS treatment information network. Anderson credited AIDS activists and doctors who risked their own futures to provide experimental treatments with adding four years to his life.

"He learned that activism saves lives," a close friend says. "He saw the enormous personal sacrifices that men and women were making to try to help people with AIDS."

And he saw that the people he called the "real-life heroes" of the gay community all too often go unrecognized, unrewarded.

Before he died last year at forty-three, Anderson established a $1.25 million foundation to reward heroic efforts to improve the quality of life for gay men and lesbians.

The brilliant commodities trader saw his no-strings-attached Stonewall Awards as the gay equivalent of the MacArthur "genius" prizes, which have never gone to a gay activist. This year the MacArthur Foundation did honor two individuals working to help people with AIDS, however.

During his life and in his will, Anderson contributed to good causes. But with the Stonewall Awards he decided to give directly to a few good people.

"He wanted to reward individuals, not the institutions they have grown," says Delaney, who received a 1991 Stonewall Award because of his work with Project Inform. "You reward behaviors. That's how you make things happen. He wanted to say, 'People who make contributions to this community will be rewarded.'"

The Stonewall reward is a check for $25,000. Cash-strapped cartoonist Howard Cruse and his lovemate of fourteen years, New York activist Edward Sedarbaum, were floored when they opened a letter announcing they'd won one of this year's four Stonewall Awards.

"We called to make sure it wasn't a practical joke," Cruse recalls. "It came at a time when we really needed it. This was a real case of the cavalry appearing over the ridge."

Best known for his gay comic strip *Wendell,* Cruse has been working for two years on an illustrated novel about a white gay man who learns through the civil rights movement of the 1960s that "we can create tragic consequences by doing nothing."

Anderson hoped his Stonewall winners would use their windfall to pamper themselves a bit. In 1991, when the first prizes were awarded, he said, "I'd sort of like it if they went out and bought new cars."

Cruse is thinking more in terms of groceries.

But Earnest Hite, Jr., plans to splurge on a New Orleans vacation. He's co-founder of Image Plus, a Chicago program designed to bolster the self-esteem of other black gay men and lesbi-

ans. The Stonewall Award, he says, "is a really marvelous validation of the work I've done."

This year's other winners are Pat Norman, head of the California AIDS Intervention Training Center, and Suzanne Pharr, a
political organizer from Little Rock who helped defeat Oregon's
anti-gay referendum last November.

Betty Anderson says her son taught a great many people
that, "yes, nice people do get AIDS. And, yes, nice people are
gay."

Futures trader Paul Anderson left us all another valuable legacy as well: The long-term prospects of the gay community are
excellent. Invest all you can.

JANIS IAN BURSTS OUT OF THE VINYL CLOSET AS GAY SOCIETY'S CHILD

JUNE 25, 1993

J anis Ian was just fifteen when she held a mirror in front of
white America and made us look racism in the eye. Declaring herself "Society's Child," the young songwriter sang a
heart-crushing ballad about a white girl who listens to her elders
and tells her black boyfriend she can't see him anymore.

In the last verse of her 1966 Top Ten hit, which was banned
on many radio stations, Ian says that maybe one day she'll stop
letting others tell her whom to love.

In reality, Ian always loved as she pleased. Yet she became
"society's adult" by going along with the conspiracy of silence
that allowed gay singers to become successful in the mainstream
music world only if they stayed in the Vinyl Closet.

And succeed she did. In 1976 she won the Grammy Award for
Best Female Vocalist and was nominated for both Best Record and
Best Song for capturing the ugly-duckling despair common "At
Seventeen."

Musical success gradually turned the working-class prodigy from South New Jersey into a star with a seven-figure bank account. The money "made me feel like I could write for the rest of my life and not feel worried," Ian recalls.

Her financial security vanished in the Eighties along with her bankbook when the IRS demanded payments due. The family friend entrusted with Ian's finances had failed to pay her taxes for seven years. She lost virtually everything, even her piano.

She gave up on Los Angeles, moved to Nashville and started over. "I made an active decision not to be bitter," Ian recalls. Ironically, she says not having money was "really freeing." Five years ago she decided that if she ever cut another album she'd be forthright with her fans.

Breaking Silence (Morgan Creek), her first album in a dozen years, is now out—and so is Janis Ian.

She is simply letting the world know something she realized at age nine. "I was sitting on a hill in the fourth grade looking at my teacher. And the thought popped into my head, 'This is not a phase.' I was pretty advanced, obviously.

"My next thought was, 'I'd better not tell anybody.' "

Just as her social conscience brought Ian fame at fifteen, it has brought her out of the closet at forty-two. She wants gay kids— and the rest of the world—to get a healthy dose of gay reality to counteract the sick stereotypes she confronted in library books as a child.

What she would have given then to read about a famous lesbian, a singer perhaps, who breaks into a proud grin when showing off the ring symbolizing her five-year relationship, which had "better last forever!"

Ian's justifiable fear about coming out was that her songs would be too narrowly interpreted. Many of her lyrics are intentionally ambiguous, but "Jesse," which Roberta Flack took to the top of the charts in 1973, really was intended to be about a man, Ian insists.

Mixed in with her new album's songs about the Holocaust, child abuse, wife beating and simple survival—"This Train Still Runs"—is one to Pat, the woman she has been with "Through the Years."

But where's the gay equivalent to "Society's Child," the song that will force the nation to look bigotry in the eye yet again? "I'd love to be the one to write it," Ian says. "I've tried for years."

Ian thinks she can foster understanding without ever penning a gay hit. "In a sense I've already been in people's living rooms for two generations. I've been in their bedrooms. That's what they say to me.

"I think a lot of people are scared of gay people because they think they don't know any of us. If the person who wrote 'At Seventeen' who's already touched you can say 'I'm gay,' then maybe that's less scary."

Ian is finding that "people would rather shake the hand of a lesbian celebrity than not shake the hand of a celebrity." She knows that if society can embrace openly gay stars the future of every other lesbian and gay man will shine much brighter.

Chapter

7

WHY ANGRY MEN CAN'T SPELL

WHEN I WAS LITTLE, MY FAVORITE TV SHOW, EXCEPT FOR *Captain Kangaroo*, of course, was *The Popeye Club*. Between cartoons, Officer Don, a nice pudgy guy in a police uniform, played games with the children lucky enough to be in the Atlanta studio audience. I planted myself in front of the screen every weekday afternoon in hopes of getting to watch one particular game again.

A lazy susan sat on a table that came up to most of the contestants' noses. Officer Don arranged paper lunch sacks around the lazy susan. Even standing on tiptoes, none of the players was tall enough to see into any of the bags. Into all but one bag, Officer Don dropped all kinds of little treats—toys, candy, gift certificates for ice cream. But when he came to the last bag, he broke a raw egg and dropped it in, shell and all, then added flour, molasses, anything sticky. Finally, he gently spun the lazy susan to try to confuse the young contestants.

One by one, each player reached up and, after a moment's hesitation, plunged a hand down into one of the bags. Usually, the next sound was a shout of delight from the child who'd just won a tiny water pistol or flavored-wax false teeth. Those of us watching weren't much interested in the winners. Sooner or later, though, a kid would reach in and grab a handful of sticky glop. At that instant, children all across Georgia would shout, "Ooey Gooey!"

Reaching into a sack of Deb's mail is exactly like playing "Ooey Gooey." That's why Deb decided that I should be the one to open the letters.

Actually, I appointed myself to the task when the column was just a few months old. In the very beginning, Deb had opened her mail as soon as it arrived at *The Detroit News'* Washington bureau. Then she'd share it with me over lunch. Every batch contained wonderful treats, letters like the one from the Niagara Falls father who said, "My daughter is a lesbian. It was difficult for us at first. Now we are comfortable with her life. We're very proud of her. She's in medical school at this time. I wish your newspaper column had been available when we were trying to understand." At first, almost every letter made a permanent impression on us. I remember what kind of sandwich I was eating—bacon, lettuce and tomato—when Deb showed me the letter from a Michigan man who wrote, "Between the two of us, John and I have five children and three grandchildren. We are very family oriented, with the same family values that we were lucky enough to grow up with. It has been a constant struggle to explain to our children how people who don't even know us could deny us fundamental rights. . . . Thank you for being one of those brave souls to bring these concerns to the light in our nation. . . . I love you for what you are doing."

Looking back, I wish I'd been quicker to notice how much Deb was affected by the really nasty letters. A two-page missive that began "Hi Pig Shit" before deteriorating into unrepeatable filth could throw her off stride for an afternoon. I soon decided that, no matter how many trashy letters arrived, Deb would never have to read another. Now my favorite weekly pastime is planting myself in front of a mound of mail. I'm the first to read how the column has touched readers' hearts or opened their eyes, how it made them laugh out loud or helped them build a bridge. Heartwarming little treats get sorted into the read-and-reply stack, the civil (and quite predictable) criticism goes into the read-only stack, since Deb doesn't have time to answer everything. And the trashy mail is just tossed—unread by Deb—into boxes and saved.

Why do I enjoy playing Ooey Gooey with Deb's mail if I so often end up with several pages of slime on my hands? Why doesn't reading it upset me? Long before Deb's column started I knew from firsthand experience how even the most minor public figure becomes what Deb calls "a lightning rod for hostility." Given the way much of that hostility is expressed, the metaphor I prefer is "fireplug." Before becoming a columnist, Deb had never been in the public eye. She'd never been on the receiving end of strangers' anger. But at twenty I discovered that being editor of the University of Georgia's daily student newspaper, *The Red and Black,* turned me into a handy target. I walked into my campus office one day and found that an anonymous reader had left a little something on my desk—a bullet. Etched on the shaft was a political slogan. On the tip were my initials. My roommates were totally unnerved and talked of moving out. I never took the apparent threat seriously; I never forgot it either.

But what really toughened me toward hate mail is that I've seen it all before. In college I interned in Congress for a smart and funny liberal, U.S. Representative Mo Udall (D-Ariz.), and often helped sort mail in his Washington office. I quickly became acquainted with the Crayon Crowd, folks who returned Udall's newsletters with rude notes scrawled across them in crayon or Magic Marker. Every congressional office regularly gets uncivilized feedback. An Atlanta Democrat once received a box of ripe manure, which might sound funny if you've never been the flunky opening mail.

Perhaps if it were my name—rather than some twisted version of Deb's—on the envelopes, I wouldn't be able to get any emotional distance from the column mail. Yet I think that, being a social scientist at heart, I'd keep on reading every word. I try to piece together patterns and decipher the messages that the letter writers unconsciously convey.

Deb's gay audiences invariably ask specifically about hate mail, a question that reflects the understandable but unfortunate tendency to focus more on our foes than our potential allies. The most important things I've discovered about Deb's hate mail are: (1) There's much less to it than meets the eye. Sorting through almost three years' worth, I've found that the worst of it comes from people who write quite regularly and usually anonymously. (2) The hate mail sent to a lesbian columnist isn't much different from other hate mail, particularly hate mail sent to other women in the public eye. Reading a *New Yorker* magazine article about Constance Baker Motley, who as an NAACP attorney fought for school desegregation, I was struck by how similar an unsigned letter she received decades ago is to Deb's vilest mail: "Mrs. Motley: When you made your plea before Judge Tuttle, how many windows did you raise to let your stinking body odor escape? How much cologne did you use to saturate your clothing with to prevent others from smelling your stinking body? . . ." Compare that with the Ooey Gooey letter a Michigan man wrote Deb: "Hi Freak of Nature: . . . Does your breath always smell of pussy? Are your lips dry and scaley [sic]? Do you have herpes? Do you like raw oysters? If you answered yes to these questions you are indeed a stinking maggot faggot!"

While it's important to understand the sources of the toxic venom in our society, I'm more interested in mail from good-hearted people raised to believe that homosexuality is wrong. Where are the cracks in their anti-gay armor? How can they be educated to see that sexual orientation is no more a moral issue than eye color or freckles but that bigotry is a moral issue? I believe a great many heterosexuals can be converted into allies by being introduced to loving gay couples. To me, the San Jose woman who wrote Deb anonymously after reading about our visit to the Metropolitan Community Church in Dallas represents the hope of a gay-friendly future:

Dear Ms. Price,

. . . Although I have never written to a columnist before, I felt I had to write to you to tell you what you have done for me.

No, I am not gay. I'm a straight, married mother and grandmother. I still believe that the Bible teaches that a sexual relationship between two members of the same sex is sin. I pray and struggle with the issue, but I can't come to any other conclusion. I don't think I'm homophobic, what-

ever that is. I can't think of a single person I hate, gay or straight or I-don't-know-which.

Today, I felt your love for your partner, I felt your commitment to each other and I felt your joy as you worshiped together. . . .

I'm sure as you read my letter you won't agree with the way I feel about homosexual lifestyles. I hope you will know that I am struggling to understand. I hope you will know that you have helped me today. I hope you will know that I loved you today as a sister.

I would gladly plunge my hand into a hundred envelopes full of slime for the chance to be first to read such a lovely letter.

Unlike the look-alike paper bags in the Ooey Gooey game, envelopes addressed to a gay columnist give fairly reliable clues about their contents. If it's written in pencil, beware! And a fake return address along the lines of "Normalville, U.S.A." definitely is not a good sign. But the most common clue as to whether a letter is putrid is how Deb is addressed on the envelope. The vast majority of Deb's negative mail comes from readers outraged simply by having a gay voice included in their newspaper. They refuse to recognize the right of gay people to speak. They would even deny us the power to determine how we're addressed.

So much of Deb's hostile mail comes addressed to "Debbie Price" that we've joked about bundling it up and forwarding it to our ex-colleague Debbie Price, now executive editor of the Fort Worth *Star-Telegram.* Deb and Debbie met at *The Washington Post* when their paychecks and mail got scrambled. Debbie accidentally opened a personal letter addressed to Deb. That's how Debbie, who is straight, discovered Deb is not. Debbie became a columnist after leaving the *Post* for less-sexist pastures. When Deb joined the ranks of columnists a little later, she worried that Debbie would be upset if people confused her with the new gay columnist. But Debbie reassured her, "I think it's a hoot!" Debbie added that readers accuse her of being a lesbian anytime she knocks deer hunting.

When *The Detroit News* officially began Deb's column, Debbie commented in her own column, "This is a gutsy move and one long overdue in the newspaper world. But I have to tell you, I do not want to get Deb Price's mail now. As a straight person who occasionally writes about gay issues and AIDS, I've received enough homophobic hategrams to last a lifetime. I can't imagine setting myself up for a steady diet of it." If Debbie won't take all the "Debbie Price" hate mail that I've got boxed up, maybe I can unload some of Deb's negative correspondence on someone who goes by the second most common name concocted by her critics. But where will I find a "Mr. Deb Price"?

Once an envelope is open, Crayon Crowd messages are the easiest to spot. There must be a lot of angry Americans who read their daily paper while tightly gripping a sharp object—a pair of scissors. If something offends them, they cut it out, mark it up and send it back. A few of these people seem to have lost their crayons because they don't write anything at all. They just send little cutout magazine pictures of mixed couples or of a bride and groom cutting a cake or of a man, woman and child together. Is looking at a heterosexual photo supposed to make Deb exclaim, "Oh, my, I'm supposed to be with a man!"? It's amazing what some people will waste a postage stamp on. To me, each truly goofy letter represents thirty-two cents that didn't get contributed to Senator Jesse Helms or Pat Robertson. I figure Deb is costing the Radical Right plenty. Someone from Michigan once mailed Deb a cutout of a long-haired woman standing face-to-face with a large chimpanzee. Guess I'm supposed to be the chimp. That stuff is too mindless to be classified as hate mail.

Once members of the Crayon Crowd find their pencil boxes, though, look out! They scribble on Deb's photograph or draw cartoon balloons and put words in her mouth like "Look at me I'm a sicko and proud of it." They often have her saying raunchy things about Hillary Clinton. Others just scrawl across the entire column: "It's better to be a bigot than to legitimize scum like you." "Harvey Milk got what was coming to him. Too bad you were not with him, then we would have one less queer." "The best thing that ever happened to you queers is AIDS. I love it!!!" And under a *San Jose Mercury News* column headlined "Taking our place at the front of the bus," was the reply: "Boy I'd LOVE to get you in front of a bus." But the Crayon Crowd's frustration is best epitomized by the reader who wrote across Deb's column in giant Magic Marker letters: **"WHY DON'T YOU GO HAVE**

A BABY!" If any of her readers think that would make a gay columnist shut up, then Deb hasn't written enough about the lesbian baby boom.

When Deb hears from anti-gay women, usually their letters are polite, handwritten notices that she's headed to a hellishly warm place. A five-page message from a well-intentioned but misguided Springfield, Missouri, woman is typical: "I used to be disgusted with gay people. I had a real hard time with it. But I feel like the Lord has changed my heart. Now it just makes me sad when I hear or read about the gay lifestyle. . . . Because you won't be going to Heaven. I can't imagine anything sadder than that. . . . I'm going to be praying for you. So, when you feel a tugging at your heart, know that it's the Lord." Having reread and categorized all Deb's mail in my search for patterns, I can testify that Deb almost never gets such a kind letter from an anti-gay man. Oh, plenty of men quote scripture, but they seem much less concerned with tugging at Deb's heart than shutting her mouth. They turn the Bible into a weapon.

How do you get a woman to shut up? I say "woman" rather than "gay person" or even "lesbian" because so many of Deb's most vociferous critics are obsessed with her gender. Their letters delineate the very large intersection between misogyny and homophobia. For example, after Deb wrote about the ongoing Presbyterian struggle over the place of gay people within that denomination, a Virginia man wrote, "What is amazing is how a 1976 national Presbyterian task force on homosexuality could conduct two years of theological study and conclude that homosexuality is not sinful and that openly gay people should be ordained as ministers. . . . But the results do not really surprise me. A denomination that allows women in the pulpit is not following God's Word anyway."

The nonviolent methods of trying to silence an opinionated woman haven't really changed since the days of the suffragists. Deb's outraged male readers routinely write that she's ugly, that she's fat, that they don't find her sexually attractive (this is supposed to upset a lesbian?), that she's acting like a man. Of course, even today one of the most effective methods of shutting up women is to accuse them of being lesbians. The truly dim bulbs among Deb's critics actually try that tactic: "I have not read but two of your columns (the other was all baloney, too) and I hazard a guess that you are a lesbian." "I fail to see why you are going all out for gays. I can only assume that you are gay also. . . ." "Finally, in your story you state, 'Yet the U.S. Constitution promises all Americans equal protection under the law. And that is all we gay people want. . . .' You do not state you are stating the opponents' point of view. I read that as an admission that you are homosexual. If that is the case, aren't you biased to be writing about this?"

Deb's vilest mail comes from straight white men who claim to be Christian. They hate blacks, Jews, women, people with AIDS. The anger they spew at everyone who isn't just like them is truly unsettling. Even though Deb's column is never explicitly sexual, the grossest mail it draws almost always is. Letter writers carry on endlessly and in the most disgusting manner about sex, often weaving in their racism: "Since you work in the murder capitol [sic] of the world, have you had a chance to eat a nigger pussy . . . ?" Some of these men bizarrely argue that Deb should become heterosexual because women "stink" and men are "cleaner." (Pity the women who are involved with those men.) Then there are the self-appointed religion experts: "According to God—They (gays + les) [sic] are abominations. Of course, if you don't believe God—your [sic] anti-Christ." Occasionally, one of these rude men actually knows how to spell: "You and the newspaper ought to be arrested for obscenity and indecent exposure just for showing your ugly mug in public. . . . Some day that filthy tongue of yours which you use for all of its filthy, immoral, ungodly, wicked practices, is going to confess that Jesus Christ is Lord. Then, as he who created you and every other human being a heterosexual casts you headlong into the lake of fire, you will use that filthy tongue to beg for mercy, but it will be too late."

Playing Ooey Gooey with Deb's mail has given me plenty of time to ponder why angry men can't spell. My theory: Straight white boys growing up in a society that revolves around the desires of straight white men expect to become kings. Instead, many become uneducated and powerless—life's pawns. They feel cheated. They think their birthright as straight white men has been stolen by women, gay people, people of color, Jews. And they're damn angry about it. They try to prove they really are powerful, despite all the evidence to the contrary, by writing dirty letters to strangers. By contacting Deb, they get a double thrill, venting their anger by simultaneously rebuking a woman and a gay columnist. These fellas are really twisted, and their letters are sic, sic, sic. "You have contributed greatly to a cause you must beleive [sic] in namely the destruction of the United States. . . . I could write hogwash like this all day but its [sic] true hogwash," declared a man from Anoka, Minnesota.

Originally, I'd hoped that Deb's negative mail would provide thought-provoking arguments that she could use as springboards for future columns. That's not proven to be the case. Most anti-gay feedback doesn't rise above the level of "You always will be a minority." Or, "My son has a doctorate. . . . And he KNOWS homosexuals are not the norm!" One Michigan woman put it another way—"Ms. Price: Or is it 'Mr.' Price? . . . 98% of the people in this world cannot be wrong! 2% CAN be!" Moving beyond simple numbers, the theme that there is one correct sexual orientation was expanded upon in a letter from California: "Homosexuals are defects of nature for whatever cause just as are cripples, blind and other handicapped persons that enter the world in their condition and they are not the 'norm.' . . . You're smart enough to know you're a defective heterosexual and you'll have to live with it. Be thankful Heaven doesn't have an instant recall program for gender defects." Letters to the editor about Deb's column haven't been much more helpful. For example, one woman offered this insight about Deb to the Palm Springs *Desert Sun:* "Every piece she writes is GAY, GAY, GAY. It's a for sure $10 bet."

Much of the criticism Deb receives makes me despair more about the quality of American education than about the future of the gay civil rights movement:

And as for other countries who have abolished gay bans, I would like to say that other countries are not the United States of America.

We have been bombarded with the term "gay bashing." It carries with it such a negative connotation.

I see you write for a Detroit News. *It appears to me you should solve Detroit's problems before you try to condemn Sam Nunn's.*

Please be aware Ms. Price it is people like you who are helping to destroy the very foundations we were founded on. . . . P.S. If you care to response [sic]—*I will be delighted.*

Believe it or not, the majority of the population doesn't care if someone is gay or not. I know, I know, we don't treat you in our laws equally, and some of us even call you names, assault you, and all that. But as history shows, like it or not, change takes time. . . . If you continually shove it in our face, it will slow the rate of change even more.

A great many negative letters argue that sexual orientation is consciously chosen and that civil rights protections should be reserved exclusively for minorities who cannot help deviating from the majority:

A Jew did not choose to be a Jew. A black did not choose to be black. You had a chooice [sic] *so quit your wining* [sic]. *You have made your bed —so go lie in it. And shut up.*

Gays and lesbians are the way they are because they choose. It is their choice to be abused and looked down on.

Homosexuality is a matter of personal choice to engage in sin. People who are male/female, white/black/brown/yellow/red, handicapped/disabled, young/old, or born in a foreign country had no choice. Their civil rights are granted to them because they had no choice and should not be discriminated against. They are not engaging in sin unless they choose to [go] beyond the life situation they were born into.

(The last writer failed to mention exactly which portion of the U.S. Constitution he thinks limits rights to people without choices.)

When Deb attacked Bush and Quayle (the Angry Man Who Put the "E" in Potato) before the '92 election because of their miserable record on gay rights, surprisingly few readers rallied to their defense. One who did was a Springfield, Missouri, reader who identified herself as a "heterosexual, married, middle-class woman who applauds the values of the right-wing Republicans." Then came the slap: "To imply that if Bush loses the election, it's because people want someone to pander to gays is self-serving, presumptuous, and laughable." For a rebuttal, here's what President Clinton told the National Gay and Lesbian Task Force ten days after his election: "I would also like to take this opportunity to thank every one of you for your tremendous support during our campaign for change—without your support our victory on November third would not have been possible."

Given how often and hard Deb hammered at the ban on gays serving openly in the U.S. armed forces, I expected many more negative replies than she received. Mainly, she heard from military people, usually retired, who seem to have been absent from civics class on the days that civilian government and constitutional rights were explained. A retired Army major who wrote from Cadillac, Michigan, was typical. "You have never worn the uniform or humped the ruck in some very interesting countries and do not have the right to state what you did. Until you have experinced [sic] it you cannot talk about it. I served twenty-seven years, am retired, and worked with some very fine Negro soldiers. . . . Queer soldiers on the other hand have only managed to distrubt [sic] the morale and cohesion of a unit. Lady, I was a company commander. . . ."

Another ex-officer wrote from Sunnyvale, California. "I spent nine years in the United States Army—five of those as an officer in the Field Artillery. (How many years were you in, by the way?) So I have some real practical experience from which to speak. I realize that makes me totally unqualified to advise the president and her assistant, Bill. . . . Lifting the ban on gays in the military is simply a bad idea. If it weren't, JFK, LBJ, or Jimmy Carter would have already done it, right?"

Then there is the ex-marine from San Jose who opposes lifting the ban because at ten o'clock one night in November of 1944 a sergeant "put his hand on my thigh. . . . I was nakid [*sic*]." Imagine if every woman in this majority-female country who had been the object of a man's unwanted sexual advance sometime in the last fifty years voted to deny all heterosexual men their constitutional rights because of it.

Deb's one column on left-handedness drew about as much negative mail as all her military columns combined. After she wrote July 30, 1993, about parallels between discrimination over the centuries against lefties and homosexuals and mentioned that there is a greater incidence of left-handedness among gay people, my right hand spent weeks dipping into Deb's stack of mail and pulling out Ooey Gooey letters from left-handed heterosexual men. They were outraged that anyone dared to suggest that anything associated with them is also associated with homosexuality. Poor boys! (Left-handed straight women apparently weren't bothered by the column.) A Missouri man wrote, "I resent your comment in your article about left-handers. . . . I am left-handed and I sure the hell am not gay nor can I tolerate being around you perverts. Also, it is not immoral to be left-handed but it is and always has been immoral to practice perversion. . . . You are fat, ugly and disgusting." A leftie from Poughkeepsie, New York, who "long ago realized that teachers tried to keep students from smearing their ink-filled pages with their sleeves by encouraging right-handed penmanship," offered a different insult: "Comparing a left-hander to a homosexual is as ludicrous as supposing you have been endowed with the ability to reason. . . . If everyone in the world was left-handed it would still be a great place to live, but if all were homosexual we would be extinct." A left-handed Rochester, New York, man chimed in, saying, "Stop being openly homosexual and your problems are solved. You can't really stop being left-handed."

The left-handed hate mail reminds me of the letter Deb received from a San Jose man in response to her May 7, 1993, column describing the role various flowers have played in gay culture: "To associate flowers with being a homosexual is not in good taste and I for one resent it very much. I am heterosexual, and feel it is too bad that a stigma of perversion is being associated with them. . . . Maybe some day your sickness will be cured, or maybe you will contract AIDS." That fellow should stick to saying it with flowers.

REALITY IS QUITE UPSETTING TO SOME NEWSPAPER READERS. THEY don't want their heterosexual illusions shattered. Deb really rattles their cages every time her column includes one very straightforward sentence: "Jesus never condemned same-sex love." I'm amazed at how many people who call themselves Christians will twist themselves into pretzels in attempting to deny the truth of that simple statement:

> *One of your recent columns stated that Jesus never condemned same-sex love. How did you come to that conclusion? It doesn't say any such thing anywheres [sic] in The Bible.*
>
> *—Buffalo, N.Y.*

> *Miss Price has stated on at least two occasions, "Jesus," (A/K/A God in the flesh), "didn't condemn same-sex love." Sodom and Gomorrah are G-O-N-E.*
>
> *—Harrison, Ark.*

> *The words of Jesus and the words of Paul carry equal weight. . . . I know that Paul spoke against homosexuality. . . . Did Jesus speak out against same-sex love? I would have to say that He did, in both the Old and New Testaments.*
>
> *—Stockton, Calif.*

For inventive religious prejudice, few can trump the Minnesotan who sent three pages of anti-gay messages that Jesus and his mother, Mary, were credited with sending to Roman Catholics by way of a Long Island, New York, housewife and "seer." A typical example: "And I repeat again: all who become part of or condone homosexuality shall be destroyed. —Jesus, June 2, 1979." Words put into Christ's mouth on June 6, 1987, called AIDS "a penance from a just God."

More typical was a Royal Oak, Michigan, letter: "I feel that I must respond to your statement that 'Jesus never condemned same-sex love.' That is not true. Same-sex love was specifically condemned by Jesus' heavenly father in Leviticus. . . ."

Right from the start, every stack of Deb's mail included letters quoting Leviticus. (According to one Kalamazoo, Michigan, man, "God did not just have an off-day at Sodom & Gomorrah. That was his FIRST judgement on this lifestyle. Aids [sic] is the SECOND! Leviticus 18:22; Leviticus 20:13.") Virtually every time Deb is a guest on a radio talk show, at least one caller quotes Leviticus. It didn't take long for both of us to become sick of the way the Bible is used selectively to try to justify prejudice. Finally, on August 20, 1993, Deb responded with a column pointing out that most admonitions in Leviticus are completely ignored in modern-day society. For example, Christians who say they believe that every word, every punctuation mark, in their English-language Bible was dictated by God don't fret about getting their hair cut. ("You shall not round off the hair on your temples or mar the edges of your beard." Leviticus 19:27.) Meanwhile, many of them embrace verses labeling sex between men as an "abomination" that carries the death penalty because those excerpts lend an air of legitimacy to their fear and hatred of people who are different from themselves.

Predictably, Deb's Bible bias column set off a new round of pretzel-making among her detractors.

They begin by defending the violation of ancient Hebrew laws spelled out in Leviticus. ". . . When the Old Testament was written, people weren't equipped to cook pork and shellfish properly." ". . . Christians believe that the old Israelite rules about dress and food were revoked by a certain dream Peter had." "Christ's teachings superseded much of this old Jewish law. . . . The overwhelming majority of practicing Christians never have given heed to those Old Testament restrictions. . . . Any good Bible student knows when to deliniate [sic] between the strict codes given to the Jews and the eternal directives handed down from God."

Then they want Deb to quit trying to understand the book that they keep throwing at her. ". . . The Bible cannot be read with mind. . . . Neither God nor his Word may be logically or scientifically analyzed."

Finally, one of the anti-gay zealots voiced a sentiment to which I could shout "Amen!" "In conclusion, I would hope that people would not quote certain parts of the Bible without reading other parts."

Deb was inundated with mail after she wrote about the Bible, but a larger portion of it than we'd anticipated was positive. More members of the clergy wrote to praise that article than to damn it. "Last week's column on the selective use of scripture was dead-on. That message has to be disseminated more widely so that the game played by the so-called 'religious' homophobes can be exposed for its hypocrisy. Your work is an important blessing to many," wrote a Catholic priest from Rochester, New York. An Episcopal priest in Palm Springs, California, complimented Deb and asked for permission to share that column with four thousand members of his denomination. A clergyman from Buffalo thanked Deb for "raising the issue to a civil, droll and thoughtful level. . . . We're justified by God's call, not by our observance of any law, ordinance or canon."

Of all the letters Deb received about the Bible bias column, two from lesbians illustrate best why we gay people cannot allow religion to be turf ruled by the likes of Pat Robertson. Neither woman had been familiar with Deb's column. Sitting a continent apart, each of them just happened to turn on a C-Span broadcast of Deb's 1993 keynote address to the National Lesbian and Gay Journalists Association conference. They heard Deb read the Bible column. And they were delighted.

One wrote from a "small, redneck little town" in Washington State, where she lives with her partner, Pam, and their baby daughter:

As I listened to you speak I was both laughing and at times crying. One of the things I am told repeatedly by co-workers, friends and, unfortunately, family is "the only problem I have with your lifestyle is the fact that the Bible says it's wrong." I have never been well read as far as the Bible is concerned and often didn't know how to respond to this statement. I loved your responses! . . . I want you to know that I have never written a letter to someone that I saw on television. Pam will probably cut me off when she sees the phone bill. The security guard at The Detroit

News *thought I was funny because it was 1 A.M. in Detroit when I called
[for the* News' *address]. . . . Thank you from across the U.S.A.*

She enclosed a sweet snapshot of her family. The other woman
wrote from Delaware:

*I thoroughly enjoyed [your speech] and was very moved by the personal
warmth you added by relating your family experiences with Joyce. My
spouse, Debbie, and I have been in a very loving lesbian relationship for
thirteen years but up until the last year have had no contact with similar
relationships. It is so validating to hear of other committed lesbian marriages. . . . Religion has been a painful subject for me ever since Debbie
and I began our relationship. We were both raised in very staunch Baptist
households. Consequently we have been beaten over the head with scripture for the last thirteen years. I actually minored in religion in college,
however, it was a Baptist College and to this day the echoes of my
parents', professors' and pastors' voices ring so loudly in my ears that I
cannot hear the actual truth in the scriptures over the pandemonium. I also
have very dear friends who are very religious and are struggling to justify
their love for Debbie and I while their church is condemning us. I would
love to become active with the religious community again but feel I need to
be able to defend myself against the biblical mudslinging that I am bound
to encounter.*

The best defense against those who would hurl the Bible at
gay people is the Bible itself. If you don't believe me, just take the
suggestion of a Rochester, Michigan, reader: "Look at Proverbs
20:10 to see that 'diverse weights and measures' are an 'abomination.' So there you have it. Homosexual behavior ranks right up
there with using the metric system in terms of odious behavior."

MANY OF THE BEST LETTERS THAT I GET MY HANDS ON WHEN I DIP
into Deb's mail come from friendly heterosexuals. Deb is the first
gay person that many have come to know. Others write about gay
friends, relatives or colleagues. Some talk about seeing the similarities between their lives and those of gay people. A few offer Deb
what they consider helpful hints.

I particularly cherish letters from gay-friendly veterans whose voices were ignored during the din over the ban on openly gay members of the armed forces. "I am a veteran of WWII, and the presence of gays in our unit was not disrupting," wrote a Hollister, Missouri, man. Another veteran of World War II, one who served overseas three years, wrote from Winthrop, Massachusetts, that he "never heard or noticed anyone being annoyed by gays. However, our frequent concern while in the shower was to make certain that our limited funds or possessions of any interest were not stolen. Incidentally, I have written to Senator Nunn of my personal concerns during military service while in the shower. Yes, indeed, it was our money and not men having sex with men!"

I'm also heartened by the number of heterosexuals writing about parallels between gay lives and their own. One California husband wrote about violating gender norms by being less ambitious than his wife and by encouraging her to make all the financial decisions. Unmarried straight couples wrote that they, too, struggle to find a comfortable term to use in introducing each other. A gay-friendly Rochester, New York, woman declared: "No one should have to explain what they do in the privacy of their bedroom—gay or not. Shouldn't our bedrooms be off limits to the hate-mongers?" And a Detroit nurse with a one-year-old daughter wrote she was "simply horrified and outraged by the court taking a child away from a lesbian mother. Personally, I'd rather have my daughter raised by a lesbian who loves her than by a judge who strips people of their humanity simply for being gay. What next? . . . Will smokers lose their kids? Will someone take my kid if they find out I lived with her father a year and a half before we were married? . . . Will they take kids from people simply for not being Christian? Where does it end?" Some of these people remain anonymous because they fear the possible repercussions of reaching out to a gay columnist:

No, I am not gay myself. I belong to an equally mistrusted segment of society. I am a single female well beyond marriageable years—i.e: an old maid. I deal with the public constantly, and, since I do not have a handy male escort, I frequently have to explain that I am not gay. In many instances, I would be more accepted if I were. . . . I am not going to sign this letter. I am ashamed that I am not doing so.

Again and again, straight readers confirmed that knowing gay people makes them like gay people and support equal rights for us:

When I was thirty, I shared a house with two schoolteachers who thought three women living together looked "less suspicious" than two. Happily, ten years later they are recognized as a couple and one of them has become an elementary school principal. . . . I can only look foward to the day when people are accepted for what they are, not what they are expected to be.

—*Stockton, Calif.*

Since moving to Santa Cruz in 1989, it seems that most of our new friends are gays & lesbians, most "just folks" rather than stereotypes. Issues affecting them affect me & my husband, as we don't want to see friends lacking things we take for granted. . . . I hope Hawaii . . . sets a precedent [legalizing gay marriage] that is followed.

—*California*

I am a straight woman, in her mid-forties, married, etc. A few years ago I worked for a company that became a victim of the recession, and I was forced to find other work. The only job that was available was as a retail clerk in a very new-age type of retail store. My boss was a lesbian. . . . I was so impressed with her. She was fair . . . reasonable . . . extremely kind and compassionate. . . . I have worked for some bitches in my time, all very straight, very married, very mean. . . . I keep her in my prayers. I hope that she never experiences the attitudes of people without an ounce of understanding in their hearts.

—*Bermuda Dunes, Calif.*

I have had to help my lesbian friends avoid "witch-hunts" by being their apparent companion, even at the cost of being told I was having several affairs. This started in the Army—I just didn't think it was Uncle Sam's business—and continues to this day with several friends in government positions. My wife has helped with gays. We both wish it wasn't required. . . . A [lesbian] couple my wife and I really like broke up because they couldn't be open.

—*Chapel Hill, N.C.*

Right from the first, Deb has heard regularly from supportive relatives—usually parents—of gay people. "Tony's Mom" wrote from Palm Springs, California:

It has almost been two years but really more like twenty for me. Maybe I knew before he did. I did know but knowing & accepting are two worlds. When he finally told us, a wall exploded. It was a wall we all helped build. . . . I mail him your columns & reread the ones I tape over my wall desk. Thank you for building a bridge from knowledge to understanding and acceptance. P.S.: My favorite is your Bible verse article.

A Kimberling City, Missouri, woman who reads Deb's column in the *Springfield News-Leader* wrote:

I guess our greatest fear is that someone will injure or kill our son and son-in-law just because they are gay, without ever coming to know what fine young men they are. I believe your column can change someone's mind about how they feel about homosexuality.

Opening a letter from someone whose mind has been changed is an extraordinary reward. Deb, her hands unsullied by Ooey Gooey-grams, tries to snatch those letters away while I'm still reading them:

I am a white, forty-four-year-old male—very straight, very narrow-minded and was very scared about talking about gay people. That is until I started reading your column in The Saratogian. *. . . (Your piece on Janis Ian—outstanding.) Please keep writing. There are so many people who think like I used to.*

—*Saratoga Springs, N.Y.*

Your column has greatly affected the way I look at gay human beings and caused me to reexamine the way I've looked at the world. . . .

P.S.: I am probably not your average reader. I am forty-seven years old, married, Republican, male and retired from the U.S. Army.

—*Rogersville, Mo.*

Judging from readers' responses, Deb's column usually seems to erode prejudice and misunderstanding slowly, like a drop of water and another and another falling on a stone week after week. But sometimes a single article will wash away a lifetime of hostility or indifference. A Dickson, Tennessee, woman, who "would be saddened if any of my sons announced they were gay," was nevertheless touched by the October 16, 1992, column noting that evil triumphs when bystanders do nothing. "I cannot see myself actively supporting the gay movement," she told Deb, "but because of your article I will now stand up for them if I see them being discriminated against in my area." I believe tens of millions of Americans can, with encouragement, reach a similar destination. No, they may never be eager to embrace gay people or dance at our weddings. We don't need them to. We just need them to stand up for our civil rights.

Having never played Ooey Gooey as a child, Deb sometimes gets confused about which letters are treats. I actually caught Ms. Thin-Skinned trying to put the following New York State fan letter from a woman with old-fashioned handwriting into the hate mail stack: "Dear Ms. Price, You write a fine column, and I'm sure you are a very smart gal. You would sure be more attractive if you would cut your hair and have it styled. Long hair is not for everyone. It's OK for Whistler's Mother." That letter represents the ultimate mainstreaming of gay issues! Finally, an openly gay columnist is getting unsolicited hairstyling advice just like Dave Barry, Ann Landers and almost every other columnist in America.

THE MOST CONSISTENT REWARD IN READING DEB'S MAIL IS HEARING from gay people—slightly more gay letters come from men than women—who are delighted to have the column in their family newspaper or, in many cases, to know that it exists even if they cannot read it regularly. Most understand that Deb's role makes her a lightning rod and just want to offer an encouraging word.

Despite the extraordinary diversity of Deb's gay readers, almost all who write seem to share our belief in the importance of taking a positive yet realistic approach to gay issues. After reading Deb's mail for years, I can tick off on the fingers of one hand the negative gay letters. And most of those were just from grouchy readers attempting to be helpful. One lesbian, for example, said, "I think your column is too happy. . . . I am glad you are being published; I just hope you will use the exposure you possess to enlighten the gay and straight population to the fact that our life is full of discrimination. . . ." I'd like to introduce her to the gay man who wrote to accuse Deb of not having a sense of humor. Another gay man complained about Deb's hair. (Heaven help us if the common ground we're always searching to find for gay and straight America turns out to be inside a beauty salon!) The only gay letter that ever made Deb angry came from a fifty-two-year-old lesbian who urged: "Don't get into any rompin'-stompin' gay activism or AIDS-related stuff. We're associated too much with AIDS already." For a gay columnist to ignore AIDS would be more than unprofessional; it would surely be a sin.

The closet is such a handy metaphor for concealing homosexuality that it's easy to slip into thinking that everyone living "in the closet" is in a similar situation emotionally, legally, socially. When I hear someone is closeted, my immediate reaction is to think of how my own life was in the years that I knew I was gay, had a loving relationship with a wonderful woman and had a few gay friends but wasn't explicitly out to my parents or my bosses. I was quite consciously trying to move toward the openness that's such a joy now. Millions of gay Americans do have walk-in closets that pretty closely match that description. But some of Deb's saddest mail reminds me that other closets look quite different:

> For over sixty of my years of life, long, long before I knew what a "homosexual" is or had even heard the word, I have been one. I have and do live otherwise. That one monstrous duplicity has been followed by others and the guilt has had me under care for stress, anxiety and, finally, severe chronic and clinical depression.
>
> —a Hawaii husband, married forty-plus years

I am a closeted gay individual who has hidden my sexuality since I can remember. I fought for many years when I was younger to rid myself of this perceived "curse" but to no avail. After several years of counseling, I married and now have a family, always keeping my sexuality a secret. My life is essentially normal, void of any real feelings or the ability to share intimately with anyone around me.

—no name, no gender, Rochester, N.Y.

About the column: I am enjoying it immensely! . . . I also appreciate your willingness to share tidbits from your relationship with Joyce. You two are so very lucky. I do envy you. I have neither the courage (I am a public school teacher) nor the motivation (the woman I love, have been in love with for twenty-nine years, is heterosexual) to come out. Sincerely yours, Jane Doe.

—Detroit

Not all the correspondence from the closet is heartrending, though. This lovely anonymous letter postmarked Buffalo arrived just a month after features editor Terry Murphy and Dr. Anonymous succeeded in generating enough positive feedback to keep Deb's column running in Niagara Falls. Deb wishes she could tell its author that her column runs in The Key West Citizen:

Dear Deb Price,

Love your articles in the Niagara Falls Gazette. Hope they continue forever.

I admire your openness about gay life. I'm an older person from the OLD school and I guess I'll never come out of the closet. There are a group of us from western New York, we meet at each other's homes for dinners and small parties. We vacation together and enjoy life as best we can. All of us are professional people and the youngest is forty-six.

I always wanted to find a "valley" [as in the July 24, 1992, column] where me and mine could live together and enjoy the people around us who were also gay. Sort of a "gay paradise." A place where we all help each other, care for each other and—if and when alone—you are not left out. No bar scenes and no hanky-panky.

You are doing all of us a big service with your column.

I head south in the winter and have found a church that is friendly and open to all gays. The people are much like myself, OLDER, QUIET and SECLUDED. This is my first step into an openness of sorts. I'm thankful for it.

Your column is well written and informative. Do you write for any of the west coast Florida newspapers? I'd like to pick one up each time you write.

Keep up your good work. I'm not putting an address or a name, but I wanted you to know how I felt.

Sincerely,

A happy, retired, gay person

Many other readers have written that they'd be happier if they were less closeted. Deb responds to the signed letters with suggestions on how to contact gay groups or P-FLAG (Parents, Families and Friends of Lesbians and Gays).

Any advice on breaking the news to my family? Mom and Dad come from a small town in northwestern Michigan, very Roman Catholic, very Polish. I'm not sure how they'll react, but I know I can't continue to lie and cover up.

—Troy, Mich.

The lesbian bars, if they exist in and around Detroit, don't seem to do much advertising in the News. *How does one plug into the social clubs, the gay subculture, the non-traditional underground? . . . Just where are the clues? This may be the Nineties, but the closet is still full. I am happy for you and for Joyce. The* News *has two new readers faithful on Fridays.*

—[signed] Delighted

When the column was exactly one year old, a New Yorker who follows it in both *The Niagara Gazette* and the *Rochester Democrat and Chronicle* wrote:

Dear Deb,

Happy first anniversary. . . . You make me very proud—first as a woman facing discrimination and second as a gay woman facing two forms of discrimination. I'm also proud of you for being out—wish I was. . . .

Me? I'm a twenty-nine-year-old gay man who still lives at home for financial reasons. . . . Thank you very much for fifty-something articles. . . . I have no gay friends, and you are my window on the world. . . . (Hi Joyce.)

For a few readers, writing Deb becomes part of their coming-out process. Deb heard from a "gay-friendly" college student from San Jose three times, including once when she needed help with a gay-rights term paper. Then Deb happened to write a column on September 24, 1993, about how disrespectful we are to our partners and ourselves if we deceive others about the nature of our relationship. A fourth letter arrived:

I said I was a straight girl whose best friend is gay. That is true, my best friend is gay. What I didn't tell you is that I myself am gay. . . . I felt the need to set the record straight (so to speak), because I need to start somewhere. . . . I've dated women exclusively for the last couple of years. . . . The only person I was fooling was myself. Your articles and letters really helped give me the guts to finally come out.

A bisexual man from Minneapolis wrote to thank Deb for "sweeping out the closets and letting in the sunshine." He added, "Now maybe the closets can be used to store those unseasonable items we're not ready to part with but we no longer actually need. Now that we don't need to live there."

Whenever a newspaper picks up Deb's column, the first letters from gay readers usually focus on the column's sheer existence:

The gals here in the Twin Cities are delighted to have your column running in the Star Tribune. *When I told friends about it, I was accused of hallucinating, but now they've seen it for themselves.*

—Minneapolis

It is nice to see the subject of homosexuality treated casually for once. . . . I know I'm not alone when I say how nice it feels to be included in the mainstream in a way, outside of the witch-hunt military ban and bogus hetero studies. Those people who got all upset and threatened to cancel their subscriptions should do just that. That way they can keep themselves deep in the caves wrapped up in the "family values." Oops, looks like that darn soapbox snuck under my feet again.

—Minneapolis

I think it's wonderful to finally have a news reporter that not only covers the serious issues about being gay but the fun ones as well. Many times when I see an article about my lifestyle I think, "Who's suppressing me now?" I was overjoyed to see your article on gay rodeos, not just because I'm a horse fan but also because it's a positive and productive activity of the gay community. Many times the articles I read about the gay community focus on sex, AIDS or whether our lifestyle is "deviant." Besides the fact that some of these articles are written by homophobic heterosexuals, they sometimes portray gay people as bitter and corrupt individuals. As a gay person I know this isn't true. I love my lifestyle and believe that gay people are the most outgoing and accepting people on earth (this statement may be a little biased). So I give you a pat on the back for reporting on everyday events in the gay community.

—Ithaca, N.Y.

Thank you for your columns on gay issues and history that appear in the San Jose Mercury News. *They have opened a new pathway of communications between my mother and myself. Since Christmas she has sent me several of your columns and commented on the subject in her letters. Before that I had never expected to hear her say the word "lesbian"—and now she writes it!*

—West Linn, Ore.

In the original Ooey Gooey game, all the prizes were small. But when I reach into Deb's mail, every now and then I pull out a major treat, a handmade work of art that crystallizes some aspect of gay life in twentieth-century America. Opening one of my favorites, postmarked Rochester, New York, triggered an Ooey Gooey alert. It was a fabulously false alarm:

Dear Deb,

I want to call you Deborah, a beautiful name, but if you prefer Deb, drab as it may be, then Deb it is.

John and I read your column every Thursday in our local Democrat and Chronicle. *The first one I saw, and my favorite, was the "couples things" column [June 12, 1992] where you spoke of your lover's love of gardening and the problems you've encountered with it. Oh how this hit home! However, our case is a bit different than yours as we're both gardeners. I'm flowers and bushes; John is vegetables. We curse when we trip over the other's pots, tools, etc. In early March, we compete for the grow lights for our indoor seedlings. Outdoors, in summer, I become furious when his zucchini vines start strangling my pansy bed and he becomes likewise when I cut them back. What he grows is rambling, naughty and in need of constant spanking. What I grow is beautiful and well behaved.*

You're a gifted writer, Deb, but your writing's major significance is being there, there in a conventional newspaper to be read by all. Who knows how many doors and windows you have opened.

Where was your column during my growing years? It didn't exist, of course, nor any other like it. In the late Fifties and early Sixties, there was no positive media. If our local newspaper addressed homosexuality, it usually did so with malice and disgust. Now, here you are, a delight for adult gays and lesbians and an inspiration to young ones. The gay youth of today can read your words and perhaps hate themselves a little less. Some may even take pride in being different.

I indulged in sex at a very early age and hated myself for it; and the guilt, always the guilt, the constant guilt. Had there been a gay person to confide in, I may have felt differently. There was none.

I was seventeen, almost eighteen, when I first met gay people socially who had other interests than sex. They liked me. I liked them. It was a glorious event in my life.

I was nineteen when I met John. He was twenty-one. This May 30 [1993] we celebrate our thirtieth year together. Our relationship is strong and complete and, pardon my smugness, more rewarding than any other gay or straight relationship I've seen. We are very fortunate.

This former ugly duckling, now a swan, thanks you for the pleasure you bring to us each Thursday morning.

Sincerely,
Dick

P.S. I know, I know, Dick is a drab name compared to Richard, but I'm too old to change it.

When I opened that first letter from Dick, Deb and I had been together not quite eight years. Getting acquainted with a couple who've still got humor and a spark after almost four times as long was quite inspiring. Now I never look at an aggressive zucchini vine without thinking of John, who dropped us a note after their benchmark anniversary: "Our thirtieth was nice, but it was quiet. Every day of our life together is a celebration, even on those nights when we hardly say anything to each other."

While Dick was trying to imagine what it would have been like to have had Deb's column around during his growing years, Kim Casey found that the column was helping her to blossom:

Dear Miss Price,

It's funny, as gay people, the weapons we use to defend ourselves against the world. Tonight, after a youth group meeting held around the theme of "coming out," I began to think about my own weapons. I remembered the day I made the decision to tell my parents, standing outside their room with my hands trembling on the knob until I decided to take a walk. I remembered my voice, slow and methodical after that walk, and how my hands were steady as I talked and, after a while, handed my parents the two pieces of paper I had carefully folded and hidden away that morning. One was a celebration of National Coming Out Day, an article on gay youth with a picture of my lover on the front. The other was a newspaper piece detailing the horrors of homophobia. This was yours. As a weapon, the picture of my girlfriend gave me the strength I needed, but it was your article that gave me the reasoning behind my request for the love and support of my parents. It struck fear in me, as it did my parents, but above that stood out the message that I looked for—that understanding and openness are important not only between gay people, but between everybody else as well.

Having your column to look forward to each week, as I eagerly awake early to grab the front section of The Desert Sun, *has helped me find much more than a defense against arguments. I realized this tonight. It also gives me a frame of understanding through which I have been able to see my culture, my pride and my identity, things I had so sorely lacked and so desperately needed. Your insights have encouraged me to explore myself as a lesbian woman and homosexual through your references to books, articles and famous people who I could call heroes. In other words, after the support of my lover, I consider your work the most important aspect of my coming out.*

Now as a member of the board of directors at G.A.Y. (Gay Associated Youth), I am proud to be the only young adult and the only lesbian assigned to direct and encourage other teens in their efforts to find themselves.

Our group, centered in Palm Springs, holds weekly meetings discussing gay issues, particularly those important to young people. The information in your column also provides our group with a connection to our gay culture, a shot of reality amongst the palms in our little gay world. It's an exciting place to emerge with all the tourism and events that give residents a little more respect and understanding. We are, perhaps, more free, as the picture [of her lover and herself] I have sent shows.

It was taken at this year's Homecoming dance at Palm Springs High School, where I escorted my lover. The event was fairly quiet with very little name-calling or harassment, even when we slow danced before what seemed like a thousand staring high school eyes. The rumors that emerged were much more exciting than the actual dance. (Neither I nor Melissa is fond of school functions, particularly fancy ones.)

Through all this, I look happily, even gayly to what the future holds —days of love and friendship, the Dinah Shore golf tournament, the Palm Springs Gay Pride Festival, the march on Washington and coffee in the morning, curled up on the couch with my copy of Deb Price.

> *Respectfully yours,*
> *Kim Heather Casey*

Kim knew at sixteen that she was gay and told her parents on National Coming Out Day, 1992, when she was eighteen. I met Kim a year later during a trip to Palm Springs. She was training horses, taking college courses and hoping to become an English professor. After Kim told me over lunch that her parents took her sexual orientation very much in stride, I gave her mother a call.

Twenty minutes later, Kim's mom and I were chatting beside her backyard pool in La Quinta. The oldest of six children, Kim is named after her mother, who doesn't mind being called Kim Sr.

She says her oldest daughter's 1992 announcement surprised her. "Looking back on it, there were probably things that should have tipped us off. My husband would tell you that he knew."

The night Kim broke the news, Kim Sr. recalls, "She came to us and said, 'We need to have this little talk.' And . . . she goes, 'You know I'm eighteen, I'm your daughter, I love you and I'm gay.' And we were like, 'Eeeek! Okay, well, that's one way to tell us, dear.' "

Kim Sr. and her husband read the clippings Kim handed them. But, Kim Sr. says, "I don't think we really needed the arsenal of what she had to back her up. I think it helped her more than anything."

She believes that she and her husband reacted calmly, after a moment of shock, because "we'd been exposed to gay people in the past. We know them on a one-on-one basis, and they're just people." She says Kim has "always been a different kid," really curious, hardworking, bright, independent. Her sexual orientation "is nothing to get upset over. It's just part of her, and she's a package. If she weren't gay, she wouldn't be who she is. She'd be a different person, and I like the person she is."

The letters Deb and I most treasure turn strangers into friends we simply haven't met yet. That's how we immediately felt about Linda Marquez and Juanita (Johnnie) Hernandez:

Dear Deb Price,

Just wanted to tell you how much we enjoy your column in The Desert Sun *newspaper in Palm Springs, California. We read your column every Tuesday. It certainly is great to read about cities that allow us to be ourselves [Provincetown, Massachusetts; August 14, 1992, column]. I didn't think any such place existed. We loved your [August 7, 1992] article on [*Fried Green Tomatoes*]. Believe me, we all saw the same movie you did. We love the way you include your partner in life in your column. That is just nothing short of great. You have shared so many wonderful stories with us, I would like to share a story with you.*

Johnnie and I are forty-three years old. We have been together twenty-six years. Way back in 1966, her fiancé asked me to take care of her while he did his stint in the Army. (Germany.)

Well, we were still in high school, and we were just friends. Well, actually, she had already knocked my socks off when I saw her in the P.E. showers. She was gorgeous! Well, we hung out together. Finally after six months I kissed her. She kissed me back! It was a glorious night! Yes indeed! I realized that this was just a temporary thing. When [her fiancé] came back, she would go with him. As all straight girls did. Well, I continued to see my other "friends" and a few months passed. Johnnie tells me that she doesn't want me to see anyone else. I told her that I couldn't burn my bridges behind me. She would leave me when [her fiancé] returned and I would be left alone. Well, she removed her engagement ring, threw it over the fence, wrote [her fiancé] a letter, stating the engagement was over, and the rest is history. Here we are in 1992 still committed to one another. The honeymoon still isn't over. I always tell Johnnie that I wished there was a place where we could walk hand in hand or arm in arm and not be sneered at. Just be accepted as another couple in society. Well, thanks to you, Deb Price, Johnnie and I and a few other couples are planning a vacation trip to Provincetown, Massachusetts.

Thank you for your column and all of the information you give us through your articles.

Hope you liked our little story. Thought you would like a story with a happy ending. Since you give us so much, we thought we'd give you a little something to read. And a great big embrace to you both and a great big thank you!

Sincerely,
Linda Marquez

In the fall of 1993 Deb and I finally met Johnnie and Linda face-to-face when they attended a speech Deb gave in Palm Springs. Deb had to head back to Washington almost immediately, but I stayed in town a few days and heard more of the Linda and Johnnie story over dinner.

They'd been Earth-bound with zero interest in boarding an airplane to anywhere until Deb wrote about the joys of walking hand in hand through Provincetown. "We always said, 'We're never going to fly.' I'm not flying; she's not flying. Then this article—she says, 'I'm flying to this.' I said, 'Okay,' " recalls Johnnie, who's generally much quieter than Linda.

They flew to P-town with four friends, returning home just the week before our dinner interview. Together Linda and Johnnie excitedly showed me photographs, already arranged and labeled in an album. (If only Deb and I could ever be so organized!) "We never knew a town existed where we could go and be ourselves. Without that article, we would never have known," Linda says. "It was great to walk down the street and have Johnnie put her arm through my arm. Nobody staring or making faces at you. It was great! And I held her hand at the table—no big deal."

Linda and Johnnie are loyal to Deb's column because it gives them gay information they've never found elsewhere. "It's a window for us," Linda explains. "It's a window to the outside world."

After more than a quarter century together, Linda and Johnnie still can't get enough of each other. Driving forklifts and filling orders, they are the entire staff of a telephone company warehouse. They are together constantly. When relatives descend on them on the weekend, Linda and Johnnie often flee to the movies just to spend more time alone. "A lot of people ask, 'How can you stand it?'" Johnnie confides. Linda answers, "It works because Johnnie is real happy. She's just real mellow all the time. And if I get riled up, she just is like, 'Yeah, well, there's nothing we can do about it so, you know, calm down.' I rant and rave like a maniac, then everything is okay. So if I get excited, she's the buffer. So it works out real good. We're real compatible. . . . Every year it feels like I'm more passionately in love with her."

Linda was a sophomore in high school before she had a label —"homosexual"—for herself. By then, she'd known for years that she was different from most of her classmates. "I asked the nurse in elementary school to give me a shot to make me like everybody else because I knew I wasn't chasing little boys and letting them chase me. I just didn't fit in." She soon quit searching for a cure: "I couldn't feel what they wanted me to feel. I just knew I was different and there was nobody that was going to tell me that I was going to live like Mom and Dad did. I couldn't do it."

During high school, Linda helped her father every day from 4 to 7 A.M. and again after school. "My dad was a gardener," she relates. "And he was checking out women on his side of the truck. . . . And I was checking out women on my side. Of course, Dad didn't have a clue. He was busy."

She was dating other girls when she fell in love with Johnnie. The evening Johnnie threw her fiancé's ring over the fence, Linda recalls, "I got on the phone and made some calls and said *'adios'* to everybody else."

Unfortunately, Linda and Johnnie didn't have a healthy relationship of any sort to model theirs on. Linda had grown up not knowing there could be home life without breaking furniture, without screaming. She tried to be as macho as her male relatives; Johnnie as subservient as her female kin. Looking back, Linda says, "I went out drinking and I left her at home and I expected her to be there when I got back. Thing is, Johnnie never expected to be treated otherwise because all her brothers-in-law treat their wives like that. . . . When I came home, she'd ask if I was hungry and fix me something to eat. And I was just a rotten person. When I turned twenty-six was my turning point, was when I stopped and evaluated during a hangover: 'I've got to make some changes here or Johnnie is not going to stick around much longer.'

"I quit drinking, not completely but not leaving her home and going drinking with my buddies. And then I told her, 'We're going to buy a house and go the whole nine yards. If we're going to go with this relationship, we're going to do it.' We were living in a house that leaked every time it rained. . . . The house we live in now is the house we bought," Linda says.

Over the years, Linda and Johnnie have tailored their roles so that their relationship is much more equal. Johnnie, who's learned to be more assertive, now handles all the bills, for example. Being part of both the gay and Latino communities is especially challenging, they say. "The Latinos are very narrow-minded. It's either right or it's wrong. There is no in-between," Linda explains. She and Johnnie left the Catholic Church because they tired of its anti-gay dogma. And, gradually, they've come out to all Linda's relatives and most of Johnnie's, who are quite religious.

"Little by little, I tell the young ones before they are totally corrupted," Linda explains. Shortly before my visit, she'd told Johnnie's fifteen-year-old nephew: " 'Me and your Aunt Johnnie have been living together twenty-seven years, right?' And he goes, 'Yeah.' And I said, 'Well, I think it's time that you know we're lesbians. . . . Does it make any difference?' And he said, 'No, I don't think so.' And I said, 'Well, I'm the same person I was five minutes ago.' . . . And he said, 'I never expected you to tell me that.' 'Well, tell me how you feel.' And he said, 'Well, I still love my Aunt Johnnie a lot. And you guys are still really important.' And I said, 'That's all I wanted to know.' "

Linda and Johnnie dote on each other, flirt with each other and clearly have built a strong, healthy life together. Their home in Cathedral City includes a music room, studded with an amazing array of Elvis Presley photos, where Linda practices the romantic songs she's hired to perform at local fraternal lodges. With Johnnie smiling in the doorway, Linda serenaded me in Spanish and English. A mellow alto, she ended by crooning a ballad whose title she translates as "If They Let Us." Linda, who never forgets having had to seize her forbidden love, gave Johnnie a knowing look and said, "They'd never *let* us."

Many people spend their entire lives dreaming of the kind of love and companionship Linda and Johnnie have found. Finding a soulmate is never easy, but it's especially hard for older people in this youth-oriented culture. If you're also gay and closeted, the prospects of even finding a dear friend can seem bleak. That's why Deb jumped at the chance to write about a national organization for older lesbians in search of women like themselves. Several of the papers that ran the resulting column omitted the group's address. Soon polite requests for the address flooded in. Older lesbians use very nice stationery. And they know how to spell.

COLUMNS

JULY 2, 1993–JANUARY 7, 1994

> ### *GOLDEN THREADS* HELPS WEAVE
> ### CONNECTIONS FOR LONELY LESBIANS

JULY 2, 1993

L ike many successful professionals married to their jobs, Christine Burton awoke one morning and realized she was deeply lonely. Never shy about grabbing life by the collar, the lifelong lesbian fired off a check and a description of herself to a service that promised to help like-minded women connect.

Less than a week later her check was returned with a note: "Unless you made a mistake about your date of birth, we can't do anything for you. Nobody is looking for lesbians older than fifty."

Burton, a very precise and deliberate woman, had made no mistake. She was born in 1905.

Appalled by the arrogance of youth, Burton, then seventy-four, vowed not only to find friendship—and maybe more—for herself but also to help other mature lesbians keep from being cast aside.

She had to defer her dream for four years, until she sold her twenty-one-employee tax-preparation business in Massachusetts. Only then did she have time to start *Golden Threads,* a quarterly newsletter for lesbians over fifty who want to correspond with one another.

"I conceive of humanity with each individual like a thread in a fabric," says the original Golden Threader, now an eighty-seven-year-old feminist who emphasizes her points by rolling up a tight fist and slugging the air. "Each of us is essential to the fabric."

Over the years, *Golden Threads* has knitted together sixteen hundred older lesbians around the globe. The current newsletter that proclaims "You're never too old to love or be loved" contains 120 notices from would-be pen pals. All are assured confidentiality.

Burton says she's received countless thank-yous from Golden Threaders who say, "I'll never be lonely again." She shares that sentiment, declaring, "I've never had so many friends in my life!"

Her aversion to age limits means that lesbians under fifty are welcome in the network for our older sisters. Anyone with a birth certificate proving she's at least eighty receives a free lifetime membership.

Every member gets a strong dose of Burton's philosophy that happiness is the best tonic for an ailing society. "Every contact I have I try to make a person feel better about themselves, feel warm, friendly and happy," she explains. "It's not Pollyannaism. It's simply good mental health because happiness is normal." Burton's philosophy is not, well, merely philosophical. She lives it by being everything American culture tells old people, especially old women, they can't be—from fiercely independent to romantic.

In addition to producing her non-profit newsletter, Burton is matriarch of the *Golden Threads'* annual celebration in gay-friendly Provincetown, Massachusetts. At the recent seventh gathering, which drew 180 women, she was the dancer in aqua socks and Birkenstock sandals.

Asked about her current wooing of Joy Griffith, a dynamic

fifty-eight-year-old teacher, Burton laughs: "If you're going to blame me for robbing the cradle, I'm going to say, 'What do you want me to do—rob the grave? Everybody my age is dead!' "

An ex-Michigan horse farmer who spent five years in a convent, Burton has lived more fully than most of us. And now she lives more openly than most lesbians or gay men one-third her age.

But she knows that the women most in need of *Golden Threads* are extremely isolated. In hopes of reaching them, Burton asks her Golden Threaders to leave lavender business cards with the address of her "discreet contact publication" on grocery store bulletin boards, on bus seats and inside library books. "I can tell when there's an active Golden Threader in an area. All of a sudden I start getting a whole lot of inquiries from one town," Burton says with satisfaction.

Gradually, the lesbians "nobody is looking for" weave their lives together. With *Golden Threads,* the indomitable Burton is embroidering her credo on heart after heart: "I refuse to stop living before I'm dead."

———

For information on Golden Threads, *write: P.O. Box 60475, Northampton, MA 01060-0475.*

Laws Are Unfair When Lovers Are Partners in Crime

JULY 9, 1993

We are a nation of sexual outlaws. And I don't mean we gay people. I mean we Americans.

Virtually every modern American couple has found sexual pleasure, research shows, in ways that would have offended the delicate sensibilities of Julie Andrews' prissy missionary husband in *Hawaii.* And when in the privacy of our bedrooms we deviate from the idea that sex is exclusively for married people attempting to produce the next generation, we become criminals in many states.

But since every lawbook contains bizarre, unenforced bans on things like setting a mousetrap without a hunting license, why should we care about moldy, misguided rules on so-called crimes against nature?

Well, in part because sometimes they are enforced. William C. L. Fry, for example, was sentenced to ten years in a North Carolina prison for consensual sodomy with a woman in 1987.

Sodomy, usually defined by lawmakers as oral and anal sex, remains illegal in the military and twenty-three states. Sodomy laws tend to apply to everyone. Even married couples are in jeopardy in twelve states. Unmarried heterosexuals, meanwhile, also confront fornication and cohabitation laws in many states.

Actual prosecutions are rare, but antiquated anti-sex laws are used with surprising frequency as an excuse to deny child custody, turn away would-be renters and reject job applicants.

Secular prohibitions on non-breeding sexual activity ironically date from the reign of English King Henry VIII, hardly Mister Fidelity. They were adopted by the American colonies and remained universal in this country until 1961, when Illinois enacted a model penal code decriminalizing private non-commercial sex between consenting adults.

State after state followed Illinois' lead until the AIDS crisis hit. Suddenly, state lawmakers were too timid to touch legislation that could be construed as "promoting" gay sex even if most of the people affected by it would be straight.

The already slowed decriminalization drive slammed into a brick wall with the U.S. Supreme Court's *Bowers v. Hardwick* decision in 1986. The court ruled 5 to 4 that the constitutional right to privacy does not protect the lovemaking of gay men and lesbians. The decision was silent about heterosexual sodomy.

In an impassioned dissent, Justice Harry Blackmun wrote that "the right of an individual to conduct intimate relationships in the intimacy of his or her own home seems to me to be the heart of the Constitution's protection of privacy."

The *Hardwick* decision tossed sexual-freedom issues back to the states. Kentucky's top court threw out its sodomy law in September. Courts in Texas, Tennessee and Louisiana are considering similar action. And this summer, for the first time since 1983, a state legislature has lifted a sodomy ban, thanks to Nevada State Senator Lori Lipman Brown.

"If people in my district don't believe enough in privacy to re-elect me because of this, I'm probably not the person they want up here," says Brown, a freshman Democrat. She pushed repeal of the gay-only sodomy law as a public health issue because fear of prosecution was discouraging gay men from getting AIDS tests.

But the piecemeal updating of America's sex statutes creates strange laws for bedfellows. Illinois, for example, forbids unmarried heterosexual "fornication" but not gay sex. Similarly, New Mexico and North Dakota outlaw male-female "cohabitation" but don't restrict same-sex relations.

Hoping to erase all such laws, Spectrum Institute of Los Angeles is trying to craft a national coalition for court challenges. But, realistically, some consensual sex laws will survive until we get a few more Supreme Court justices who respect individual liberty.

Even Russia, which in April dropped its ban on gay male sex, has stopped policing bedrooms. Isn't it time we demanded our own government recognize that what's really criminal is prying into the rightfully private lives of free men and women?

WE'VE MASTERED SEAT BELTS— NOW LET'S TRY SAFE SEX IN THE BACKSEAT

JULY 16, 1993

Remember diving headfirst over the front seat of a car barreling down the highway and getting hollered at for accidentally kicking the driver? What about sitting in a grown-up's lap and steering while barely tall enough to see over the hood?

Those were the days when astronauts seemed exotic for being strapped into their vehicles and when—to the ears of a six-year-old—"car safety" meant trying not to sit on the french fries. Only the french fries haven't changed.

Today, childhood begins in a rear-facing infant seat, progresses to ever-larger car seats and ends with the click—or automatic whoosh—of the shoulder harness that's become standard equipment for adulthood. Even Clint Eastwood's Dirty Harry now buckles up.

My generation's recollections of treating the inside of a car like a trampoline must sound as harebrained to today's kids as tales of standing on a running board did thirty years ago. Yes, our late-blooming national infatuation with auto safety has made youngsters experts on staying alive in the fast lane.

If only we were teaching today's twelve-year-olds as much about avoiding a fatal accident in the backseat of a parked car as we are about being safe in the front seat of a moving car.

The young people now on the brink of puberty came into this world just as the AIDS crisis surfaced. But in a dozen years no national AIDS prevention plan has been adopted to try to keep them safe from the disease that has already killed more than 179,000 Americans.

Seventy-five percent of today's twelve-year-olds will be sexually active before high school graduation. And if they follow the example of their older sisters and brothers, most will flirt with disaster by failing to use condoms regularly.

The car seat crowd, which was consistently taught to accept passenger restraints as natural, still thinks of condoms as optional equipment. Thousands of those children will pay with their lives for the truth about AIDS transmission.

The shame of the nation is that, unlike with traffic fatalities, we've not yet learned that too many people have died of AIDS. Complacency fuels the ignorance on which the deadly pestilence thrives: Widely dismissed as the scourge of gay men and intravenous drug abusers, AIDS is expanding among heterosexuals.

And even after so many deaths, the dying has barely begun. Characterizing the epidemic now is "like trying to take a snapshot of a tidal wave," warns the National Commission on AIDS. The lethal virus is already ticking away inside at least a million more Americans.

There is no known cure, no vaccine. Our only immediate hope is prevention through education.

Thanks to auto-safety campaigns, it's no longer common to hear "I only wear my seat belt on long trips." Yet supposedly smart folks in a nation where one in four people contracts some sexually transmitted disease foolishly try to calculate when unprotected sex is safe.

The fault lies largely with the federal government, which changed behavior and saved lives by championing seat belts, yet shies away from lifesaving lessons about AIDS.

The final report of the AIDS commission is a lamentation, a cry about warnings unheeded and deaths undeterred. As it has since 1991, the panel begs the White House to lead.

President Clinton, who seeks a $500 million boost in AIDS funds, has appointed the first AIDS czar. Kristine Gebbie, Washington State's ex-secretary of health, says: "He wants me to make this a coordinated national effort, pull the agencies together. . . . He's delivered the message loud and clear."

Gebbie, a nurse with gay friends, adds that she'll gauge her success in part by whether "we achieve a sense of community around this disease," by whether we can learn to fight a virus, not each other.*

Many of us who loved to jump around inside cars now eagerly pay extra for air bags and anti-lock brakes. Uncle Sam helped us grow up about car safety. It's way past time to help us grow up about AIDS.

---

* Wielding little political influence despite the title of her ill-defined job, Kristine Gebbie submitted her resignation July 8, 1994.

CLINTON'S LACK OF LEADERSHIP ROBS GAY SOLDIERS OF THEIR RIGHTS

JULY 20, 1993

Y ou have the right to remain silent.

That's what President Clinton, who for months allowed his strings to be pulled by the very military men sworn to obey his commands, finally told the gay men and lesbians serving this country. Forget freedom of speech. Forget equal protection under the law. And, while you're at it, forget candidate Clinton's "Not one person to waste."

The compromising we've heard so much about was really with the principles of the Constitution. The military brass, which balked at racial integration and still openly discriminates against women, essentially gets to keep the fifty-year-old ban that serves as a gag order for the gay men and lesbians in their ranks. Gets to keep it for now.

U.S. military leaders claim Vietnam taught them not to get into a war they cannot win. Yet they are doing just that in propping up a rule that is an affront to everything this nation tries to represent.

The president's long-overdue explanation Monday of why he

proposed lifting the ban simply underscores that this country could have dealt with this issue in an adult manner if he had chosen to lead. Instead, his "substantial advance" means only celibate or silent gays may serve.

Despite trying to craft a plan that can withstand constitutional challenges, Clinton ran afoul of the First Amendment: A serviceman will not be investigated for saying, "She is my girlfriend." But if a gay servicewoman dares to utter those words, the presumption will be that she is violating the Uniform Code of Military Justice. Expulsion or imprisonment will follow unless she proves celibacy.

Meanwhile, the vast majority of heterosexuals engage in sexual acts prohibited by the military code, yet are presumed innocent.

The White House and Pentagon now are giving gay people in uniform the warning normally reserved for accused criminals: If you choose to speak, anything you say can and will be used against you.

Although Clinton seems to support gay Americans, he has not yet learned that as commander in chief he cannot win a battle he does not fight. Clinton's "honorable compromise" was the best he could get only because he never rallied the nation to rise above prejudice.

The argument is widely heard that we gay folks don't deserve equal rights because we "choose" to be gay. I've never known anyone with a chosen sexual orientation. But the strangest part of that bogus argument is its assumption that all of us who are not straight white men would be, if we could be. Don't ask what I think about that idea. I'm sure I don't need to tell.

This is a shameful hour in the history of the United States. We lecture other nations on human rights yet do not even pretend to offer the gay citizens serving aboard our aircraft carriers and in our missile silos the chance to be judged solely on the basis of their job performance, loyalty and character.

The U.S. military's dinosaur will continue to chew up gay careers, but the armed forces of most Western allies live in the modern world. A recent report by the General Accounting Office, an investigative arm of Congress, highlights just how far behind we are.

The GAO studied as examples the experiences of Canada, Germany, Israel and Sweden, allies chosen because of their large militaries and involvement in regional conflicts or U.N. peacekeeping missions. Of the four, only Germany still somewhat limits gay military service.

"Military officials from each country said that, on the basis of their experience, the inclusion of homosexuals in their militaries has not adversely affected unit readiness, effectiveness, cohesion or morale," the GAO says.

Our allies not only point us toward fairer treatment of gays in the military, they also show how to get there: by dropping archaic laws on consensual sex and by banning anti-gay bias in employment.

Clinton's disappointing directive means the battle over gays in the military moves to the courts. It shall not end until gay men and lesbians no longer have to compromise their constitutional rights to serve the country they love.

GAY CARTOONISTS BRING CHARACTERS OUT OF THE CLOSET

JULY 23, 1993

If there's a Hall of Fame for home wreckers, Joyce wants to nominate Alison Bechdel.

She's the one who told us approvingly that Harriet and Mo (a short-cropped Monica) were "dykes to watch out for" and eventually introduced us to them. She's also responsible—at least in Joyce's mind—for their shocking breakup.

Perhaps Harriet and Mo wouldn't have seemed like such a perfect couple if they hadn't reminded us so much of our own relationship.

Like me, Mo is compulsively intense and intensely compulsive. Incapable of chitchat, she's also incapable of reading a newspaper or watching a movie without launching into what uncharitable folk could call a feminist tirade.

The world rests more lightly on the shoulders of Harriet and Joyce. The word "relax" is not foreign to them. And "sensible" describes more than their shoes. I can recall Harriet saying on a sweltering night, "Mo, stop. It's too hot to rave."

So I was doubly floored recently when Joyce, who'd calmly been reading a book of comic strips an hour before, met me at the front door raving: "Terrible news! Harriet and Mo split up! Call Alison Bechdel! #@*&! How could she do this? Call her right now! Something happened! We're missing the crucial strips!"

That's how I ended up calling Vermont to quiz the most popular gay cartoonist in America about why her characters Harriet and Mo are no longer joined in the strip. "I got sick of them. Harriet was like an ex-lover of mine," says Bechdel, who is quite Mo-ish herself. "They drifted apart," she says with the finality of an undertaker.

But Bechdel, a thirty-two-year-old who hopes she and all her *Dykes to Watch Out For* will grow old together, insists she isn't in total control of her two-dimensional lesbians. "They sort of take on a life of their own. And my job is to respect that as much as I can," she explains. Joyce, however, remains convinced that Bechdel drew Harriet and Mo apart.

Beyond the cultural confines of the Sunday funnies, gay cartooning is flourishing. The art form exploded—KABOOM!— in 1980 with publication of *Gay Comix,* a collection of gay cartoons and comic strips for adults. The publication was also a milestone for its first editor, Howard Cruse, a successful mainstream cartoonist best known for his *Barefootz* strip.

Cruse showed other cartoonists the way out of the closet.

"I saw early *Gay Comix* issues," recalls Bechdel, "and I didn't have to think about being a lesbian and drawing cartoons about my life. Somebody was already doing it—it was an option."

The industry in which superheroes competed with gangsters and zombies for drugstore shelf space has never quite recovered from McCarthy-era craziness. In 1953 psychiatrist Fredric Wertham charged that Batman and Robin were lovers and that Wonder Woman—who whipped foes into line with her golden lasso of truth—promoted lesbianism, says comics historian Andy Mangels.

Outraged parents burned comic books, and the U.S. Senate held televised hearings. (And you thought Senate hearings these days featured cartoon characters!) For years afterward, the industry "voluntarily" banned such pseudo-threats to youth as homosexuals and zombies.

It took the counter-culture Sixties to revitalize comics and create room beyond the mainstream for gay cartoonists.

With her "feminist, anti-nuclear, vegetarian view of the world," Alison Bechdel likes keeping her dykes out of daily papers. But, through them, she voices frustrations anyone can understand.

> *First Dyke to Watch Out For:* Wanna see a movie?
> *Second:* Well . . . I dunno. I have this rule, see.
> . . . I only go to a movie if it satisfies three basic requirements. One, it has to have at least two women in it
> . . . who, two, talk to each other about, three, something besides a man. . . . Last movie I was able to see was *Alien*.
> *First:* Wanna go to my house and make popcorn?
> *Second:* Now you're talkin'.

Eventually we'll be watching out for dykes and gay men every day in the funny papers. Just don't tell the U.S. Senate.

IT'S TIME TO GIVE A HAND
TO PEOPLE SOCIETY HAS LEFT OUT

JULY 30, 1993

Stigmatized as evil, defective, social misfits, they've never been a majority of any culture. Bias against them is reinforced by almost every religion.

Scientists argue over whether their mere existence signals some flaw in nature or nurture. "Cures," even brutal ones, fail to change their basic orientation. And our civilization, like others throughout history, is designed to remind them in a thousand different ways that they just don't fit in.

Left-handers.

"Being gay is just like being left-handed." For years I joined countless gay men and lesbians in offering that comparison to explain that homosexuality is simply a natural human variation, not a moral issue. The analogy is far more apt than I, a right-hander long oblivious to most rightward bias, realized.

Nobody knows exactly what causes left-handedness or homosexuality. Although inheritance patterns haven't been deciphered, genes seem to play a major role in both. Other prenatal influences might contribute to left-handedness, which is more common among twins, men, gay people of both genders and blonds than the rest of the population.

Gay lefties may soon find that their sexual orientation is less mysterious than their manual orientation: The National Institutes of Health just found that one or more genes on the X chromosome predispose some men to be gay.

Like gay people, left-handers have been mistreated for centuries. We've all heard tales of left-handed first-graders getting their knuckles rapped. Yet until recently I failed to notice how uniformly everyday life is geared to the dominant hand of the majority.

The right-handedness of scissors, power saws and car stick shifts is easy to see. But what about rulers, doorknobs, playing cards and corkscrews? To me their design had just seemed sensible, much as the shape of our society's laws and customs may seem sensible to the heterosexuals they are designed to fit.

Even my favorite tool, language, makes left "gauche" and "sinister" while right is, well, "right." Lefties don't even get a fair shake with "ambidextrous," which turns out to mean "right-handed on both sides," says Jack Fincher in *Sinister People*.

Rooted in fear of difference, unconscious prejudice against lefties interlocks with other mindless biases. In a study reported in 1969, college students were asked what they associated with "left." They chose "bad, dark, profane, female, unclean, night, west, curved, limp, homosexual, weak, mysterious, low, ugly, black, incorrect and death," according to the book *Neuropsychology of Left-Handedness*.

Lefties needn't bother looking to Christianity or Judaism for moral support. From the serpent to Satan to the damned lined up on Judgment Day, the left side is associated with evil and sin. Even the custom of throwing spilled salt over the left shoulder grew out of the superstition that the devil lurked there.

The Old Testament book Leviticus forbids blemished rabbis, a rule that long exiled lefties. The New Testament seats Jesus at the right hand of God. Islam's pro-right bias even outlaws public use of the left hand, according to Stanley Coren's *The Left-Hander Syndrome*.

Yet left-handedness is with us always. American teachers, thinking left-handedness was a choice—and a perverse one at that —forced generations of students to write "right." But handedness turned out to be a fundamental orientation, not a behavior ripe for change. Adults who rate themselves "successfully switched" to right-handedness do most tasks with the left, Coren says.

Pressuring anyone to switch now seems old-fashioned. The case of the Riverside, Missouri, police officer fired in 1980 for wearing his holster on the left was as rare as it was outrageous.

When it comes to hands, difference doesn't mean deviance. How long before our nation learns that the lesson also applies to hearts?

VISITING SAM NUNN TERRITORY, WHERE ANY WORD ABOUT GAYS IS BLISSFULLY IGNORED

AUGUST 6, 1993

Perry, GA.—If ignorance is bliss, Senator Sam Nunn must want us to have a deliriously happy military. As chairman of the Senate Armed Services Committee, he forged the "don't ask, don't tell" policy that commands our troops to march with their heads in the sand.

Where does a politician like Nunn come from anyway? Ignoring the fact that my question was rhetorical, Joyce—my native Georgian—offered to show me.

On a morning so blistering that I kept mistaking the gasoline prices on electronic billboards for the temperature, we turned off I-75 about 110 miles south of Atlanta. Sam Nunn Boulevard took us right to the heart of Perry, Georgia.

We thought gays in the military would be the hottest topic in an already hot town. That notion quickly wilted.

We headed first to see Jim Kerce, editor of the twice-a-week *Houston* (County) *Home Journal.* Perry doesn't debate the gay ban, Kerce says. "The only mention is supporting Sam Nunn's view."

That's also the only mention in the *Journal,* since Kerce believes a newspaper should be a "mirror," reflecting what its readers already think. "In this town of ten thousand, if we had four thousand gays, then gays would be something we would cover," he says.

Well, are there openly gay people in Perry? "If there are, I don't know about them," Kerce replied. "The sexuality of someone is not an issue at all to me. It mystifies me to see it develop as an issue, just as it has mystified me to see handicapped people make a big issue out of being handicapped."

Leaving the *Journal,* we scoured the nearby bookstore for anything a fair-minded Perry resident could read to better understand gay people. Again, we struck out.

Could the saleswoman at the office supply store tell us where to find openly gay folks? "I've never known anyone openly gay, and that suits me just fine," she told us. We decided not to introduce ourselves.

Then we stumbled upon Seeds of Truth, a Christian bookstore. Two friendly clerks quickly located four books hostile to homosexuality.

Why didn't they stock any gay-friendly Christian books, especially since Jesus didn't condemn same-sex love? Out came a very large Bible. Clerk Debbie Davis read aloud from Galatians.

After Joyce pointed out the verse didn't mention homosexuality, I whisked her out the door. Down the street we found the public library, where an unflattering portrait of Sam Nunn hangs in the main room.

The sixty-thousand-book card catalog contains four entries under "Homosexuality." Two are by Anita Bryant. All date from the Seventies.

We found two groundbreaking gay works only because we knew the author's name, Randy Shilts. His *Conduct Unbecoming: Gays and Lesbians in the U.S. Military* had been checked out once.

Not one of the ninety library books given in Nunn's honor is about gay issues. (Anyone wishing to rectify that can send a book to: Perry Public Library, Sam Nunn Collection, 1201 Washington St., Perry, GA 31069.)

To boost gay visibility in the library, Joyce shifted *Newsweek*'s lesbian issue to the top of a stack of magazines. Perhaps she accidentally set off an anti-gay alarm: Within minutes Davis rushed in, armed with four more Bible verses. In truth, all were condemnations by the apostle Paul, not Jesus.

Then, with our shoes melting, we walked to the county courthouse to see if gay people were busy being turned down for marriage licenses. We wondered because Nunn keeps solemnly declaring that "homosexual marriage" must remain grounds for a military discharge.

Actually, one male couple from nearby Warner Robins, home of a major Air Force base, was turned down. That was back in the Sixties, recalls Probate Judge Frances V. Annis, an Ann Richards look-alike.

We told her we'd not found anyone openly gay in Perry. "You won't," she responded. "They just wouldn't fit in socially."

All day we used our best manners, but folks kept saying they'd never before been "confronted" about homosexuality. They're happy to know nothing about their senator's whipping boy.

"Blissful" can mean oblivious to inequities. For an army or an electorate, such contentment is dangerous. Knowledge—even when it's unsettling—is power.

"DON'T ASK, DON'T TELL" HAS LET MANY PASS AS SOMEONE THEY AREN'T

AUGUST 13, 1993

Only two photographs exist of the real President Franklin D. Roosevelt. He spent his White House years passing as someone else, someone able to stand unassisted.

FDR's presidential library overflows with carefully orchestrated pictures of an iron-willed man determined to be seen as physically fit or, perhaps, just a wee bit disabled by polio. When challenged, he lied to maintain his fiction: "I don't use a wheelchair at all, except a little kitchen chair on wheels to get about my room while dressing . . . and solely for the purpose of saving time."

Yet the two exceptional photographs reveal the truth. FDR always had to use a wheelchair or be carried by strong men.

Reporters, photographers, even cartoonists cooperated, explains historian Hugh Gallagher in *FDR's Splendid Deception*.

Newspaper readers weren't told, for example, that when FDR appeared to be walking up steps he actually was being carried upright by Secret Service agents gripping his elbows. And when he pitched forward off a stage because the lectern that he was using to hold himself up wasn't bolted to the floor, moviegoers didn't see it in the newsreels.

Despite his declaration that "the only thing we have to fear is fear itself," Roosevelt must have been terrified of being judged unfit to lead, not just unfit to walk, if voters realized he was paralyzed.

Where would we be if FDR hadn't gotten the nation, knocked flat by the Depression, back on its feet? And what if he hadn't been president when the time came to stand up to Hitler?

Roosevelt's Herculean effort to appear non-disabled was physically exhausting but amazingly successful. It illustrates the pressure that members of stigmatized groups feel to try to pass themselves off as part of the dominant culture. Gay men and lesbians are far from the first group to be given the message that the only way we'll get equal opportunities is by disguising our identity.

Female writers used male pen names to be taken seriously. Female warriors dressed as men to get into battles. Jews took Gentile names to scale barriers to colleges, resorts, neighborhoods. Light-skinned blacks crossed the color line to escape racism.

The "tragic mulatto," who finds passing as white psychologically devastating, was a movie staple from the 1930s to the '50s. In the 1959 remake of *Imitation of Life*, a little girl is caught trying to pass at school. Her exchange with her much darker mother eerily foreshadows the national struggle over gays in the military.

Sarah Jane: They didn't *ask* me. Why should I *tell* them?

Mother: Because that's what you are, and it's nothing to be ashamed of.

Passing is an attempt to avoid hatred. Yet, within the person trying to pass, it breeds self-hatred as well as disrespect for others who cannot or will not deny their identity. I cringe every time I read a gay personal ad in search of a "straight-looking, straight-acting" mate.

Essence senior editor Linda Villarosa came out in a 1991 magazine article because "part of me felt guilty about having the luxury of being able to pass for straight, thus reinforcing the myth that there are only a few lesbians in the African-American community."

What Villarosa didn't tell readers was that her family had been humiliated by her grandmother's obsession with seeming white. "She did not want my father to marry someone who was obviously black," Villarosa says.

Her blue-eyed grandmother, who lived in a white neighborhood, told Villarosa's mother to use the back door and leave the room if neighbors dropped by. "My mother did leave the room," Villarosa recalls. "My father did allow her to leave the room."

Despite her grandmother's insistence that "it's better to be white than it is to be black," Villarosa refused to deny being her mother's daughter.

Years later, *Essence* ran a handsome photograph of the real Linda Villarosa, a young black lesbian unwilling to pass as anything else. Beside her was Clara Villarosa, her proud mother.

BIBLICAL VERSES ARE USED
AS CRUTCHES TO PROP UP BIASES

AUGUST 20, 1993

An engineering professor is treating her husband, a loan officer, to dinner for finally giving in to her pleas to shave off the scraggly beard he grew on vacation.

His favorite restaurant is a casual place where they both feel comfortable in slacks and cotton/polyester-blend golf shirts. But, as always, she wears the gold and pearl pendant he gave her the day her divorce decree was final.

They're laughing over their menus because they know he always ends up diving into a giant plate of ribs but she won't be talked into anything more fattening than shrimp.

Quiz: How many biblical prohibitions are they violating?

Well, wives must be "submissive" to their husbands (I Peter 3:1). And all women are forbidden to teach men (I Timothy 2:12), wear gold or pearls (I Timothy 2:9) or dress in clothing that "pertains to a man" (Deuteronomy 22:5).

Shellfish and pork are definitely out (Leviticus 11:7, 10), as are usury (Deuteronomy 23:19), shaving (Leviticus 19:27) and clothes of more than one fabric (Leviticus 19:19). And since the Bible rarely recognizes divorce, they're committing adultery, which carries the rather harsh penalty of death by stoning (Deuteronomy 22:22).

So why are they having such a good time? Probably because they wouldn't think of worrying about rules that seem absurd, anachronistic or—at best—unrealistic.

Yet this same modern-day couple could easily be among the millions of Americans who never hesitate to lean on the Bible to justify their own anti-gay attitudes.

Bible verses have long been used selectively to support many kinds of discrimination. Somewhere along the way, Jesus' second-greatest commandment gets lost: "You shall love your neighbor as yourself."

Once a given form of prejudice falls out of favor with society, so do the verses that had seemed to condone it. It's unimaginable today, for example, that anyone would use the Bible to try to justify slavery.

Yet when the abolitionist movement began to gain momentum in the early nineteenth century, many Southern ministers defended the owning of human beings as a divinely approved system: "Slaves, obey in everything those who are your earthly masters . . ." (Colossians 3:22).

In an influential anti-abolitionist essay, South Carolina Baptist leader Richard Furman declared in 1822 that "the right of holding slaves is clearly established in the Holy Scriptures."

Meanwhile, anti-slavery crusaders were taking an interpretative approach to the Bible, since a literal reading "gave little or no support to an abolitionist position," author Carl Degler says in *Place over Time: The Continuity of Southern Distinctiveness.*

Nearly one hundred years after the Emancipation Proclamation, a Virginia court defended racial segregation by saying, "The

Almighty God created the races white, black, yellow, malay and red, and he placed them on separate continents. . . . He did not intend for the races to mix." The U.S. Supreme Court rejected that ridiculous reasoning in 1967 when it struck down laws in sixteen states forbidding interracial marriage.

Like advocates of racial equality, suffragists found the literal reading of the Bible was their biggest stumbling block. Many ministers even condemned using anesthesia during labor because pain in childbirth was punishment for Eve's bite of forbidden fruit (Genesis 3:16).

Susan B. Anthony eventually declared in frustration: "I distrust those people who know so well what God wants them to do, because I notice it always coincides with their own desires."

Studying the Bible is often akin to looking at Rorschach ink blots, says biblical scholar Joe Barnhart, author of *The Southern Baptist Holy War*. "What we get out of it is sometimes what we put into it," he explains.

The punishment the Bible metes out to all men for Adam's downfall is toiling "in the sweat of your face" (Genesis 3:19). Yet, Barnhart notes with a laugh, there's one bit of progress never denounced by preachers hot under the clerical collar: air conditioning.

THE SCAPEGOATING OF THE SALEM WITCH-HUNTS IS STILL WITH US

AUGUST 27, 1993

A late-summer visit to Salem, Massachusetts, conjures up images of Halloween. Witches ride broomsticks across gift-shop coffee mugs and key rings, on T-shirts and newspaper boxes, even on police uniforms.

Salem repeats its witch-trial history somberly at museums, then candy-coats the past for fun and profit in the rest of town. The seaport just north of Boston quickly begins to seem ghoulish.

Want to help trivialize the suffering caused by Salem's undeclared war on women? Tourists can buy little pieces of wood taken from trees on Gallows Hill. Nineteen people were hanged there as witches. A twentieth victim was crushed to death by rocks.

Unfortunately, even Salem's least commercial retelling of its obsession with executing witches makes the events of 1692 seem like isolated madness, something that did not happen elsewhere and certainly could not return three centuries later.

In fact, hundreds of thousands of suspected witches—the vast majority women—were executed in Europe during the sixteenth and seventeenth centuries, according to *Riding the Nightmare,* by Selma R. Williams and Pamela Williams Adelman.

Shortly before being crowned in 1603, England's King James declared that witches tended to be female because woman "is frailer than man is, so it is easier to be entrapped in . . . snares of the devil." He applauded "swimming" witches—binding their thumbs to opposite big toes and tossing them into water, Williams and Adelman say. Floaters were declared guilty and hanged. The "innocent" drowned.

In the American colonies, the first convicted witch was hanged in 1647. By 1725, another thirty-four New Englanders had shared her fate, Carol F. Karlsen says in *The Devil in the Shape of a Woman.* Eighty percent were women.

Ordinary Puritans thought of witches as criminals who used supernatural powers to harm neighbors, often attacking men in their bedchambers, Karlsen explains. Clergymen preached that witches were the devil's handmaidens.

The colonists' superstitions made witches handy scapegoats. A storm at sea? Blame a witch. Beer disappeared? Witchcraft. A child is born with a clubfoot? The midwife is a witch. A man becomes impotent? Must be bewitched.

In Puritan society, women were expected to produce children, remain dependent and never challenge male authority. Those who stepped outside that narrow path risked prosecution as witches.

Simply living beyond her child-bearing years put a woman in jeopardy. So did inheriting more than her neighbors thought proper for a woman, becoming self-supporting or displaying a "manly" skill, like preaching. The first English Quaker women who headed to Boston to preach were arrested as witches even before reaching shore, Karlsen says.

The notion that uppity women are witches hasn't quite vanished. Last year, Pat Robertson warned that the equal rights movement "encourages women to leave their husbands, kill their children, practice witchcraft, destroy capitalism and become lesbians."

Although Salem doesn't push visitors to see the link, twentieth-century superstitions about gay people are quite like those about unsubmissive seventeenth-century women. Both have been portrayed as sexually predatory, godless and dedicated to luring children into evil.

No wonder we gays have become America's most wanted scapegoats. The family breaking down? Point a finger at gay people. Moral values declining? Must be those homosexuals. The AIDS virus? Blame gay men.

The scapegoating is now taking the shape of ballot initiatives in more than a dozen states that would codify our outcast status. One Georgia county recently passed a non-binding resolution just to go on record condemning homosexuality. How far are we from Salem?

Fear of being branded a witch eventually silenced the Puritans' assertive women. Fear of being similarly misunderstood has long kept gay people quiet. But now we've begun to speak the truth of gay reality as if our lives depended on it. Perhaps they do.

PRETENDING EMILY DICKINSON WASN'T GAY IS WITHOUT RHYME OR REASON

SEPTEMBER 3, 1993

The dainty white dress, given shape by a headless manne-quin inside a transparent exhibit case, invites a visitor to Emily Dickinson's Amherst, Massachusetts, bedroom to fill in the unseen poet.

Was she a mousy little recluse who morbidly locked herself away in this small room when heterosexual heartbreak left her holding a pen, not a bridal bouquet? Or was she a strong-willed artist who reveled in being unmarried and poured thirty-five years of passion for Susan Gilbert into more than three hundred of her poems?

The questions that come to mind when touring Dickin-son's Homestead reflect the century-long custody battle over the image of America's greatest female poet. The struggle, fiercest in academic circles, raises the same issue as the de-bate over gays in the military: Must our society pretend not to see someone's homosexuality in order to appreciate her talent?

"Emily is sort of the sweetheart of America," says Dickinson scholar Martha Nell Smith. "It's interesting how scared people get talking about Emily's love for Sue and the very idea that you may be able to call that love lesbian."

In her newly released *Rowing in Eden: Rereading Emily Dickinson* (University of Texas Press), Smith bolsters the argument first articulated by Rebecca Patterson in 1951 that the poet's sen-sibility was lesbian.

Take, for example, the last stanza of the spirited "Wild Nights," which an early editor dreaded to publish "lest the malig-nant read into it more than that virgin recluse ever dreamed of putting there."

Rowing in Eden—
Ah, the Sea!
Might I but moor—Tonight
—In Thee!

"If you've got a female speaker, try to make sense of that heterosexually," says Smith.

But for Smith, it is the poet's 150 letters to Sue—her next-door muse, audience, critic and sister-in-law—that most clearly reveal she harbored lesbian desires. Still enthralled after decades, Dickinson writes: "Susan knows she is a Siren—and that at a word from her, Emily would forfeit Righteousness."

Emily's letters to Sue are scattered over nine volumes. Smith is pulling them together in a book due out in 1995 so that readers can more easily sense the strength of the women's relationship.

"I think [Emily] was passionately in love in an erotic way," Smith says. "Whether they actually had sex I do not know. . . . But we can be sure there were attempts to heterosexualize her."

Those long-successful attempts began soon after the poet's death in 1886. Slicing, dicing, the people entrusted with much of her writing thrust it into a literary Veg-o-matic to make her sentiments conventional.

Editors lopped off half of one four-stanza poem and slapped on the title "Wedded," making it praise marriage. Yet "if you leave the last two stanzas," Smith points out, it is "about a woman being powerful and strong precisely because she's not wedded and doesn't want to be."

Similarly, Emily's letters to her brother, Austin, were "mutilated" to delete her pursuit of Sue, Smith says. Sometimes half pages were chopped out; other times just the "s" that kept "she" from being male.

When Austin won Sue for himself, Emily responded angrily. A censor later tried to rub out the source of the sibling rivalry and turn "Susie" into something unexplosive: "Dear Austin, I am keen, but you a good deal keener, I am something of a fox, but you are a hound! I guess we are very good friends tho', and I guess we both love [S]us[ie] just as well as we can."

Sue married Austin and moved into the Evergreens, beside

Emily's Homestead. Seven years later, writing in the room now occupied by an empty white dress, the poet declared that when she "hoped," she "stood at a window facing west," facing Sue.

To truly understand Emily Dickinson and her poetry, we must appreciate her orientation.

GAYS' PARENTS BREAK OUT OF THEIR OWN EMOTIONAL CLOSETS

SEPTEMBER 10, 1993

The warning left in my New Orleans hotel room came straight from the bishop: He was disguising himself, he said. He would find me; I would not be able to find him.

Yet it still came as a shock a few hours later to find myself interviewing Louis XVI. He was on his way to a lavish Mardi Gras–style banquet with Marie Antoinette. On more common evenings, Their Royal Highnesses are known as retired Methodist Bishop Mel Wheatley and his wife, Lucile, of Orange County, California.

I'd not expected so much gaiety at the twelfth annual international convention of Parents, Families and Friends of Lesbians and Gays (P-FLAG), a four-day gathering of 550 folks "Celebrating Family."

Yes, there were four dozen serious-minded workshops on topics like "Confronting Anti-Gay Groups" and "Homosexuality and Biology." Many reflected P-FLAG's growing emphasis on advocating equal rights.

But a lighthearted streak also ran through the conference. Many parents who joined P-FLAG to find a shoulder to cry on have moved light-years beyond merely accepting their children's homosexuality: They crack delightfully disconcerting jokes about it!

After a comedy show by leather-loving lesbian Lynn Lavner,

P-FLAGers packed into an "up" elevator. As the doors opened for the first stop, a father intoned in his best department-store voice: "Leather. Lingerie. Leather lingerie." The car shook with laughter.

P-FLAG members learn the importance of putting human faces on our civil rights struggle. Borrowing a gay phrase, P-FLAG members tell of "coming out" as the parent of someone gay. Some announcements are wonderfully casual: "My son came out and all I got was this lousy T-shirt."

Like many parents, Jane Smith, a conservative Houston Republican, remembers being "heartbroken" about her son. With P-FLAG's help, she says, "Slowly I've come to realize that I was homophobic. Now I'm out to most everyone because we shouldn't hide it as a secret. There is nothing wrong with homosexual people."

Disguising himself only at costume parties, Bishop Wheatley came out to his Council of Bishops in 1978 as the supportive father of a gay son. He and his wife became P-FLAG members.

"We never went through the agony that most P-FLAG parents went through," Mel Wheatley recalls. "We knew immediately that if John was gay, the stereotypes must be false."

John Wheatley died of cancer in 1984. "We feel very close to John when we're doing this," the bishop says of working with P-FLAG. "We wouldn't feel comfortable being anywhere John wouldn't be welcome."

P-FLAG conventioneers showed that the gay fight is their fight. As a button worn by Sally McLeod of San Jose, California, declared: "I'd rather have a bigot think I'm a lesbian than a lesbian think I'm a bigot."

Like their children, most P-FLAGers were long afraid to take a public stand for gay rights. Harriet Dart, Detroit's P-FLAG dynamo, now helps other parents evolve into advocates. "It used to be if they saw a TV camera, they wanted to hide," she says. "Now they're all wearing stickers saying, 'Please interview me!' "

Parents like the Wheatleys—never upset about having a gay son or daughter—are streaming into P-FLAG. As anti-gay attacks have escalated, so has P-FLAG's membership. For P-FLAG membership information, call (202) 638-4200. Oregon has jumped from three chapters to twenty-two. "That's a result of people coming out of the closet and saying, 'I can't sit on my duff anymore. These people are out to get my kids,' " reports Vice President Bob Bernstein.

New Orleans' gay community saluted P-FLAG with a gender-bending Mardi Gras extravaganza. Countless ostriches got plucked for the glorious fifteen-foot costumes.

When the locals judged the masked out-of-towners, the most original honors went not to the Wheatleys but another royal pair, "a queen and his mother." That's just the kind of convention it was.

Long live P-FLAG!

THANKS TO TWO GAY MEN, WOMEN AREN'T LOCKED OUT OF WRESTLING ANYMORE

SEPTEMBER 17, 1993

Gay men are passionate fans of strong women, tough cookies like Joan Crawford, Bette Davis, Mae West, Marlene Dietrich. The list wouldn't be complete without the New York City gals who recently gave me a little something to remember them by. They're the Knights Wrestling Club for Women.

The club exists because two gay men, Bob Hofmann and Ed Unger, thought women should be encouraged to unleash their physical power. "Most women don't realize how much strength they have. And they are afraid to use it," says Hofmann, who jokes he's the only male president of a lesbian group.

The idea of starting a women's wrestling team originated at Gay Games III, an Olympic-style international competition that drew 7,300 athletes to Vancouver in 1990. Only wrestling was closed to women.

After the all-male wrestling team he founded put a hammerlock on first place, Hofmann came home and joined gold medalist Unger in working to see that women wrestle in Gay Games IV next year.

The inclusive Games—open to everyone regardless of sexual orientation or skill level—are expected to draw fifteen thousand athletes from forty countries. From June 18 to 25, good sports of all ages will be in New York City to test their abilities in badminton, Rollerblading and golf as well as in traditional Olympic events, like diving and ice hockey.

For the first time, an international competition will include figure skating for same-sex pairs. Women's wrestling will also debut.

Yet the very notion of one grown woman trying to pin another's shoulders down on a wrestling mat might seem bizarre at first. Contact sports, after all, have been an almost exclusively male preserve.

For women, wrestling is "a sport where all the things you were brought up to be—that good little girl, that person who should be passive—all that is taken away. When I'm in practice, I'm told to win," says Juanita Harvey, a vice president of the two-year-old Knights Wrestling Club for Women, the nation's first such club.

"Wrestling is a lot like chess—anticipating not only the next move your opponent is going to make but the fifth move," adds Harvey, who says her hard-won strategic skills even help in business meetings.

Somehow during our initial interview Harvey maneuvered me into agreeing that Joyce and I would wrestle her team. "Just promise not to hurt her!" I insisted with the macho protectiveness Joyce hates.

Although as a child Joyce saw the Fabulous Moolah, queen of pro wrestling, neither of us knew what to expect from the female Knights. Once inside a padded room, we joined women of all shades and sizes in taking off jewelry, putting on kneepads and checking to make sure our fingernails were clipped short. (We aced that test.)

Coach Unger warmed us up with stretching exercises, including R-rated postures that really loosened everyone up. Then we got down to the rougher business of practicing techniques for wiping the mat with other cities' teams in Gay Games IV.

By then I was really worried. Joyce was pitted against the formidable K. C. Clayton. Their matchup lasted an eternity, fifteen seconds. Joyce escaped unbroken.

I was much less concerned about my assignment: moving newcomer Donna Swan out of a four-foot circle. Task mastered. We reversed roles. No problem—until she grabbed my left leg and twisted, twice, like breaking the seal on a soda bottle cap. Owweee!

Seeing me put out of commission, Joyce might have wanted a tiny opponent for the day's last match. When she instead pointed again to Clayton, I blanched. Everyone else chanted, "Joyce! Joyce!"

Clayton had twenty seconds to crawl across the room. Her only obstacle was Joyce. On "Go," my mild-mannered mate leaped on Clayton and pressed her flat until time ran out.

Even Clayton liked Joyce's flat-iron style: "She moved her body weight great." Wrestling, Joyce says, should be called "squash."

When the historic Gay Games wrestling matches begin, Joyce and I hope to be right there among the strong women—watching.* Participatory journalism has its drawbacks. I've got the knee bandage to prove it.

---

* At the 1994 Gay Games, Juanita Harvey and three other members of the Knights Wrestling Club for Women won four of the six gold medals awarded in women's wrestling. Gay Games V is tentatively scheduled for August 1–8, 1998, in Amsterdam. For information, write the Federation of Gay Games, 584 Castro Street, Suite 343, San Francisco, CA 94114.

WEDDING BANQUET SERVES UP
A LESSON ON THE MESSY NATURE
OF STRAIGHTENING UP

SEPTEMBER 24, 1993

Straightening up. We all do it when company's coming. But in many households the focus isn't on remembering to put out the guest towels. It's on sweeping every sign of gay life under the rug.

Down come the photos that might make the "roommate" seem like more than just a friend. Away go the gay books and magazines. Off comes the layer of dust that announces the second bedroom is never used.

Within minutes the home that should reflect individuality instead becomes a minefield of schemes. The point of the deception, of course, is for the heterosexual visitor to feel comfy presuming that the hosts are straight.

It's a dangerous game that I played well into my twenties. My integrity and first relationship were undermined by it. As Sir Walter Scott warned in 1805, "Oh, what a tangled web we weave, when first we practice to deceive!"

The messy hazards of straightening up have reached the big screen in *The Wedding Banquet.*

The movie, playing in one hundred artsy theaters around the country, explores the extraordinary efforts of one gay man, a naturalized U.S. citizen from Taiwan, to straighten up his life to please his parents.

Wai-Tung and Simon, his lover of five years, go far beyond simply taking down a few gay posters. They decide Wai-Tung, under constant pressure from his parents to wed, should marry a Chinese woman who needs a marriage license to get a green card. The in-name-only bride is so desperate to remain in America that she accepts their proposal.

The nightmarish scheme, mostly played for laughs, naturally starts to damage the men's life together.

As soon as Wai-Tung's parents fly in from Taiwan for a pre-wedding visit, Wai-Tung introduces Simon as his landlord. (Wham! A sledgehammer hits the honest underpinnings of their relationship.) When evening comes, Wai-Tung and Simon head to separate bedrooms. (Wham!) Again and again, Simon is shoved aside to make way for the fraudulent bride. (Wham, wham, wham!)

When the lies become too much for Simon, he screams at Wai-Tung over breakfast. Wai-Tung's confused mother, who understands no English, whispers to her husband, "Are we staying over our welcome? . . . Did Wai-Tung pay his rent?"

By the final scene, Wai-Tung's parents know that what he didn't pay to Simon was the respect due a mate.

The Wedding Banquet is loosely based on the tangled life of Nicky, a thirty-nine-year-old native of Taiwan drawn here by the 1975 *Time* magazine cover story on gay Air Force Sergeant Leonard Matlovich. In the United States, Nicky thought, he could avoid marriage and find a rewarding gay life.

For the last decade, Nicky has loved a China scholar named Bob. Nicky's friends and co-workers know he's gay. Unlike Wai-Tung, he's never had a sham marriage.

But, he told me over dinner, he's spun complicated tales for his parents about why he lives with Bob. There was "The Homesitting Story," "The Renter," "The Tax Break." His parents, unlike Wai-Tung's, still don't know the truth. "That's the biggest irony," Nicky says.

Another irony is that Nicky's childhood pal, straight screenwriter Neil Peng, is publicly leading the gay movement that *Wedding* has sparked in Taiwan.

But the saddest irony is that, despite his elaborate ruses, Nicky has failed to please his parents. Nicky says his father recently told him that "I'd been irresponsible all my life. And his conclusion about why I didn't want to get married is that I don't want a family responsibility."

Nicky adds, "I told him you're all wrong. I couldn't tell him the real reason." Through tears, Nicky says he wants his parents to know what Bob means to him.

When we try to avoid pain by straightening up, we often just postpone it. Life, after all, isn't tidy. And the cornerstone of any relationship worth having is honesty.

A GAY FAMILY CAN BE LOVING— EVEN WHEN NO ONE IS THE MAN OF THE HOUSE

OCTOBER 1, 1993

Centuries of misunderstanding were distilled into a single question about the young mother's lesbian relationship: "Who is the man in your house?"

The attorney quizzing Sharon Bottoms as she tried to regain custody of her two-year-old son, Tyler, was hired by the state of Virginia to represent Tyler's interests. Yet the lawyer understood so little about the boy's family that he thought of Tyler's mama and her partner, April Wade, as an imitation heterosexual couple.

No one is the man, Bottoms informed him.

"So there is no one dominant figure in the relationship?" attorney David Boone persisted.

"No," she replied.

Last month, in Richmond, Boone gave Judge Buford M. Parsons, Jr., his assessment of whether Tyler should remain with his heterosexual grandmother, who gained custody March 31.

"I believe that a homosexual should be allowed to raise a child," Boone began. But then, with logic worthy of a pretzel, he said, "Whether April was a man or woman, I would have the same problem." He couldn't abide "two adults raising a child without benefit of marriage."

A gay couple, of course, can't legally marry. Boone's solution: Punish Bottoms, Wade and little Tyler for failing to meet an impossible standard. Keep Tyler with his grandmother, he urged.

The now-infamous Bottoms case, unusual only because the gay parent lost custody to a third party rather than to the other biological parent, illustrates how unprepared most U.S. courts are to deal justly with gay families.

Judge Parsons let Bottoms be grilled about the most private details of her love life. She admitted oral sex, a felony in Virginia.

Parsons denounced Bottoms' conduct as "immoral" and illegal before officially declaring her "an unfit parent." The family-busting judge now lets Bottoms and her son be together each week only from Monday morning to Tuesday evening—and never in their home or around Wade.

With Smokey and Bandit—Tyler's cat and puppy—roaming their Richmond town house, Bottoms and Wade tell of working to preserve their young family. In calls to Tyler, "I let him know that I love him," Wade says.

"He always wants to see April," Bottoms says, "but he can't see her. . . . I just think that maybe he feels he's done something wrong."

Sharon Bottoms' adulthood got off to a rocky start when she left home at seventeen without a high school diploma or job skills. Her brief marriage died shortly before Tyler's birth. She perpetually relied on her mother, Kay, for weekend child care.

Ironically, Bottoms's publicized troubles began when she tried to get her life on track. She says she sought counseling to heal emotional scars caused by being sexually abused from twelve to seventeen by her mother's live-in boyfriend. Eventually, she confronted her mother, saying Tyler could not visit unless the boyfriend left.

Kay Bottoms' response was to file for custody. She has testified that she kicked out her boyfriend of seventeen years shortly before her first court date simply to improve her chances of winning Tyler.

The life of forty-two-year-old Kay Bottoms was not subjected to the same scrutiny as Sharon's in court. Despite Virginia's fornication and cohabitation laws, she was not branded a criminal. And she was not asked whether she, too, violates the oral sex statute.

As for Sharon Bottoms, she'd have had a better chance of keeping Tyler if she'd been sleeping with every man in Richmond. Instead, the judge rebuked her for exposing Tyler to what most of us—regardless of sexual orientation—seek: a committed, affectionate relationship.

That relationship will be blessed this fall in a church ceremony. "We're going to be married in God's eyes," Bottoms explains.

Meanwhile, she and Wade keep fighting for Tyler. "He's going to know," Bottoms says, "he has two mommies who love him very much."

But, for now, who can tell a little fellow why some grown-ups care less about how much he's loved than whether his home has one man, no man or two?*

---

* In the ongoing custody battle, the Virginia Court of Appeals on June 21, 1994, ruled unanimously that a parent cannot lose custody simply for being gay. While the court ordered that Tyler be returned to his mother, his grandmother blocked that order by appealing.

FORMER ASTRONOMER THANKS HIS LUCKY STARS HE TURNED TO A LIFE OF ACTIVISM

OCTOBER 8, 1993

Decade after decade, federal workers fired for being homosexual left quietly, without protest. That was until 1957, when Uncle Sam decided to kick out Frank Kameny, then a meek astronomer working for the Army Map Service.

"I took that as a declaration of war by my government upon me," Kameny recalls. "And I don't grant my government the right to declare war on me."

Suddenly radicalized, he did the unthinkable: He fought back.

He poured his meager financial resources into a long-shot appeal. Despite a doctorate from Harvard, he was impoverished by the federal blackball, which kept him from entering the young aerospace industry or returning to academia. For months he survived on twenty cents' worth of food a day.

Teaching himself the intricacies of law, he pursued his case in the courts, finally writing his own petition to the Supreme Court. Turned away by the "supreme injustices," as he calls them, he never was reinstated. His career as an observational astronomer was over. Yet he ultimately won what turned out to be an eighteen-year war.

Federal personnel officials "surrendered to me on July 3, 1975," Kameny says gleefully in his Washington, D.C., home. The Civil Service Commission announced homosexuality was no longer grounds for dismissal.

That historic change followed years of successful battles that Kameny waged for other gay workers fired from their federal jobs or denied security clearances. The nominal fees he charged his gay clients for his renowned expertise largely supported him.

"I've stabbed myself in the back," he jokes in his booming voice. "By killing the [anti-gay] issue as an activist, I have deprived myself of an income as a self-characterized paralegal."

Kameny credits his days as an Army private at World War II's front lines for his pit-bull activist style. "I dug my way across Germany slit trench by slit trench," the ex-mortar shell loader says.

That tenacity has served Kameny well in his many protracted battles to ensure gay people full equality. Now sixty-eight, the cheerfully dogged Kameny, surrounded by stacks of documents from his paper wars, ticks off his awesome victories with the pride of a four-star general.

His most recent triumph was the September 14 repeal of Washington, D.C.'s sodomy law. While actual prosecutions are rare, sodomy laws are indirectly used to tar gay people and deny them jobs and even their own children in custody disputes. He began that fight thirty years ago as the first person to publicly denounce the law in congressional testimony.

Even in his defeats, Kameny gained gay ground by staking out new territory. In 1971, for example, he became the first openly gay person to run for public office when he competed for D.C. congressional delegate. Today, 128 openly gay people hold public office.

Kameny laid the groundwork for his most profound success in 1961 when he founded the D.C. branch of the Mattachine Society, an early gay-rights group. The gay movement of that pre-Stonewall era was "apologetic and unassertive," he recalls. He opted instead for "militancy and activism."

Kameny soon realized that a major stumbling block was the mental illness theory. Drawing on his formidable scientific skills, he dived in and found "shoddy . . . and just plain sleazy research in which moral, cultural and theological value judgments were cloaked in the language of science."

And so began his ten-year war with the American Psychiatric Association. "They surrendered about noontime on December 15, 1973," Kameny notes with his characteristic precision, when APA's trustees voted that homosexuality is not an illness. "In one fell swoop, 15 million gay people were cured!"

Today, with his eyes fixed not on the stars but on the earthly territory yet to be won, the former astronomer is mapping a new strategy for his thirty-one-year-old assault on the military's gay ban. "I tend not to lose my wars," he says confidently. Friends of justice should take heart.

A WOMAN'S FAITH TURNS INTO HOPE AND LOVE FOR GAYS

OCTOBER 15, 1993

The Bible is filled with people who were going along their merry way until called upon by God to walk a more difficult path. Just as with the saints of old, Virginia Davidson's openhearted devotion to God has taken her on an unexpected journey for the past twenty-five years.

Davidson was a traditional wife and mother in her early fifties when her life forked.

A family friend had struggled to confide in her. He couldn't find the words. His secret finally dawned on her moments before he found the courage to speak.

"Tears were streaming down his face, and he told me he was struggling with homosexuality," recalls Davidson, who had never before heard such a confession. "I was absolutely numb for three days."

Davidson could never again look at sexuality in the same old way. "When you begin to have eyes that see, you see," she says. "When you've heard, you hear more. It's really very biblical."

She believes that "through this dear friend of ours, God had enlarged my heart and my understanding."

With her friend's revelation, the lifelong Presbyterian began a deeply religious journey in which she gradually became her denomination's foremost advocate of permitting openly gay ministers.

Now seventy-seven, the snowy-haired elder of the Downtown United Presbyterian Church of Rochester, New York, is at war with her faith's national governing board over its refusal to honor her congregation's call of Jane Spahr as a co-pastor in 1991. Spahr is gay.

Davidson headed the search committee that after eighteen months settled on Spahr as the best candidate. The panel decided it couldn't ignore her remarkable gifts simply because she is a lesbian.

"The Downtown Church . . . didn't really call Janie Spahr," Davidson says. "It was God's call to Janie, through us, to join us in ministry. We didn't set out to do this thing; God chose us and we said 'yes.' "

When the national board countered with "no" last year, it was overruling Davidson on homosexuality just as it had in 1978.

In 1976 she had headed a national Presbyterian task force on homosexuality. After two years of theological study, the panel concluded homosexuality is not sinful and openly gay people should be ordained as ministers.

Unwilling to see or hear the truth, the Presbyterian General Assembly vetoed the task force's findings.

Feeling battered by Bible-wavers, Davidson, then sixty-two, entered seminary. She also prodded her home church in 1979 into becoming a More Light congregation, one that reaches out to gay men and lesbians. Now 53 of 20,023 Presbyterian churches emit More Light. Other faiths also have small but growing clusters of gay-friendly churches.

"We say as a More Light church that all who wish to profess their faith are welcome," Davidson explains. "Now the [church] law may say—just as the [civil] law once said this park is segregated—that you may not ordain to office anyone who is gay. . . . We say that is unjust."

Becoming a More Light church revitalized the aging Downtown Presbyterian, now a seven-hundred-member congregation that is 15 percent gay. Beneath Tiffany windows and tremendous organ pipes, gay folks, retirees and young straight families exchange hearty hugs.

To keep some link to Spahr, Downtown Presbyterian dubbed her its evangelist. Her cross-country mission is to spread the good news that an inclusive congregation expresses God's pervasive love.

Being barred from calling Spahr as a pastor has both hurt and empowered the church, says Rose Mitchell, one of its three current pastors. "It has caused people to think more theologically, to really talk about justice and do more biblical reflection.

"The transforming moment is when you totally realize this has nothing to do with sin."

Davidson's journey is to continue leading her fellow Presbyterians to that realization. "I feel I was called to do this," she says.

God bless Virginia Davidson for answering that call.

FINDING WHOLENESS WITHOUT BECOMING HALF A COUPLE

OCTOBER 22, 1993

The lesbian scholar announced with gusto that she was embarking on playing-the-field research in San Francisco. She intended to prove through personal experience that gay women, despite our instincts for rapid nesting, can indeed date.

A few months passed. Just as Joyce and I began to wonder how our friend Linda's social experiment was going, a festive card arrived from California. Inside, Linda—single-minded no more— announced the creation of a domestic partnership.

Well, so much for dating.

Most lesbians we know just aren't comfortable being single for a really long time, say six weeks. Lesbian couples often form faster than an infatuated woman can whisper, "Are you allergic to cats?"

No wonder the world's most famous lesbian riddle is "What does a lesbian take on a second date?" Answer: "A U-Haul."

Lesbian culture has always centered on couples. But although some male couples have been together since Oscar Wilde was in diapers, the gay male world didn't much revolve around longtime companions before the AIDS crisis hit.

Now, however, a great many single gay men scramble to find Mr. Right and settle down. For years, Chuck Collins was one of them.

Now forty-two and a trainer of Kodak engineers in Rochester, New York, Collins recounts his many attempts to find a life partner: "I dated men of all sizes, shapes and personalities. I joined a gay gym and attended lots of gay social events. I fell in love several times and broke more than one heart during my quest. I listened to tons of advice, observed lots of couples, read books on gay coupling. And still I am single."

Collins saw singleness as a problem to be solved until his older sister Judy shifted his perspective. "Judy just looked at me and said, 'Have you ever thought that maybe you're just the kind of person who is not going to couple?' "

Momentarily, Collins felt insulted. But, almost as quickly, he began to embrace the rich possibilities of a contented single life. His role model was a widow almost twice his age whom he had long admired.

"I realized," Collins recalls, "that part of what's beautiful about her is her independence, her love of all people and her freedom to move easily among people and not have to be with a husband."

No longer obsessed with becoming half a couple, Collins appreciates the wholeness of his action-packed life. He sings, swims, bikes and leads church workshops on how homophobia stifles the lives of everyone, straight or gay. Muscular and strikingly handsome, he's perfectly cast as a Roman centurion in his church's Christmas play.

Collins still dates but also enjoys being alone in a crowd. He says he will "go to a movie alone and laugh with the couple next to me when they spill popcorn and be a part of their world for just a moment. I love doing that."

Unfortunately, when it comes to more than momentary encounters, Collins finds gay couples often tightly bolt the doors to their worlds. "Single gay people are increasingly ostracized," he says, voicing frustration long felt by unattached women of all sorts.

After chatting with Collins over breakfast in Rochester, Joyce and I revised our thinking about single lesbians. No, we didn't see them as threats or misfits. But we plead guilty to one count of making an unsolicited attempt to fix one friend up with another.

Bonded tightly enough to star in a Super Glue commercial, we would-be matchmakers unconsciously viewed singleness as something in need of fixing. Collins helped us repair our attitude instead.

For so many people, Collins notes, "the only vision for happiness is coupleness. It's hard for some people to imagine someone can be happy single. We need to open up our acceptance for other kinds of happiness."

While we're busy telling straight society that one pattern of living doesn't fit all, let's be sure to hear the message ourselves. Every single one of us counts.

Russo Spliced Together His Celluloid Fantasies and Love of Being Gay

October 29, 1993

Finding her little boy Vito, that was never a problem for Annie Russo. He was always at the picture show.

"He practically lived at the movies," she recalls. "Saturdays, he never came home. We had to go look for him, that's where he was. He'd be there seeing the same movie over and over again."

When only seven, Vito was turning the dimes he earned doing errands into celluloid fantasies at the movie house down the street from his Italian Catholic home in New York City's East Harlem.

Already he had begun a lifelong study of film. And when, years later, he discovered that his other passion was his gay identity, Russo spliced the two, becoming the leading authority on the depiction of homosexuality in the movies.

Eager to share his insights, Russo turned his New York apartment into a mini-theater and entertained friends with a running commentary on the night's feature.

Novelist Dorothy Allison fondly remembers those evenings: "To watch a movie with Vito was to have the language continually interpreted for you. He would point out things you would never notice," things like women kissing far in the background.

In 1981, Harper & Row published his eye-opening work, *The Celluloid Closet: Homosexuality in the Movies.* Gay people are not missing from movies, he explained, if you know where and how to look.

"Gays have always been visible," Russo wrote. "It's how they have been visible that has remained offensive for almost a century."

Now, three years after Russo's death at forty-four, Academy Award winners Rob Epstein and Jeffrey Friedman are fulfilling his dream of turning his book into a documentary.

Finally, Russo's message will play to a bigger audience.

Even before talkies, Hollywood toyed with homosexuality through the use of comic sissies. Because filmmakers associated anything feminine with inferiority, sissy sidekicks and butlers soon were being used to make heroes seem larger than life.

Predominently heterosexual audiences could howl over the antics of Oliver Hardy's doting buddy Stan Laurel or root for the Cowardly Lion in *The Wizard of Oz* without realizing—or, at least, acknowledging—that the film was playing with homosexuality. The subject simply was not dealt with overtly.

That's because a 1930 movie code banned mention of homosexuality. More than ever before, moviegoers needed to be in the know to understand veiled references.

In the 1938 comedy *Bringing Up Baby,* for example, Cary Grant dons a fluffy nightgown. Asked if he always dresses that way, Grant shouts, "No! I've just gone gay . . . all of a sudden!" The joke escaped the censors' scissors only because "gay" wasn't a well-known term.

After the code was relaxed in 1961, the anti-gay hostility that continues even today exploded on the big screen.

In what Russo called "kill 'em or cure 'em" films, homosexuals appeared as crazed villains or pathetic freaks. Either way, they tended to end up dead.

Yet Russo never lost his love for the movies. He interpreted even the bleakest scenes of his own life in movie terms.

In the AIDS Quilt documentary *Common Threads,* Russo describes finding a purple spot behind his knee. While he feared Kaposi's sarcoma, his lab test was negative. Two days later his doctor called back: The lab had been mistaken. He did have KS.

"At that point," Russo said, "I sort of felt like Susan Hayward in *I Want to Live.*" Her character's death sentence was commuted, then reinstated and carried out.

But while the final reel of Russo's life ended far too quickly, his story is one of triumph, not tragedy.

Finding meaning in her son's life is easy for Annie Russo. "I honestly believe," she says, "that God put Vito on Earth for the gay issue, to fight for their rights and stand up for people."

And like his boyhood matinee idols, Vito Russo fought right to the end.

> # SOONER OR LATER, THE COURTS WILL MAKE UP FOR CLINTON'S BROKEN VOW ON MILITARY GAYS

NOVEMBER 5, 1993

If a year ago a fortune-teller had predicted that in the fall of 1993 the president would be arguing in federal court that the gay ban is essential to military readiness, I'd have declared: "Are you crazy? George Bush lost the election!"

Little did I know that the Man from Hope would quickly turn into the Man from Flimflam.

Yes, the faith that many of us had in Bill Clinton—that he would help bridge the gap between gay and straight—was misplaced. But the faith we had in the American political system was not: The prohibition on gay men and lesbians serving openly in the military will be lifted by the U.S. Supreme Court.

As Boston attorney Mel Dahl puts it, "The question is not *if*" the court will remove the ban. "The question is *when* and under what circumstances."

Dahl, now thirty-four, has spent more than a decade challenging the gay ban. He enrolled in law school in part because he wanted to defend an ousted gay sailor—himself.

In many ways he was still a kid when he enlisted and became a Navy cryptographer. Gradually, he decoded his own sexual orientation. Then, in 1981, during a routine security check, Dahl was asked whether he was gay. He was discharged for telling the truth.

Dahl argues that the gay ban unconstitutionally infringes on his right to equal protection for one simple reason: It is based on prejudice against homosexuals. In a ruling issued after the announcement of what Clinton so wrongly called his "honorable compromise," U.S. District Judge Milton L. Schwartz agreed with Dahl.

Schwartz found that the only gay-related threats to military readiness, if indeed there are any, "arise solely from heterosexuals' adverse reactions to the presence of known homosexuals . . . not from the behavior of homosexuals themselves."

Rather than forbidding biased heterosexuals to act on their irrational fear and hatred of homosexuals, the military brass— along with Congress and President Clinton—are expelling anyone in the armed forces who acknowledges being gay.

That solution, Schwartz ruled, is flagrantly unconstitutional. He noted that in 1984 and 1985 the Supreme Court declared that government policies may not be based on mindless prejudice against any group. "The Constitution cannot control such prejudices," the high court stated, "but neither can it tolerate them."

Many gay-ban challenges like Dahl's are moving up through the federal court system. In one, Judge Terry Hatter, Jr., not only reinstated Navy sonar instructor Keith Meinhold but also blocked anyone else from being kicked out simply for being gay.

Discharges resumed recently because the Supreme Court decided Hatter had overstepped his authority. That ruling, which did not assess the merits of Hatter's reasoning, came in response to one of the most disgraceful performances of the Clinton administration.

Solicitor General Drew Days III argued on behalf of the president that ending gay discharges would cause "irreparable injury." As proof, he pointed to 115 dismissals that were being held up. Clinton just couldn't wait to destroy the military careers of the gay soldiers, sailors and airmen who had heard his campaign promise and naively thought it was finally safe to tell the truth.

The Dahl and Meinhold challenges are now before a federal appeals court in California. One of them—or a very similar case

—is likely to be heard by the Supreme Court during its 1994–95 term.*

With luck, a majority of justices will swiftly declare that a military policy built on irrational prejudice is intolerable. That decision is inevitable but, realistically, could be decades away.

Even when the ban is removed, the taint on President Clinton's record will remain. He will be forever remembered as a politician who won by promising equal justice for all Americans but ended up using taxpayers' money to fight for special rights for bigots. Funny, I'd have sworn that bigotry lost the '92 election.

---

* In August 1994, the Ninth Circuit Court of Appeals ruled Meinhold cannot be discharged for being gay. On November 28, 1994, the Clinton Administration decided not to appeal to the Supreme Court.

SLEEPY TOWN AWAKES TO FULFILL DREAMS OF EAGER COUPLES

NOVEMBER 12, 1993

The sleepy-eyed justice of the peace clearly wants to tell the couple at his front door to come back at a more reasonable hour. But their eagerness to be legally joined is so touching that he beckons them in from the night.

Within moments, the justice of the peace and his wife have pulled together the sweet, makeshift wedding ceremony that's a staple of old Hollywood movies.

Because Joyce is a stubborn romantic, I've watched more than my share of big-screen elopements. Yet I never expected we'd star in what felt like a Gay Nineties remake of those classic scenes:

The alarm clock rang so early that our canine companions, Jazz and Eddie, doggedly refused to get up. But we jumped into nice clothes and quickly drove to the town hall. We were intent on being first, on making a tiny bit of history. Four equally eager couples lined up behind us.

The ten of us were greeted by Takoma Park, Maryland, officials as if we were guests at a party they had forgotten they were throwing. Yes, this was the first day unmarried couples could legally register their domestic partnerships, but town officials clearly hadn't expected anyone to show up—at least not so soon.

Quite a bit of good-natured bustling ensued as the officials found the application forms, double-checked the $25 fee and determined that permanent certificates had not yet been printed. What about a notary? A frantic call went out.

If you don't want to wait for the notary, an apologetic official told us, just come back later. We'd all already waited years for legal recognition. No one budged.

Soon, Joyce and I signed a declaration "that we are in a familial relationship characterized by mutual caring and the sharing of a mutual domicile." As the notary's seal bit into the document, my government-approved domestic partner and I felt an unexpected surge of pride and, yes, validation.

Unlike a marriage license, our domestic partnership certificate really will be just a piece of paper: no tangible benefits, no legal responsibilities. Yet all ten of us felt we'd taken a major step.

"Politically, it's a really important step for the culture to be forced to reckon with us," says Marilee Lindemann, who registered with her partner of nine years. "Psychologically, it's extremely important for us to have certificates and rituals. The older I get, the more important that becomes to me."

After Berkeley, California, voted in 1984 to recognize domestic partners, a dozen cities followed suit. I wasn't surprised when Takoma Park, the most progressive suburb of Washington, D.C., joined the list. But Joyce's proposal that we sign up floored me.

Joyce had always been far more stubborn than romantic about domestic partnership registration. "No second-class citizenship for gay couples!" she'd declare. "Marriage or nothing. Our own commitment is what matters."

Her attitude abruptly changed, she now tells me, after we began using a joint checking account. If having our creditors see us as a couple felt good, she reasoned, wouldn't having the recognition of our little town feel terrific? Takoma Park, after all, was offering everything it could. It cannot change the state marriage law.

Many Americans believe a sexually active couple must be legally married to be "honest." Even the attorney trying to help lesbian Sharon Bottoms regain custody of her son is ensnared by that myth. "She can't make herself an honest woman and marry April Wade," he told a Virginia court this fall.

But isn't it our lawmakers and judges who aren't honest? They see gay couples wedded to a lifetime together yet refuse to recognize our right to marry. By slamming the door in our faces, they tell us this isn't a reasonable time.

As the hour changes, we'll knock again on justice's door. Domestic partnership is not enough for a first-class relationship. Honest.

LISTENING TO EXPERTS WOULD YIELD WISER GAY-PARENT RULINGS

NOVEMBER 19, 1993

Two women argued over which of them had given birth to the infant. Each demanded to raise him. Asked to settle one of history's first recorded custody disputes, the Bible's King Solomon had but one concern: Who is really the child's mother? Once he ingeniously answered that question, he swiftly reunited mother and child.

In what passes for modern-day Virginia, Judge Buford M. Parsons, Jr., was asked to decide which of two women should have custody of the two-year-old boy both wanted. Lacking the wisdom of Solomon, Parsons had a very different concern: Who is the lesbian? After Sharon Bottoms testified that she is gay, Parsons swiftly denied her custody of her son, Tyler.

Fortunately for Tyler, the ruling that forces him to live with his grandmother might yet be overturned. Parsons' ruling is based on two groundless assumptions: First, gay men and lesbians are unfit to be parents. Second, living with a gay parent places an "intolerable burden" on a child because much of society condemns homosexuality.

Both assumptions are tackled head-on in a powerful friend-of-the-court brief filed Monday with Virginia's Court of Appeals. The American Academy of Child and Adolescent Psychiatry declares with the American Psychological Association and the National Association of Social Workers that lesbians and gay men "have parenting skills comparable to those of heterosexual parents."

Pointing to twenty years of research, the brief adds that "any presumption of unfitness rests on prejudice and false stereotypes."

As for the well-being of the child, the mental health professionals' brief states that "the fear . . . that children of lesbian or gay parents would suffer psychological trauma as a result of 'social condemnation' is not borne out in the research." In fact, research "strongly suggests that a court does far more harm than good when it removes the child from his or her gay or lesbian parent to 'protect' the child from the possibility of future taunting."

University of Virginia psychology professor Charlotte Patterson agrees, adding that "the costs of separating a child from a parent are enormous. They're tremendous psychologically."

During the Bottoms hearing, Patterson told the court that studies of the children of gay parents consistently find they are quite similar to other children. Judge Parsons ignored her testimony.

Perhaps the appeals court will pay attention to Patterson's conclusion now that it is being echoed by the leading professional groups concerned with the emotional development of children and adolescents. Their brief, which should dispel the fears of anyone worried about gay parents, concludes:

♦ "There is no social science evidence that even suggests that lesbian or gay parents are more likely to sexually abuse their children or to allow them to be molested by others."

♦ "There is no evidence that children develop their sexual orientation by emulating their parents."

♦ "Research suggests that there is no significant difference in the overall psychological health of children raised by lesbian or gay parents and children raised by heterosexual parents."

♦ Studies of popularity and self-esteem also find no significant differences between the two sets of children.

♦ "Parent-child bonding . . . is crucial to a child's development and well-being. Disruption of this relationship should be based only on compelling reasons . . . certainly not on a parent's sexual orientation."

In custody rulings involving gay parents, judges often forbid the child to spend time with the parent's mate. Little Tyler, for example, cannot see his mother's partner, April Wade.

Ironically, research suggests the home life of lesbians' children is richer with two parents—the mother and her partner.

Gay parents can count on fair treatment only when judges truly put "the best interests of the child" first. Like Solomon, our courts stop short of resolving custody disputes by slicing children in half. Is slicing up healthy families any more civilized?

THE INS AND OUTS OF COMING OUT
TO YOUR PARENTS

NOVEMBER 26, 1993

All across America during this holiday season, closeted gay adults who've bought expensive plane tickets or driven for hours just to be with their parents are performing a painful stunt: talking without saying anything at all.

"So how's everything going?" a father sincerely asks.

"Just fine," comes the self-protective reply. "Mid-November

was unusually warm, but I'm expecting snow in the mountains soon."

A mother then tries to start a real conversation. "You've seemed really happy lately. What's new?"

"Well, it's been a lot less rainy this fall," answers the stranger she raised.

Are you, too, hiding your life behind weather bulletins? Perhaps it's time to look in the mirror and ask: "Do I really want my folks to suspect I'm a meteorologist?"

In many ways, the stress-stuffed holidays aren't the best time to come out to parents, but the truth is that a lot of us do it this time of year because it's when we see our folks.

Like other special occasions, the coming-out conversation is much more likely to turn out well—at least in the long run—if proper preparations are made.

The most important thing to prepare is yourself: Be certain you're comfortable with your sexual orientation. And be sure you're capable of coping emotionally and (if you're still in school) financially with whatever immediate reactions you receive.

Otherwise, your parents are likely to mistake your fear of rejection for confusion about whether you're really gay. Having heard the myth that sexual orientation is a choice, they might well think that showing disapproval would force you to straighten up.

"One of the common mistakes people make is coming out to others in the hopes that the other person will approve of them and thereby short-circuit their own personal self-acceptance," says psychologist Rob Eichberg, author of *Coming Out: An Act of Love.*

As the subtitle of Eichberg's book emphasizes, coming out to parents is a loving act, an attempt to tear down the wall of silence. Yet on the parents' end of the conversation, coming out often seems like a hostile act, one that instantly puts up a barrier.

Be prepared to help your parents begin to rid themselves of the misconceptions that we all absorb simply by living in this anti-gay culture. Perhaps for the first time, you'll be leading the way.

Immediately after breaking the news, give them the phone

number of a parent now comfortable with having a gay child. P-FLAG (Parents, Families and Friends of Lesbians and Gays) at (202) 638-4200 can put you in touch with the chapter nearest your folks and provide two helpful pamphlets: *Read This Before Coming Out to Your Parents* and *Is Homosexuality a Sin?*

Also, hand your parents a letter and a book to be read once the emotions of the moment ebb. The letter should explain again that you want them to know who you are because you love them. The book should forthrightly address all the reasons that few parents break out the champagne when finding out a son or daughter is gay. Two of the best such books are *Now That You Know: What Every Parent Should Know About Homosexuality* and *Beyond Acceptance: Parents of Lesbians and Gays Talk About Their Experiences.*

But why roll back the fog that surrounds our lives if a clear view of us as adults will likely upset our parents? In many families it's easier to just keep yakking about the weather.

"That's also the policy the Defense Department codified— Don't ask; don't tell," Eichberg points out. "If we don't like it being established as law, then why live it in our personal lives?"

Besides, your parents might find it refreshing for you to bring honesty home for the holidays. If you keep them guessing about who you really are, don't be shocked to end up with a gift-wrapped barometer.

STUDY OF GAYS IN UNIFORM GATHERED DUST— INSTEAD OF SUPPORT

DECEMBER 3, 1993

Who on earth would spend $1.3 million on a "how to" book and then ignore its simple, sound advice? If the only answer that comes to mind is "some rich idiot," perhaps an old outrage will provide a clue: Who thought nothing of spending $640 for a toilet seat and sending the bill to the taxpayers?

Yes, those Lords of Discipline at the Pentagon are up to their old tricks again.

Last winter the Defense Department commissioned RAND's National Defense Research Institute to analyze how to best go about "ending discrimination on the basis of sexual orientation in the armed forces."

RAND's three-pound report hit the desk of Defense Secretary Les Aspin in time to have provided President Clinton the ammunition he needed to keep his pledge to end the ban on gays in the military. Instead, the Pentagon and White House locked it away, releasing its recommendations only after interest in Clinton's broken promise waned.

But now that five federal courts have ruled against the gay ban, maybe someone in the Pentagon is dusting off the $1.3 million road map that RAND drew for the route the military must surely follow someday.

The military's chief argument against lifting the gay ban boils down to this: Heterosexuals won't like serving with people who acknowledge being gay.

Just as judge after judge is responding, "So what? That's no justification for unconstitutional discrimination," RAND needed only what it calls a "commonsense observation" to demolish the military's excuse. "It is not necessary to like someone to work with him or her," RAND bluntly points out.

RAND urges the Pentagon to declare the sexual orientation of its troops irrelevant and to order everyone in uniform to treat each other with civility and respect. The focus, RAND emphasizes, must be on ensuring professional behavior, regardless of private prejudices.

"Attitudes may change over time," RAND says, "but behavior must be consistent with the new policy from the first day."

In reaching its conclusions, RAND draws on the experience that foreign militaries as well as U.S. police and fire departments have had in blending openly gay employees into their units. But much of RAND's optimism comes from the pride our own military takes in its successful racial integration.

Just five years before President Truman's 1948 military integration order, 88 percent of white soldiers opposed racial integration of the military. So did 38 percent of black soldiers.

Yet, despite dire predictions like the ones now heard about the consequences of lifting the gay ban, "unfavorable attitudes toward [racial] integration did not necessarily translate into violent or obstructionist behavior," RAND reports. "Military personnel were able to separate their personal feelings from their conduct," it adds.

RAND finds that on-the-job experience with a member of a minority group is a powerful antidote to poisonous stereotypes. For example, two-thirds of white officers who fought in Korea in integrated units thought blacks and whites made "equally good soldiers." Only one-third of the officers in all-white units agreed.

Similarly, RAND reports that privacy is a major concern for police officers and firefighters who have not worked with a gay colleague. Those who have worked with someone gay say privacy isn't a problem. RAND also points to a 1992 study showing that Army men and women who know someone in their company is gay are more apt to oppose the ban.

Since we taxpayers paid for this grand report, let's heed RAND's advice and focus on requiring civil behavior, not on eliminating barbaric attitudes.

Let's send a forceful command to our highest-ranking public servants—whether in uniform, in Congress or in the White House: You have to allow gay men and lesbians to serve our country proudly and openly. You don't have to like it.

GAYS HAVE THEIR WORK CUT OUT FOR THEM IN JOB FAIRNESS

DECEMBER 10, 1993

Back when horse-drawn laundry carts were considered quite modern, San Francisco enacted a tax on laundries. Those with two horses paid four dollars. Those with one horse paid two dollars. But laundries with no horses at all paid fifteen.

It doesn't take a math whiz to figure out that the government had a special animosity toward the owners of no-horse laundries. The tax was, in fact, a thinly disguised attempt to drive Chinese laundries out of business. Only white-owned laundries could afford horses. With two heavy baskets hanging from a bamboo pole, Chinese laundrymen made deliveries on foot.

Early in the gold rush, white men happily let Chinese men do "women's work," like laundering. But soon, driving Chinese laundrymen out of work was seen as a way to drive them back to China.

Between 1873 and 1884, the San Francisco Board of Supervisors responded to a rising tide of anti-Chinese sentiment by directing fourteen ordinances at Chinese laundries. The supervisors made those ordinances appear to apply equally to all people. Laws that were explicitly anti-Chinese—California's tax on Chinese laborers, for example—had already been ruled unconstitutional.

In attacking Chinese laundries, the supervisors "looked for characteristics that were true only of the Chinese, then made those characteristics illegal," explains professor Sucheng Chan of the University of California at Santa Barbara.

Although stereotyped as meek, Asian immigrants "fought hard to defend their right to earn a living," Chan writes in *Asian Americans: An Interpretive History*. Chinese laundrymen took their fight to the U.S. Supreme Court and won historic equal-protection decisions.

Job discrimination—then as now—expresses one crude sentiment: "Their kind just doesn't belong around here." Depending on the circumstances, "here" can be as small as a boardroom or as large as a nation.

In San Francisco 120 years ago, "their kind" meant Chinese people. In much of America today, it means gay people.

Listen to County Commissioner David Hays explain why he voted November 30 against encouraging Apple Computer, which prides itself on treating gay workers fairly, to build in his part of Texas: "If I had voted 'yes', I would have had to walk into my church with people saying, 'There is the man who brought homosexuality to Williamson County.' "

The right of gay people to earn a living is under attack nationwide. In the guise of wanting fairness, "no special rights" initiatives are under way in a dozen states. Their real intent is to ensure that unfair treatment of gay men and lesbians remains legal.

Thirty years ago many businesses made no secret of barring women from the best jobs. Now many bosses freely admit antigay prejudice. In a 1988 poll of Alaska employers, nearly one in five said they'd fire a suspected homosexual. Among those employers without a gay friend or relative, 40 percent would fire, 57 percent wouldn't hire and 52 percent wouldn't promote a gay person—no matter how qualified.

Fashions in prejudice change with the seasons, but passage of the 1964 Civil Rights Act acknowledged that, year in and year out, certain traits make workers especially vulnerable to unfair treatment. That federal law prohibits job discrimination on the basis of race, color, religion, sex or national origin.

"Age" became a protected category in 1967; "disability" in 1990.

In all those cases, our government was trying to put a stop to special wrongs. It was not providing special rights.

Now the federal government needs to follow the lead of eight states in outlawing special wrongs against gay workers. But as San Francisco's no-horse tax illustrates, governments are just as likely to fan the flames of popular prejudice as to douse them.

It's important to remember how women finally won job protection: "Sex" was added to the 1964 Civil Rights Act initially to try to sabotage it. Yes, the Land of Opportunity embraces job fairness slowly, grudgingly. How's that for dirty laundry?

> # GAY BLACK MEN TRY
> # TO BE VISIBLE IN TWO WORLDS
> # THAT CHOOSE NOT TO SEE THEM

DECEMBER 17, 1993

The doubly invisible man travels in two worlds but rarely finds his image in either. The doubly invisible man is black and gay.

"Where is my reflection?"

Joseph Beam's cry echoes throughout his anthology, *In the Life* (Alyson Publications). The historic collection of twenty-nine black gay authors' works grew out of twin frustrations: Almost nothing in either the black community or the gay community affirmed the existence of black gay men.

Within the black community, Beam wrote, "I am most often rendered invisible, perceived as a threat to the family, or am tolerated if I am silent and inconspicuous. I cannot go home as who I am and that hurts me deeply."

Turning to books by white gay men, he found, "All the protagonists are blond; all the blacks are criminal and negligible."

Seeking solace and reality, he dived into the rising river of black lesbian writing. "Their courage told me that I, too, could be courageous. I, too, could not only live with what I feel, but could draw succor from it, nurture it and make it visible," Beam declared in 1986.

Seven years later, despite a few scattered images in works such as Beam's, black gay men continue to ask in righteous bewilderment and rage, "Where is my reflection?" And the most courageous find ways to make visible their dual identity.

Marques McClary of Michigan didn't expect to need courage to connect with other gay students at predominantly black Howard University in Washington, D.C. All he thought he needed was the right phone number.

Early in his freshman year McClary thumbed through Howard's directory of student organizations to find the number of the gay club. Instead, he found he was isolated: There was no such group.

Dorm life deepened his alienation. He made friends quickly. But his sense of camaraderie turned to fear when his new pals laughed over the beating of a gay man.

"I felt like, 'These are my friends. What are they going to say or do to me when they find out I'm gay?' " McClary recalls. "It wasn't so much a fear of getting beaten up as that they'd turn on me. That scared me the most."

Unable to find any positive reflection of being a gay black man, McClary desperately gave heterosexuality the old college try. "I regressed into thinking maybe I could change," he says. His heart quickly reminded him that he could not.

McClary wouldn't wish his miserable freshman year on anybody. Now a senior, he's working to make sure other gay students don't have to feel so alone. This fall McClary founded the Howard University Lambda Student Alliance, an officially recognized group believed to be unique among the nation's 117 black colleges.

In making his true identity visible, McClary overcame not only fear but ridicule, harassment and threats.

The first step, taking out a newspaper ad to propose forming a gay social group, was one of the hardest. He walked past the student newspaper's office fifteen times before getting the nerve to go in.

Then the calls began. A few came from students eager to join. Others from folks far more timid. "Maybe once it's started, I'll have the guts to come," one anonymous caller said.

McClary's positive phone messages mingled with hateful, mocking, even menacing ones. "Someone actually said, 'If you bring this up here, we'll get all of you,' " he says. "That's when I sat down and said, 'Oh, wow, what am I doing?' "

But then he got angry and "realized more than ever that the group was needed."

McClary now rejoices in already bringing together seventeen men and women: "Just seeing other people who are like you, that's the most comfortable feeling in the world. . . . Knowing you're not the only one."

Doubly invisible men who create their own reflections should be doubly proud. When will they be honored in two worlds?

"JUST MAUI-ED" COULD SOON APPLY TO GAY COUPLES

DECEMBER 23, 1993

A Hawaiian tidal wave powerful enough to reconfigure the nation's social and political landscape is headed for the mainland. Triggered by the attempt of three same-sex couples to obtain marriage licenses, the slow-moving titan is likely to cause quite a splash by 1995.

Just a year ago the Hawaiian couples' lawsuit seemed unlikely to create much of a ripple. For decades courts in other states had flatly denied gay couples the right to marry legally.

But Hawaii is not like other states. It's a delectable tropical mixed salad of cultures and races with nearly as many Buddhists as Baptists. Accommodating diversity is the norm.

When the Hawaii Supreme Court agreed to hear the marriage case, it accommodated gay couples by really listening. The court heard the merits of their argument, that refusing to issue a marriage license to two people simply because they are the same sex is, at heart, sex discrimination.

In a monumental but preliminary ruling last May, the Hawaii Supreme Court declared that state officials must prove that the marriage ban "is justified by compelling state interests." Otherwise, the ban must be lifted.

The Hawaii court quoted from the 1967 U.S. Supreme

Court ruling overturning laws against interracial marriage: "The freedom to marry has long been recognized as one of the vital personal rights essential to the orderly pursuit of happiness."

Comparing interracial and same-sex marriage taboos, the Hawaii court noted that, as late as 1949, thirty states outlawed interracial marriage. Today the marriages of 45 percent of Hawaiians would be illegal if the state had such a law.

In the same-sex case, arguments about supposedly compelling "state interests" must now be heard by a lower court before heading back to the state's top court. The final ruling—the one expected to flood gay hearts with joy—will probably come in 1995.

Dan Foley, attorney for the gay couples, finds nothing compelling about the arguments the state plans to offer. They focus on procreation (an activity not limited to heterosexuals), the cost of fairness, and tourism. "We are confident we will prevail," Foley says.

Meanwhile, the case is being debated in Hawaii's court of public opinion. Throngs of islanders testified at hearings before state House Judiciary Committee Chairman Terrance Tom. The Japanese American Citizens League, Afro-American Lawyers Association and the Hawaii Women's Political Caucus are among the groups supporting legal gay marriage.

In newspaper ads, opponents warned of unleashing the "wrath of God" and perhaps another hurricane.

But the issue before the court is not a religious one. As the Hawaii Supreme Court pointed out, "Marriage is a state-conferred legal status." Churches make their own rules about which couples to bless. Some turn down divorced or mixed-faith couples; a growing number unite gay couples.

The Reverend Maggie Tanis has performed fifty gay weddings at Ke Anuenue O Ke Aloha (Rainbow of Love) Metropolitan Community Church in Honolulu. Only the words "by the power invested in me by the state of Hawaii" are missing from those ceremonies, she says.

Chairman Tom wants to ensure Hawaii continues to recognize only mixed-sex marriages. Even though the state dropped impotence and sterility as bars to marriage in 1984, he wants to make clear that "the state issues licenses to those couples who appear to present the biological possibility of producing offspring."

Tom, of course, outraged childless and elderly couples and much of the rest of the state.

The coming tidal wave will not be held back by anyone's less-than-compelling arguments. Gay Americans will win the right to wed legally in Hawaii. After all, why should mixed couples be the only tourists buying T-shirts that proclaim: "Just MAUI-ed"?

FOR ONCE, THE LAW OFFERS A SAFETY NET TO A GAY FAMILY

DECEMBER 30, 1993

Between interruptions by her playful four-year-old daughter, Laura Solomon recalls falling in love with Victoria Lane: "I just took one look at her, and that was it for me!"

They were both childless at the time, but children already occupied the center of their worlds. Lane was a clinical social worker who specialized in learning-disabled kids. Solomon was a special-education teacher.

The year was 1979. The women, then in their late twenties, were soon seeing each other exclusively. Solomon, always quick to know her own mind, wanted them to live together right away. But, she explains with a trace of amused exasperation, "Victoria doesn't make fast decisions about anything." They waited a year to set up housekeeping.

By 1983 Solomon and Lane were celebrating their commitment in a public ceremony. And they were ready to have children of their own.

Solomon gave birth to Tessa, conceived through alternative insemination, on Lane's birthday in 1985. Just when Solomon and Lane had begun to think Tessa would be an only child, a

Central American infant joined their family. They named her Maya.

Together the foursome went bicycling, visited museums, cooked, drew pictures, traveled. "Our family in a lot of ways was just really regular," Solomon says, "except that I think that Victoria and I came to parenting with far more skills than a lot of people because of the work we do."

The Lane-Solomon girls learned early about different kinds of families and to be proud of their own. After Tessa mentioned her parents at school, her classmates excitedly ran up to Lane and Solomon to ask: "Did you know Tessa has two mommies? Isn't that great?"

Legally, though, Tessa just had one parent—her biological mother, Solomon. And Maya's sole legal parent was Lane, who adopted her as a "single" woman, since an unmarried couple could not adopt.

When Maya was still little, the women petitioned a family court to allow each of them to become the second legal parent of the other's child.

On August 30, 1991, Lane and Solomon made history by becoming the first gay couple in Washington, D.C., to secure joint legal status as parents. "We were completely overjoyed. It was one of the best moments of my life," Solomon recalls. (Couples in twelve states have won similar decrees.)

Life was good at the Lane-Solomon house. Lane, the mother with the softer lap and more interest in make-believe, spent the most time with the girls because she worked a shorter day. She joked that Solomon, who was finishing her doctorate, owed "thirty thousand hours of child care."

Lane was chauffeuring the kids around town last August 9 when one of Washington's sudden, violent rainstorms hit. A tree limb smashed through the windshield and into Lane. She survived seven hours of surgery but died two weeks later of an infection.

"Her life was rich and full and, we thought, unfinished," declared the program from Lane's memorial service. "Her spirit will be in my house forever," wrote eight-year-old Tessa.

Victoria Lane's partner of fourteen and a half years, now raising two children alone, slips into present tense when speaking of her. The loss is too sudden, too complete, to yet comprehend fully.

But, unlike many grieving gay parents, Solomon has the law as an ally. Says Judge Geoffrey Alprin: "It is tragic that we had to have such obvious and direct evidence of the need [for second-parent adoption] . . . Maya is not an orphan today because of what we did."

Courts sometimes deny custody to the surviving partners of gay parents. But four-year-old Maya, who drew her four-member family for the memorial service program, needn't fear being taken from Mommy Laura.

For once, Justice sees as clearly as a little child.

OUT OF THE HORROR
OF THE HOLOCAUST, LESSONS OF LOVE

JANUARY 7, 1994

Spitting out the words "You are Jew," the Polish youngster accosted another boy on the street, then hit him. Immediately, an ordinary working man scolded the attacker, saying, "Don't do that, because he's human being and child, like you."

Stefania Podgorska Burzminski, then really only a child herself, was a bystander and heard the most important lesson of her life. "He is Jew. Look at his hands, his face and your face. Is the same. Is no difference between him and you," she recalls the workman explaining. "Only bad people make difference."

When, a few years later, the Nazis began rounding up Poland's Jews, Burzminski could not remain a bystander. Despite Hitler's vile propaganda, she knew Jews were not subhuman, were not vermin to be exterminated. They were just people, people suddenly in desperate need. And she simply had to help them.

Burzminski's reflections and those of other courageously humane gentiles are recorded in *They Risked Their Lives: Rescuers of the Holocaust,* a videotape by Gay Block. More than 8,500 such heroes have now been honored by the Yad Vashem, the Holocaust Museum in Jerusalem. Among them is Oskar Schindler, the German industrialist whose rescue of more than 1,100 Jews is powerfully retold in Steven Spielberg's *Schindler's List.*

A washerwoman, a countess, a clergyman, farmers. The rescuers seemed to have little in common, but they "kept their eyes open when so many looked the other way," the narrator of Block's video declares. Yet, perhaps a more distinguishing characteristic is that they all came to see that Jews were people much like themselves.

Rescuer Gita Bauer of Germany, for example, recalls her father steadfastly teaching her that "Jews are people like you and me, only with a different religion."

The opposite lesson continues to be preached about a multitude of minority groups by the forces of hatred and violence. They'd have us forget—or never learn—that the bridges connecting us as human beings are far stronger than whatever sets us apart, regardless of our religion, race, gender or sexual orientation.

Unfortunately, one thing we humans share is the ability to unconsciously inhale ancient prejudices against one another. How do we rid our minds and souls of these destructive lies? How do we replace those lies with truth and tolerance? And how do we find the courage to speak up for those under attack, to shelter and defend them?

Much has been made since the Holocaust of the banality of evil. But the origins of tremendous goodness can be just as ordinary. Many rescuers gradually slipped into their good works.

"We didn't sit at the table when it all started and say, 'Okay, we are going to risk our lives to save some people,'" explains Johtje Vos, a Dutch woman who hid several Jews for years.

In the beginning she and her husband agreed only to keep a small suitcase for a Jewish friend being forced into a walled ghetto. A week later they were asked to keep a child as well.

"And we said, 'Of course, bring it here,' " Vos remembers. "That's not heroic. That's just doing what your heart tells you to do at the moment."

All our hearts need to hear such tales. But publishers turned down Burzminski's memoirs, saying they had enough Holocaust books. Outraged, she replied, "That is not Holocaust. That is not killing. That is saving. And that is different. You have to show people a good example. . . . Who will teach people humanity if they see only killing?"

Psychological research indicates most people would comply with an order to administer a lethal electrical shock. Yet 90 percent would refuse if others urged defiance. In *The Way We Never Were,* author Stephanie Coontz concludes that folks can be encouraged by the example of others "to tap into their own resources of compassion and courage."

Can't we learn from the rescuers and the Polish workman? Can't we look each other in the eye and say, "Is the same. Is no difference." Wouldn't it be nice to feel good?

WALLS COME TUMBLING DOWN

As DEB AND I SLOWLY WALKED DOWN THE CHURCH AISLE TOGETHER, I felt the ground underneath a very private assumption shift. I whispered a few words to her.

Only moments before, we'd first set foot inside Downtown Presbyterian Church in the heart of Rochester, New York. I'd expected Deb to be speaking in a basement fellowship hall. Instead, we were ushered directly into the church sanctuary. I was immediately struck by how much the sanctuary, which glowed on that Saturday night in October of 1993, resembled the sanctuary of my childhood. With its shimmering Tiffany-glass windows and massive pipe organ, the gay-friendly Downtown Church is far grander than the Presbyterian church in middle Georgia where I grew up and saw so many heterosexual couples showered with rice and good wishes. But the overall look and feel of the two churches is startlingly similar. Instead of a twinge of homesickness, I felt as if I'd stumbled upon my true home. There in Rochester—surrounded by hundreds of smiling folks in their Sunday best—the past loosened its painful grip on my imagination.

Positioning myself to be within Deb's range of vision, I sat in a pew beside our newfound friend Virginia Davidson, the Downtown Presbyterian Church elder who since 1978 has fought for ordination of openly gay ministers. Deb headed to the front and, after a brief introduction, stepped to the pulpit to deliver her speech. She'd given two dozen addresses in the previous year. And along the way Deb and I had crafted a standard speech for her that was a fairly well-oiled vehicle with parts that could be replaced or retooled to fit a specific situation. Having noticed that public speakers tend to muff extemporaneous opening lines, we decided early on to wall off Deb's unscripted remarks until later, during the more relaxed question-and-answer periods. But in Rochester our well-constructed walls kept tumbling. As her unofficial stage manager, I was shocked when Deb greeted the audience and started ad-libbing: "I've got to begin by sharing something really incredible that just happened. Joyce and I walked into this beautiful church, and she turned to me and said, 'Gee, now that we're here, we might as well get married.' It took me six years to get her to give me a ring. Let me tell you, if you can get her talking marriage in two minutes, we're definitely coming back to Rochester!" The sanctuary shook with appreciative laughter.

Months before, when the Hawaii Supreme Court handed down a preliminary ruling on gay marriage, I'd finally come to believe that Deb and I will be able to marry legally someday. But up to the moment we stepped into the sanctuary of Downtown Presbyterian Church, a church wedding was unimaginable for me. Gay holy union ceremonies have been performed around Rochester for twenty years, but I literally could not imagine exchanging vows with my partner before hundreds of well-wishers in a place that really felt like a church. What my three sisters had taken for granted that they could have, I had taken for granted I could not. And I had stubbornly refused to want what I thought was impossible to ever have. But in an instant, Downtown Presbyterian made the idea of marrying Deb right there both imaginable and immensely appealing.

MORE THAN ANYONE I'VE EVER KNOWN, DEB BELIEVES IN SEIZING
the day or, in the case of Rochester, the forty-eight hours. That
makes for really hectic weekends when she's invited to speak out
of town. In Rochester we were overbooked even by Deb's standards. Deb hit the ground running with a luncheon interview for
a future column. Then I headed across town to interview Keith
Moyer, editor of Rochester's daily papers. That evening Deb
helped kick off Rochester's first gay film festival by introducing a
documentary on psychologist Evelyn Hooker, and we attended a
packed reception in Deb's honor. On Saturday, Deb had a breakfast interview for another future column, then we toured the
home of George Eastman, founder of Eastman Kodak, and the
home of suffragist Susan B. Anthony before Deb was interviewed
by the local gay newspaper, *The Empty Closet,* and we were both
interviewed for a gay TV show. That evening Deb gave her
speech, which was followed by a party in our honor thrown by
the Kodak gay employees' association. Sunday morning we were
back at Downtown Presbyterian to attend a regular church service
before driving home. The pace was frenetic, yet each of us found
Rochester emotionally soothing.

At the crowded Friday night reception, the town knocked
down one of the psychic defenses Deb had constructed during
adolescence. Ridiculed and scorned as a gay teenager, she became
accustomed to keeping her distance emotionally from all but a
very few people in order to try to avoid being injured again.
When Deb first thought of her target audience as herself at sixteen, she was thinking how reading a gay column in her daily
paper at an early age could have healed some emotional wounds.
"I could see the hurt in myself and I could see—'Oh, this would
have helped me then.' But I didn't realize that it could help me
now," she recalls. Once the column began, we both could tell
that it was a much-needed salve on the bitter wounds of many gay
people. Gradually, Deb's public appearances taught her how to
give of herself emotionally to strangers, even hug them if she felt
that's what they needed. "I would be there for people. I was
serving by nurturing, yet I desperately needed nurturing," she
recalls. "I never allowed for the possibility that I would be transformed by the column, only that other people could be." But

Rochester changed her. Gay men and lesbians stood in a slowly moving line for an hour or more just to connect with Deb for a few moments. "Suddenly," Deb told me later, "I realized I wasn't hugging people. I was being hugged by people." In a flash she understood "not just that people could heal me but that people wanted to. And that I should let down my defenses." It was a long, wonderful Friday night.

After Deb's Saturday night speech, we were whisked away to a party thrown by Eastman Kodak's developing, energetic gay employees' group, the Lambda Network. The tone of that photo-filled evening, engraved in my memory as one long communal embrace, was captured by one group member's hand-screened T-shirt: He'd written "Friend of Dorothy" but crossed out the "Dorothy" and replaced it with "Joyce and Deb." We were presented with a book chronicling the history of their beloved company that had been signed, like a school yearbook, by every one of our hosts. Deb took special satisfaction in one postscript—"Joyce, Deb seems like marriage material to me. (She gives you great looks!)"

When we returned to Downtown Presbyterian for church the next morning, the Reverend Rose Mitchell greeted us by name from the pulpit, and much of the congregation made a point of giving us hugs when it came time to "pass the peace." Downtown Presbyterian, the longtime home of rock-ribbed progressivism, takes its strength from a congregation that appeared 30 percent retired, 30 percent gay, 30 percent young families and 10 percent people with a foot in two of those groups. While we were there, the church was valiantly fighting the national Presbyterian church for the right to add an openly lesbian minister to its staff. I've been in many churches. None ever felt more spiritually alive than Downtown Presbyterian.

Although the much-maligned city of Detroit will always be special to us because it was the column's birthplace, Deb and I have come to see Rochester as its spiritual home. In the months before we actually visited Rochester and felt so uplifted, my reporting on how all the pieces necessary for approval of the first gay issues column had fallen into place in Detroit kept leading me

—to my surprise—to Rochester. *Detroit News* publisher Bob Giles and managing editor Christy Bradford—either of whom could have blocked Deb's idea—first worked together in Rochester. It was there that they were first exposed to a vibrant gay community. And it was there that they grew to love and respect J. Ford Huffman, who came to symbolize gay America to both of them. Until *The Detroit News* joined Gannett, the Rochester papers were the chain's flagship. Rochester is where many of Gannett's attempts to represent a diverse readership began. And the Rochester *Democrat and Chronicle* was one of the first papers to make a commitment to running Deb's column every week.

Rochester is also where Harriet Dart, who later moved to Detroit, learned to accept her gay son, Kevin. Rochester's P-FLAG, along with a gay-friendly Rochester nun and a gay-friendly Rochester doctor, helped convert Dart into a woman emotionally capable of founding Detroit's P-FLAG chapter and becoming its driving force.

Rochester is blessed with springtime lilacs and deep roots in social activism. The home of Kodak, Xerox and Bausch & Lomb, New York's third-largest city attracts workers who are well educated and open to innovative ideas. My first impression of Rochester, which bills itself as "The World's Image Centre," came from the initial deluge of reader responses to Deb's column. I quickly came to see a Rochester postmark as a friendly symbol, a sign of an "Oh, goody" letter rather than an "Ooey Gooey" one. Only in Rochester did an editor tell me that Deb's column is probably a circulation booster. Rochester has a proud history of being a haven for voices of reform. It's where Susan B. Anthony wrote *The History of Woman Suffrage* and where Frederick Douglass published his abolitionist newspaper, *The North Star*. Runaway slaves like Douglass were safe in Rochester because the townsfolk expelled the federal marshals sent to capture them.

IN SOCIALLY CONSCIOUS ROCHESTER, DEFENSIVE WALLS TOPPLED INside both Deb and me. Since May 8, 1992, we've lived at the epicenter of an earthquake, one that knocks holes in barriers that divide people from one another, divide us not just by sexual orientation but by age, race, gender. Its reverberations are sometimes strong enough to alter lives, perhaps none more than Deb's and mine.

When the column began shaking up our lives, I had no idea that our vision would be affected. But that turns out to be the most profound change in us. We now can see that the present is less hostile than it appears to be in most press coverage of gay issues or than it felt when we guarded our lesbianism as if it were a secret that we couldn't trust with strangers. We see how our overblown fear of heterosexual hostility kept us too isolated and prevented us from getting important emotional needs met, both individually and as a couple. And we now catch more glimpses of a gay-friendly future, a future with far more windows than walls between people of different sexual orientations.

Our vision has been corrected by having had to laugh at our own paranoia, by realizing how much gay couples crave examples of longevity, by watching a heterosexual great-grandfather gradually evolve into our friend, by seeing how many religious heterosexuals are determined to make their churches gay-friendly and by turning misty-eyed at the sight of an anniversary card—our first.

The birth of Deb's column reconfigured our lives right from the first morning when I was awakened by the call from Detroit's WJR radio. Deb often says we were like a childless couple shocked to discover that the stork delivered us triplets overnight. We felt overwhelmed, delighted, blessed. I found myself thrust into the public role of "wife of." (Knowing firsthand the burden that such public perceptions can put on an egalitarian relationship, singer Janis Ian jokingly turned the tables when we attended her concert the night after Deb had interviewed her for a column. "Oh, it's Joyce and Mrs. Joyce!" Ian exclaimed.) Meanwhile, Deb, who like many of us journalists was most comfortable around strangers when she was the one asking the questions, had to learn to give an interview, had to learn to give a speech.

Just as Deb had begun hugging readers after speeches because they needed it but found she needed it as well, she wrote about our relationship to help readers, then found our relationship benefited, too. For our first six years together, virtually all of the

positive reinforcement we received as a couple came from just the
two of us. Once the column joined our family, Deb and I started
getting encouragement to stay together from the most unexpected places: Managing editors began asking whether we intend
to have children together and, if so, how many and would we
adopt. (No, three and no.) *People* magazine's profile of Deb included a photo of the two of us sprawled in our backyard ham-
mock. The Knights Wrestling Club for Women, which we'd
worked out with when Deb was reporting a column one sweaty
New York afternoon, declared us both honorary members. In the
midst of presenting Deb a 1994 National Media Award on behalf
of the New York chapter of GLAAD (Gay & Lesbian Alliance
Against Defamation), broadcast news star Barbara Walters began
ad-libbing about our relationship—expressing hope that Deb and
I were still together and saying that if we weren't we should kiss
and make up. (That's the only time Deb has begun an acceptance
speech by reassuring an audience that I'm still her gal.) And Harriet Dart, having heard from a friend about Deb's marriage remark in Rochester, informed us we'd be in big trouble if we took
public vows in Rochester without inviting her to be there. Gradually, I came to see the value of what most gay couples have never
had: public rituals in which we share our joy in being together
and ask for the support of friends and relatives.

Deb's very personal column also had the odd and unexpected
effect of turning us into minor, out-of-town celebrities. Although
we live in a semi-gay suburb of Washington, D.C., we're still
fairly anonymous when we go out to dinner or buy groceries
because the column doesn't run in area newspapers. (It was a
shock to be walking through downtown Washington during the
massive 1993 gay-rights march and overhear: "And we even have
our own national gay columnist!") But if we drop into a place like
Detroit or Palm Springs or Rochester, we now know we'll run
into readers who feel they've known us for years. It's a weird
sensation to have a total stranger ask, "Well, who won the argument over air conditioning?" Not having had as much practice as
Deb in such situations, I usually respond: "Huh?"

Despite her sense of humor, Deb's always taken her new role
as a gay public figure seriously. Knowing all her own foibles,

though, she never presented herself as any sort of role model. She thought her only role was to do her best as a columnist each week. In her role as mother to the gay world, Harriet Dart taught Deb she was wrong. The first weekend we met Harriet, she took Deb aside and pinned an AIDS ribbon on her jacket. To Deb the message was clear: "It doesn't matter whether you see yourself as setting an example; you are." Deb never made another public appearance without that red ribbon.

Most of us in journalism chose our profession because of high ideals but tend to end up spending our days cynically focused on the worst in people—often even bringing out the worst in people. Sharing our lives with millions of readers through the column and this book allows Deb and me to focus on bringing out the best in people. Falling back on language from my Presbyterian childhood, I'll even say we both feel called to this opportunity to serve. And that by serving—by trying to encourage goodwill, understanding and personal courage—we've felt spiritually renewed. We know that we're part of something a great deal larger than ourselves.

WHEN DEB ENVISIONED HER COLUMN BECOMING A WINDOW ON GAY reality, she knew that it was a window needed by gay people as well as heterosexuals. Many of the straight readers who've written Deb since 1992 apparently think that all gay people are perfectly informed about all things gay and don't need a gay column or gay news and feature articles in their family newspaper. Naturally, that's preposterous. I've met gay people who didn't know until after they voted in the 1992 presidential election that candidate Bill Clinton supported ending the ban on gays in the military. And Jan Stevenson, head of the Detroit gay community center, says many gay people in her city didn't know there was going to be a huge March on Washington in 1993 until Deb told them. And, of course, Linda Marquez and Johnnie Hernandez had never heard of the most gay-friendly spot in the nation until Deb wrote about it. But far more important than the gay facts that Deb shares with her gay readers is the sense of connectedness she gives to gay teenagers who've never met another gay person, to gay couples who don't know any other gay couples, to gay retirees who've lost or never had a life partner. She introduces gay people locked in mental chains to gay people who've broken free. And she gives us all as clear a view of gay triumphs as of our defeats. Every time a gay American is able to envision the possibility of real equality, one of the barriers keeping us from that goal collapses. For too long, even our imaginations have been occupied territory.

For those of us who came of age after Stonewall, it's easy to focus on how much the gay civil rights movement has yet to achieve and to become disillusioned, pessimistic, bitter. Our cup doesn't runneth over. But the cup that was empty just over a quarter century ago is half full today. More than half the states have decriminalized homosexuality. The American Psychiatric Association and the American Psychological Association have stopped labeling gay people mentally ill and are working to make our society less homophobic. The number of corporations openly wooing gay dollars and offering their gay employees equal benefits is quickly climbing. And gay people in ever-increasing numbers are coming out, acknowledging our sexual orientation to ourselves, to friends, bosses, relatives, even pollsters. (National polls show that the right to marry matters tremendously to most of us. Ninety-one percent of lesbians and 79 percent of gay men told *Newsweek* in a poll published June 20, 1994, that "legally sanctioned gay marriage" is either a "very important" or "somewhat important" goal for the gay-rights movement. On a more personal level, 59 percent of gay or bisexual men in an *Advocate* survey published August 23, 1994, answered "yes" to the question "Would you want to legally marry another man if you could?" Another 26 percent said "Maybe.")

Coming out makes us hungry—hungry to understand where we've come from as a people and where we might be going as individuals. And gay couples are hungry to see other couples like themselves who are making a go of it. At the Rochester reception where Deb learned how to be hugged, a fellow in his early twenties told her, "This is my partner, and we've been together fourteen months." He said the length of time almost apologetically, as if it surely must seem insignificant to someone involved nearly a decade. But Deb saw the happiness and pride in both men's eyes.

"That's really great! Congratulations!" she told them, and they beamed.

We gay couples need encouragement, need to know we are capable of creating durable unions. I cringe whenever I hear half of a happy gay couple say, "If we stay together . . ." as if we can't have faith in our own alliances because popular American culture shows them no respect. (I've never heard a happily married heterosexual say, "If we stay together . . .") Virtually every gay couple I've ever met was hungry to meet couples who'd been together longer. A gay man named Joseph wrote from Springfield, Missouri, to say that his lover had taken to playfully calling him "Joyce" because Deb and I are so close. (I love that gay men aren't afraid to compare themselves to women.) For Deb and me, readers' responses—especially from Palm Springs—gave us our first clear view of the lives of gay couples together almost since Jesus was in sandals.

Linda Marquez and Johnnie Hernandez, who fell in love in high school in 1966, showed us how a gay relationship can continually evolve and grow over decades as interest in one another accumulates, just like money in the bank. But they are still short-timers compared with two male couples I met in Palm Springs after they wrote Deb to congratulate her on the column's birth.

"The Desert Rats," as Darrel Mortenson and J. F. Van Schaack call themselves, have been together since Linda and Johnnie were in third grade, since before Deb was born. They grew up poor, in Iowa towns just fourteen miles apart, but didn't meet until they both began working for Lockheed in Los Angeles. The year was 1957. Van Schaack, who goes by "Van," had learned to be exceedingly cautious about his private life during a McCarthy-era stint in the Foreign Service and three years in the Navy. He knew he'd be stripped of his security clearance if Lockheed discovered his sexual orientation. But when twenty-year-old Darrel, who was four years his junior, invited him bowling, he stopped proceeding with caution: He just said "yes." When they found the bowling alley full, they jumped back into Darrel's brand-new Chevrolet and hot-rodded it up a mountain. They drank and necked and promptly fell asleep in the backseat. Both men recall exactly where they had breakfast the next morning and precisely what they ate—blueberry muffins and oatmeal.

After two months, they got an apartment. Committed to a life together, they found a Methodist church in Hollywood unlocked, went inside and privately exchanged identical wedding bands. Thirty-seven years later, when I chatted with Van and Darrel on their hillside patio overlooking much of Palm Springs, they both still cherished all the little details of their time together. They talk of the importance of treating each other and their relationship with respect. If they have a recipe for longevity, it blends respect with monogamy, good sex and hard work. Or, as Van puts it: "Keep that zipper up!" With the air crackling with the electricity between them, they explain that they're both very sexual and very jealous. "One thing we've learned that's important to any relationship is that in order to have trust, you've got to have respect. If you see some hot pants and have a quickie, it blows the whole thing," Van adds. Non-monogamous relationships just don't last, Darrel chimes in, because "you think you're together, but you're not." Shaking his head in bewilderment at middle-aged guys who give up a good relationship to run off with a much younger man, Van says, "Just shoot me if I ever get a twinkie!"

Over the years they've continually renovated houses together —thirty-seven in thirty-seven years. Those real estate deals made them comfortable enough financially to move to Palm Springs in 1987 and join the semi-retired. After thirty years at General Electric, Van had found his job was being phased out. He accepted an early-retirement offer. Darrel, who'd been lighting sets for Universal Studios for a quarter century, was then working on *Murder, She Wrote*. He told his colleagues, "See you later," and took off with Van. They've been surprised by how gay Palm Springs is. But Van finds old closeted habits hard to leave behind: "I still tell white lies. I don't tell people I have a lover of thirty-seven years."

One reason he has a lover of thirty-seven years is that they both have learned to keep themselves out of harm's way. Because of Darrel's job, they were invited to a great many Hollywood parties—some gay, others mixed—in the Sixties that turned into orgies. "We'd say 'good night' and walk away," Darrel recalls. Even today they don't go to bars alone—"because things can happen," Van explains.

They are inseparable—emotionally and financially. They've always had joint bank accounts, a plunge Deb and I took after eight years together and now wished we'd taken sooner. Darrel says, "So many gays we know, even here in the desert, have separate checking—separate, separate, separate. And I say, 'Why do you live together if everything else is separate?' "

Darrel and Van head off to sea together every March. "That's the only kind of cruising we do!" Van says with a laugh. They've been taking anniversary cruises every year since 1974 and always ask the waiter to bring a cake to their table on March 10. For their twenty-fifth anniversary cruise to Mexico, Darrel surprised his lover by booking a special cabin. Van says he'd just walked in and seen the gorgeous cabin filled with long-stemmed red roses when a ship steward became quite agitated: "And he says, 'But this is a honeymoon suite! There's no room for two men!' " After arguing with Van for about ten minutes, the steward looked at Darrel, smiled and said, "Ohhhh, I understand! I understand!"

Darrel and Van don't hold hands or jitterbug together on board, but there's no mistaking the fact that they are very married. They still laugh about the time they were looking at one cruise ship's display of photos of its passengers when a little boy came up, pointed at their picture and said, "Mommy, Mommy, there's the odd couple you were talking to Daddy about!"

For those of us looking forward to cruising into retirement with the same shipmate, there's nothing odd about finding that couple inspiring. Van and Darrel don't know a gay couple that's been together longer. I'd like to introduce them to Robert Menas and Eugene Goforth, a Palm Springs couple whose relationship dates from January 1951, when they happened to meet on a street in Manhattan.

All the gay couples I interviewed who'd long since passed their silver anniversary had tremendous faith in their relationship's permanence. Not once did I hear "If we stay together . . ." That phrase is only voiced by couples who fear that, being gay, they can't succeed—and are afraid they'll sound like fools if they talk about spending the rest of their lives together.

WE MARK STONEWALL AS THE MOMENT GAY PEOPLE LEARNED TO fight back, learned to stop cowering in fear. Despite all our talk of coming out of the closet, we rarely pause to consider how thoroughly fear still controls most of us. It's largely our own fear that limits us, even those of us who say we're out of the closet. We fret about the horrible things that might happen if we make our private life as public as that of the average heterosexual. And we give too little thought to how we stunt our lives—and the lives of everyone who needs to see the gay people all around them—by yielding to such worries. A depressing number of gay people continue to conduct their lives as if this life were just a dress rehearsal: This time I'll pretend to be the person I think my parents or boss or neighbors or complete strangers want me to be. Next time I'll be myself. Next time I'll give my relatives a chance to love me for who I really am. The only winner of that foolish game is fear.

Alison Bechdel, a cartooning dyke to watch out for, poked gentle fun at gay paranoia in a 1989 strip in which Harriet and Mo go grocery shopping. We'll catch up with them in the produce department:

> *Harriet* (putting an arm around her lover to show her a piece of fruit): Mmm . . . Fresh figs! Know what these remind me of?
> *Mo:* HARRIET!
> *Harriet:* What?
> *Mo:* We're in the grocery store, for goddess' sake! Could you, like, disengage your hand from my shoulder?
> *Harriet* (playfully grabbing Mo's backside): Sure! How's that?
> *Mo:* Harriet! I'm NOT KIDDING!
> *Harriet:* Jeez, Mo! What are you so paranoid about?
> *Mo:* I'm just not in the mood to get QUEERBASHED right now, okay?
> *Harriet* (eyeing an elderly woman nearby): Yeah, that lady with the zucchini looks like a pretty ROUGH NUMBER.

. . . I bet she comes down to the produce section and
beats up dykes all the time!

Being her usual excessive self, Mo soon grabs Harriet and
plants a big kiss on her. That's just the opportunity the elderly
woman needs to say: "Excuse me, dears! You're blocking the
aisle."

Our fear polices our behavior, our aspirations, our words, far
more completely than an enemy army wielding zucchini or billy
clubs ever could. As Deb told a University of Maryland student
who worried about losing the friendship of his fellow black students if he came out in class, "The worst pain and oppression I've
ever felt was from the inside, not the outside. It was from inter-
nalizing hatred, misunderstanding and fear. It was from victimiz-
ing myself in far more inhumane ways than anyone outside me
could ever have the power to do. And the single most empowering act I ever did and believe any gay person can do is to come
out, to trust others, to be a part of the process of change."

When Deb started writing her column, I became increasingly
conscious of how much time I was spending in a defensive
crouch. Yes, Deb and I were out to our parents, our bosses and a
jillion readers. I rejoiced in feeling free at last, but I was braced for
a hateful face-to-face encounter of some sort. For example, one
of Deb's first interviews about her new column was on a local
Washington, D.C., morning news show. The televised segment
included a brief shot of her pecking away at a keyboard in *The
Detroit News'* Washington bureau.

Heading to my job at *The Washington Post* immediately after
that broadcast, I found myself tensing up, worrying about having
to deal with colleagues' reactions. Sure enough, as soon as I
stepped into a *Post* elevator, a guy from the newsroom's computer
systems office piped up: "Saw Deb on television."

Trying not to sound defensive, I replied, "Yeah?"

"Yeah," he said, "I didn't know the *News* still uses Coyotes."

He cared about the nature of Deb's computer, not the nature
of her sexuality. Suddenly, what didn't feel comfortable was being
so fearful.

Being paranoid at 35,000 feet still felt perfectly reasonable, though. I'd been a nonchalant passenger until an Air Florida flight crashed into the Potomac River in 1982. I became the Queen of Sweaty Palms. Flying with Deb, I've always grabbed the window seat so I can constantly monitor the distance between us and disaster. I watch my fellow passengers for signs of suspicious activity. Naturally, when we were flying to Hawaii in 1992 for Deb's first major speech, I noticed when the man on the other side of Deb started pretending to read his paperback novel. His pages never turned, and his eyes were fixed on the speech Deb was still pounding into her laptop computer. Suddenly, the stranger got up, opened the overhead luggage compartment and prowled around inside his large suitcase. He slipped something small into his coat pocket and disappeared. For a long time. A very long time. Finally, I could contain my anxiety no longer. Trying to sound casual, I whispered, "What do you think that guy got out of his suitcase?" Having suffered through flying with me plenty of times, Deb knew exactly what I really meant: "Do you think that guy got out a gun and is going to try to shoot you and will end up making the plane crash because he's read your speech and knows we're gay?" I never did find out what that guy had taken out of his suitcase, probably a comb or toothbrush. Eventually, he sat back down and stopped pretending he'd not read every word of Deb's speech. As he and Deb chatted, I gradually accepted that he wasn't a homicidal heterosexual. He was a Memphis florist—a gay Memphis florist. And he was fascinated and delighted to discover that Deb was writing a gay issues column for mainstream newspapers. I sheepishly stuck out a still-sweaty hand and said hello.

Even at 35,000 feet, the world is friendlier—and more gay—when we stop clinging so tightly to fear. When her column was very new and strangers asked Deb what she did for a living, she'd often cut off the conversation with a curt "I'm a journalist." Once she quit building unnecessary walls and began telling people about her column, Deb found the reaction was almost invariably positive and the conversation often amazing. And as soon as we put a gay-pride rainbow bumper sticker on our sports car, the roadways became friendlier. People now honk and wave. We're still not at ease holding hands in most public places. But we're consciously working on expanding the territory where we feel safe. It's not just downtown Provincetown anymore. After the column began, we gradually started holding hands at suburban malls, country music concerts, beaches. No one has made a rude remark to us. And at the 1994 Gay Games in New York City we walked through dilapidated neighborhoods wearing gay paraphernalia and found passersby eager to direct us to the right bus or just say hello.

We've not become terminally naive. We know there are plenty of hateful people. We know many of them despise gay men and lesbians. We haven't forgotten the Christmas of '86, when one of my sisters threw us out of her home because she didn't want homosexuals around her children. If we ever forget that painful incident, a quick round of Ooey Gooey will remind us about mindless, venomous prejudice. And anti-gay violence is not an imaginary threat.

The question is how to respond to sharing this world with hostile forces. I saw that question in a new light late one night when Deb and I were walking through a deserted hotel hallway. It was after Deb's first Detroit speech. We were feeling particularly close, but holding hands made me nervous—as if some unseen homophobe were just waiting for an excuse to pounce. Suddenly I thought how much we take for granted the fact that being women puts us constantly in physical jeopardy. For women, being hyper-alert in public simply seems like part of being alive. From birth we're rigorously trained to take precautions against being attacked by a man. Yet we'd never dream of disguising ourselves as men to reduce our risk of assault. That's not a trade-off Deb and I—or any women I've met—would be willing to make. Being female is an integral part of our identities and of how we interact with the world. Those of us who are gay must learn that cloaking our sexual orientation is just as unacceptable a trade-off as covering up our gender. And we must learn to more accurately weigh the risks of living openly and the wounds we inflict on ourselves by hiding.

In their efforts to draw much-needed attention to the political and social inequality endured by gay Americans, gay political leaders emphasize the difficulties we face. Sometimes that helps win us allies. But it also creates a bogus equation in many minds: gay = victim. More than once I've found myself reassuring the mother of a lesbian that being gay doesn't automatically turn her daughter into a hate-crime statistic.

I was raised to avoid conflict, but I now know we've got to stop giving so much power away to our most narrow-minded countrymen. I know that we gay people have to stop tolerating intolerance—which is exactly what we're doing when we render ourselves invisible. If being yourself in public feels uncomfortable, imagine how it felt to racially integrate a Woolworth's lunch counter. I'm reminded of an anonymous Ooey Gooey letter to Deb: "We have never been able to get over people like you who always go where they are NOT WANTGED [sic]. Blacks do the same thing." Bigots see the connections between prejudices. The rest of us must see them, too. Anyone who wouldn't eat in a restaurant that mistreats black customers shouldn't be eating in an anti-gay restaurant like Cracker Barrel, which in 1991 began firing its gay employees. And gay folks who still feel they must disguise their homosexuality to avoid losing a job or a loved one's affection must ask themselves if they'd be equally willing to hide their race or gender. The more of us gay people there are out in public, the safer we'll all be. For example, workers who form a gay employees' group are safer in the open together than they were crouched in individual closets.

Hiding is a dangerously addictive habit. It drugs us into feeling safe when all we truly are is isolated. "The biggest challenge in this community is the same challenge we had in 1969, which is just getting people to come out," Deb told *Between the Lines,* the gay paper in Ann Arbor, Michigan. "All of us, we collude in these little jokes and reasons why people shouldn't be out. We support each other for not being out. We need to change that— and it is changing. But what we need to do is create a supportive environment to help people come out. . . . And what we need to do as people who are out is not tear up people who aren't out, but always make clear that where we're going and where each of us should be going is to living an open, free, honest life."

AS DEB AND I HAVE INTEGRATED OPENNESS MORE AND MORE INTO our life together, we've come to understand how important it is for gay people to give straight people the chance to demonstrate that they are gay-friendly. A heartening number are ready to rise to the occasion. In face-to-face encounters, when we've presented ourselves as a gay couple, we've almost always been treated respectfully. Often, the gay-friendly heterosexual is someone wanting to keep our business—a hotel clerk, a waitress, a car dealer. For once, capitalism seems to be a liberalizing influence.

Deb's proud that her column is also a liberalizing influence. For Deb and me, one of the pleasures of being associated with the column is that it's not only a window through which some heterosexuals have looked and been changed, it's also a window that enables us to see our straight allies—in all their grand diversity—more clearly. Watching heterosexuals work to bridge the gap between the gay and straight communities makes us feel more at home in the world, makes us less wary around strangers. Despite the publicity given high-profile homophobes like big-mouth carper Rush Limbaugh and professional stumbling block Jesse Helms, the real news is the proliferation of heterosexuals willing to speak out on behalf of gay men and lesbians.

Some of our most ardent allies are religious heterosexuals. Virtually every major Christian or Jewish denomination that has not already recognized the right of openly gay people to join the clergy and to have our committed relationships blessed is being forced to wrestle with those issues. These bouts ultimately will be won, but there will be many preliminary defeats. The 1994 General Assembly of the Presbyterian Church, for example, took the first step toward forbidding ministers to bless same-sex unions. But Episcopal Bishop John Shelby Spong, who has ordained openly gay ministers and who believes the Christian church must atone for its mistreatment of homosexuals, has helped teach Deb and me that such defeats don't matter in the long run. "You raise consciousness," he once told Deb, "by forcing the debate to be engaged. When the Southern Baptist Church in 1988 condemned homosexuality as evil by a 90 to 10 vote, I thought, 'We've finally won. We've won because even the Southern Baptists have had to debate it.' Ten or twenty years ago, they would not have debated it. It would have been a universal consensus that it was evil, that the Bible said it's wrong. The fact that it got on the floor for their debate means that the consciousness has seeped down into the most conservative mainline Christian body in America."

Many religious allies of gay people are veterans of earlier civil rights wars. Back in 1965, Betty and Paul Beeman, devout Methodists, carried a banner for open housing. Now they're demonstrating their support for gay rights.

"We came out because of your column," Betty Beeman, a retired secretary, told Deb at the 1993 P-FLAG national convention. For parents and friends of gay people, "coming out" has many phases, just as it does for those of us who are gay. Betty Beeman was talking about coming out as gay-friendly in their hometown newspaper, *The Olympian,* by writing a rebuttal to the hate mail triggered by the start of Deb's column.

"As we read letters from those who so vehemently oppose homosexual relationships, we wonder who these critics are writing about. . . . Their letters represent myths and monsters created from ignorance, fear and prejudice," the Beemans wrote.

"How do we know? Because we stand proudly with our four children, two of whom are homosexual. . . . We cannot imagine what tragic losses our family would have suffered if we had operated on the principles of fear, hate and rejection, so often mislabeled as 'biblical.' Rather than experiencing what we cherish as real family values, we would all be fractured, alienated, lonely and miserable. We'll take love," they declared.

Later, at P-FLAG's convention, Paul Beeman, a retired Methodist minister, told me, "It's really important to us not to let the Radical Right have the religious ground [on homosexuality]. . . . I refuse to use the term 'Christian Right' because I don't think they're Christian." He notes that Jesus' chosen family—his disciples—was not his biological family. "There's almost nothing in the Bible that is supportive of what the Radical Right defines as 'traditional family values.' What is there is the affiliations and affirmations that come out of love for people who are in voluntary relationships. There's nothing that says, 'Mom and Dad and two kids, and Dad works and Mom stays home and cleans house.' Jesus was such a radical. He never married."

Of course, Jesus never got a chance to walk into the sanctuary of Rochester's Downtown Presbyterian Church.

AS SOON AS THE COLUMN BEGAN SHAKING UP OUR LIVES, DEB AND I began catching regular glimpses of activist heterosexual allies, usually deeply religious progressives, parents of gay adults or, like the Beemans, both. Interacting with them helps us feel much safer, keeps us from developing a siege mentality. Yet, since they're already on a wavelength so similar to ours, the encounters usually are more reassuring than thought-provoking.

But from his very first letter, Harry Guest of Oscoda, Michigan, was a worthy sparring partner, who probed, challenged, questioned, kept us on our toes. Sexual orientation wasn't the only wall between us and the man who's become such a part of our lives that we always talk of him as "Harry." The barriers created by age, gender and geography were at least as high. But the column tore a hole in all those walls. As Deb shared bits and pieces of our life with him through the column, he reciprocated and slowly showed us life from his perspective. And he reinforced our thinking that it's vital to share our life as a gay couple with heterosexual readers.

Harry's letters demanded their own special category right from the start. They were feisty, critical and barbed yet engaging, literate and fundamentally gay-friendly. Harry discovered the column in *The Detroit News* in August 1993 and began firing off weekly salvos.

O Debbie, come off it.

How far are we from Salem? Are you serious? Isn't an analogy from witch-burning three centuries ago to the current wave of homophobia overreaching just a little bit?

Are you really afraid some day some gang of heterosexual weirdos is going to truss you up like a broiler and toss you into a swimming pool to see if you'll float?

Preach to us benighted straights to help us with our prejudices, but let's don't get paranoid about it.

Aren't you concerned that your hyperbolic outbursts may be doing more to polarize us than all the Pat Robertsons and their cockamamie corps?

You have, however, succeeded in one area. You're the first thing I turn to in Friday's News. *I can't wait to see what you're going to say next. . . .*

Let's do lunch. Any place you choose. I'll pop. We're not likely to change each other's ideas about anything. I'm eighty years old and my mind-sets change with glacial speed, but we might strike a blow for tolerance and understanding.

Harry was back in the ring for Round 2 a week later, once again ribbing Deb over her choice of topics:

Why just last week, standing in line at the checkout counter in the A&P, the lady behind me tapped me on the shoulder and said, "What do you think?" Taking a quick look at the tabloids, I ventured that I thought Michael Jackson was in world-class trouble. "Oh no," she says, "I mean do you think Emily Dickinson was really gay?" Imagine my embarrassment, being caught totally unaware of this raging controversy. . . . Don't worry. The column is still the first thing I read.

The first time a topic won faint praise from Harry—"Good column. Interesting"—Deb felt like a kid finally getting an A from the toughest grader in the school. And Harry began to lose his frosty demeanor and to share a bit of his own background. He told of being lord of the manor at his house, making the major decisions for himself and his wife of fifty-eight years, Marion. He mentioned their five children, "all with spouses of the opposite sex. (Not that that's important.)," thirteen grandchildren and seven great-grandchildren. And he wrote about knowing gay people when he traveled with the circus and worked in theater in the 1920s and '30s.

Although we've not yet met him face-to-face, Deb and I think of Harry as a one-man Greek chorus we can count on to provide a running commentary on Deb's column. We sometimes speculate about Harry's reaction to a particular column even before it is written. After he'd been a devoted reader for several months, I called to ask him about his loyalty to a gay column. "It's an interesting subject to someone who's quite removed from it and, I must say, doesn't really understand it," Harry explained. He seemed both startled and delighted when I replied that, being gay, I've never quite understood the appeal of heterosexuality. He continued, "I've never thought of myself as homophobic. I just think of myself as not understanding something that's difficult for me to appreciate. . . . I suppose for most heterosexuals heterosexuality seems so perfectly natural that anything that doesn't fit in with that idea must, of course, seem unnatural. . . . If you hate oysters, you can't understand anyone who loves them, can you? Maybe it's as simple as that."

Yet, Harry admitted that by reading Deb's column he'd "acquired a considerable degree of understanding" of the gay world that's our oyster. Soon he was writing the two of us about tracking down and reading the gay books mentioned in the column and dragging Marion to see a movie that Deb had panned. He prodded Deb to write more about our life together. "I'd like to know more about the Price/Murdoch household. I think your readers would, too. . . . I think you can fill up a lot of columns with this kind of chat. Don't worry about running out of material. Old Uncle Harry will keep you supplied with ideas."

Harry's main advice to Deb is: "Remember the agenda; the purpose is to straighten out us straights. Don't waste time, energy and space on the rabid homophobics or the religious freaks who quote scripture to prove you are unregenerated sinners. You won't change them anyway. The fertile field is the great majority of stereo-straights, like me, who just need more knowledge and understanding. I don't know why I'm a hetero except that it seems perfectly natural and I wouldn't have it any other way. You have to teach me that you feel the same way."

Harry knows he feels the same way we do about gay marriage: Legalize it. "Most of the young couples I know are livin' in sin," he says. "If gay couples want to go through that outdated ritual of pledging undying love and fidelity to each other, I don't know why they shouldn't. Maybe gays will restore honor to the tradition for the rest of us."

It's wonderfully appropriate that Harry likes it best when Deb writes about the many ways in which we're ordinary people. When I talked with Harry on the phone, he mentioned that "my daughter Judy is a writer, too." As I was stifling an urge to say something patronizing, he added that perhaps I'd heard of her, that she wrote the novel *Ordinary People*. Judy, I realized to my total amazement, is Judith Guest. No wonder Harry's proud.

He sent Deb a Judith Guest essay, "The Mythic Family," that brought his background into sharper focus for us. We knew about the Michigan vineyard he operates with his youngest son. But his daughter told us about his short-lived lumber business, his Costa Rican oil venture, his envelope company. Harry had told us that his autocratic father had died young but hadn't mentioned what happened next. His mother "went to work for the Welfare Department. Her sister, Jean, moved in with her to help take care of the kids. She never left," Judith Guest writes. So after age nine, Harry grew up in a home headed by two women. Those details helped make Harry three-dimensional for us, but I felt I finally understood him when Judith Guest described growing up spending Sunday afternoons with her father and his four siblings: "My aunts and uncles were a force to be reckoned with—good-humored, energetic, very verbal. They would sit around the dining room table for hours—talking, talking, talking. . . . Kids were welcome at this table as long as they understood the rules. If you were bratty or whiny, you'd soon be removed. If you got brave and joined the conversation, you took your chances along with everyone else; you had to be prepared to support your opinions and take the heat. They loved you, but that wouldn't save you if you were full of baloney. It was something like a rite of passage in our family, and still is."

Suddenly, Harry's early, combative letters made sense to me. And reading Harry's inscription to Deb on the front of his daughter's essay, I knew Deb had survived her rite of passage into Harry's good graces. Thanks to the column, we've forged a bond with Harry that shows our shared humanity is far more important than what sets us apart. Harry wrote: "I have talked about you so often to Judy she thinks we must be good friends. I hope she is right. You have affected me profoundly, and I am grateful."

Our good friend Harry Guest was born in Detroit in 1913, before the advent of nylon and pop-up toasters, ballpoint pens and bras, AM radio and frozen food. It's difficult to grasp how much the look and taste and sound of American life has changed in his lifetime. He's certainly seen enough change to know that the shock of the new is often just its newness. He says he expects that he'd be shocked to see two men kissing affectionately. But he compares that to once being shocked to see an interracial couple walking down the street. "I'm getting used to that now. It doesn't bother me—not that it ever bothered me greatly. But I was surprised at it, and I would stop and look and say, 'I wonder what their relationship is.' But you see it so frequently now that it doesn't even cause a stir."

Deb continues to write about her life with me because we know there are good-hearted Harrys—heterosexuals capable of embracing us just as we are—out there saying, "I wonder what their relationship is." The more Deb's column fills in the fairly ordinary details and the more the rest of us gay people show heterosexuals who we truly are, the quicker we'll reach the day that our relationships don't cause even a stir. And we don't have to all begin looking like Ward and June Cleaver to make heterosexuals more comfortable with us. We just have to help them see that their fashion ideas can be a real drag.

I now fully expect us gay people to achieve full legal equality in my lifetime. Every time another gay person comes out our chances improve. Coming out has always been the key to our liberation. And people are coming out in the Nineties as never before. Yet by accentuating the negative, the news media unconsciously discourage gay people from staking a claim on a gay-friendly future by coming out. Deb consciously tries to counter that discouragement. "One of the things I try to do with my column," she told *Between the Lines,* "is talk about how fun it is to be gay. I mean, the news media projects . . . the image of being gay as you're going to be fired from your job, you're going to be beaten up, you're going to be rejected by your family. It's one thing after another. If I were a gay person in the closet reading this stuff, I would think the worst thing on earth would be (1) to be gay and (2) to be out. And that's not true. The worst thing on earth is to be in the closet and isolated."

Paul Monette, who in *Borrowed Time* wrote so beautifully of his love for the dying Roger Horwitz, later lost another partner to AIDS as well. Staring his compound grief in the face in his National Book Award–winning memoir *Becoming a Man,* Monette wrote, "I can't conceive the hidden life anymore, don't think of it as life. When you finally come out, there's a pain that stops, and you know it will never hurt like that again, no matter how much you lose or how bad you die."

The negative messages that conspire to keep gay people closeted away from one another and from our growing ranks of heterosexual allies don't just come from the news media. Word of our defeats, injuries, setbacks, travels like lightning among us. Deb knows, though, that if gay people are to be inspired and empowered, we've got to be aware of what's finally going right, not just what's still going wrong. She thunders in her column about gay victories, whether individual or international. The mere existence of her column is one such success story.

ONE OF THE MOST POSITIVE MESSAGES DEB'S EVER RECEIVED CAME IN the form of a thank-you note, one that helped us envision a more humane future—one that celebrates life and sexuality as wondrous gifts. It came from Mardell Rainey, a California housewife in her early fifties. Curiosity drew Mardell to Deb's column when the *San Jose Mercury News* began running it above Ann Landers every Thursday. At twenty, Mardell had worked with a gay insurance inspector, "a fine, kind, honorable, decent gentleman." He was kind to people and animals, traits guaranteed to draw high praise from Mardell, who confesses "a total addiction" to hummingbird-watching. But to the best of her knowledge, Mardell hadn't known anyone gay in more than thirty years when she became one of Deb's regular readers. She found herself unexpectedly moved by the January 2, 1993, column on the importance of breaking out of emotional (and fashion) straitjackets. The column toppled a defensive wall inside Mardell. "It was the nudge I needed to break loose and buy a pretty lacy pink blouse and the wildest coral print T-shirt that you have ever laid eyes on," she wrote inside a lavender thank-you card. "It doesn't matter who we are, you a young gay woman or me a silly old lady that is a bit on the large size, we all need to kick over the traces once in a while. Perhaps if we dressed like we feel about ourselves, people might get to know us better and be pleasantly surprised."

That was the first time Mardell had contacted Deb. Her card made quite an impression on me, since I am—as *The Niagara Gazette*'s Terry Murphy once described me to a colleague—"a big-boned gal." I felt proud of that California stranger, Mardell, and pleased Deb's column had given her a shot of courage.

A few weeks later Deb and I were shopping for easy-to-pack suits that we could wear to her out-of-town speeches. Eventually I found something blue that fit nicely. I tried on a very similar red suit and immediately rejected it.

"Why don't you get the red one, too?" my lanky partner asked.

"It doesn't look good on me," I replied in a tone that said, "And that is the end of this conversation."

Ignoring that stop sign, Deb continued: "It fits great. It's a fun color. It's perfect for your corporate-wifey appearances."

This wasn't a conversation I wanted to have. "It makes me look fat!" I declared.

But Deb was unyielding: "You don't look fat. If Mardell Rainey has the courage to go out and buy a wild blouse, you can buy a red suit!"

With Mardell's example leading the way, I marched to the cashier and bought the suit.

Every time I wear that suit, which has become a favorite, I think about how often we all let fear wall us off from experiences and people that might delight us. And I remember that I was able to be encouraged by Mardell because she allowed herself to be encouraged by a gay column. When I called Mardell to interview her for this book, I told her about my fire-engine-red suit. She said that after her first note to Deb she went back out and bought a provocative negligee to wear on her husband's birthday. He discovered it in a drawer, though, she says with a giggle. "He said,

'My God, are you having an affair!' " Although her husband of more than thirty years, a retired Army sergeant, is named Horace, Mardell calls him Sam, for "sexy American male."

Mardell simply believes, "People are people. What may have made me a little more sensitive is that I have a dear, dear, dear friend who is a Catholic sister and one of the things she commented to me was that she thought gay people were very, very brave because she had chosen her life and she is celibate and people think she's a bit weird and she's gotten a little bit of hassling over it, but she says gay people get more hassled. And she says she really admires them. She said, 'If this is the way a person is born, then they shouldn't be hassled over it. And if a person writes with their left hand, hey, this is how the good Lord made them.' Like when I was little, I started to write with my left hand and I still have the ruler marks on the back of my hand where I was corrected." Mardell types almost everything. "I don't write in script because I never really learned," she says. "Things like that make a person more sensitive. Hey, we're all human beings, and let's try to be good to one another."

Mardell has always been willing to buck the crowd. When only five years old, she saw her first rodeo and upset her relatives by rooting for the bull. She's still an unbridled nature lover, one who believes "we all were created and belong to a High Power that dearly loves variety." Mardell also is an equal-opportunity romantic: She roots for love, no matter the gender of the lovers.

"I don't like Hugh Hefner kind of people," she told me after saying she supports the push for gay marriage. "If people are straight, I want to see them in a good, solid relationship. If they're gay people, I want to see them in a good, solid relationship. I'm very, very uncomfortable with people who play around."

After eight years together, Deb and I received our first anniversary card—ever, from anyone—from Mardell in 1993. On the front, inside a large red heart, two teddy bears are picnicking in the moonlight. Inside, under the printed "Happy Anniversary," Mardell had penned, "Long live romance!" Deb and I were both so touched by the loving gesture that we caught each other wiping away tears. We had felt so alone for so long. We'd never dreamed of having such support for our relationship.

IN THE FIRST YEARS AFTER THE STONEWALL REBELLION, THE GAY civil rights movement focused on the right to be let alone. When we asked heterosexuals for respect—as individuals or couples—we usually just asked our closest friends and relatives. I've been blessed to receive it from my parents, just as Deb has gotten it from her mother. Now it's fitting that we gay people are demanding the same societal support, in the form of marriage licenses, that heterosexuals accept as their birthright. Getting to know people like Mardell and Harry makes me confident that ultimately we will receive justice.

Shortly after Deb and I returned from our memorable trip to Rochester, we received a letter from Chuck Collins, a member of Downtown Presbyterian Church who'd been an ordained Presbyterian minister before coming out. Chuck wrote that whenever we're feeling down or overwhelmed, we should just turn toward Rochester and remember that people there love us. Deb is terrible with directions, but she's learned exactly which way to face from our front door when she needs to reconnect with our spiritual home. We're planning a trip back to Rochester. We don't yet know the season or year. But as soon as Hawaii—or some other state—recognizes gay marriage, Deb and I will hop a plane and make our commitment legal. Then we're off to Rochester.

I already know what Downtown Presbyterian will look like on that future Saturday night. In my imagination, the Reverend Rose Mitchell and the Reverend Chuck Collins stand at the front of the sanctuary ready to ignore any Presbyterian prohibitions that remain. Deb and I walk down the aisle together, hand in hand. I can't see all the faces in the rosy light. But I know Mardell Rainey is there in a wonderfully loud blouse. Harry Guest has Marion in tow. Our Rochester friends—Virginia Davidson, the Kodak crowd and the Xerox copies—are to one side. On the other, near a jumble of my relatives, are J. Ford Huffman, Michael Hodges, Bob and Nancy Giles. Terry Murphy has driven over from Niagara Falls with her partner, Sally, and Dr. Anonymous, who is telling Deb's mother and brother his real name. Harriet Dart is parking her P-FLAG mobile out front as her husband,

Bill, loads his camera. Most of the Palm Springs longtimers have sent their regrets because they, too, had to shell out for airfare to go get legally hitched. But Linda Marquez is ready to sing at her first Anglo wedding—and Johnnie Hernandez is so proud. Russ Perry, unbeknownst to us, has wrangled press coverage. And the *Muskogee Daily Phoenix*'s Shirley Ragsdale has decided, what the hell, she'll miss a deadline to see a couple of lesbians she's never met promise to have and to hold.

Sure, it's just a fantasy for now. And I can hear some gay-rights advocates dismiss it as assimilationist. But it's actually the ultimate radical daydream: gay couples getting the love, support, encouragement and legal footing that most straight couples can take for granted if they choose to marry. Besides, Deb has finally learned how to be hugged and it would be a shame to waste that gift. Deb and I hope to grow old together. We've struggled to build a relationship that's strong but flexible enough to roll with life's punches. Now I want to make it legal. And, thanks to Rochester, I can finally imagine sealing our future married status not just with a kiss but with a church wedding.

The world really is changing in delightful and unexpected ways. Don't let fear choose your path.

Bibliography

Alyson, Sasha, ed. *You Can Do Something About AIDS*. Boston: Stop AIDS Project, 1988.

American Society of Newspaper Editors. *The Daily and Sunday Newspaper Audience: Major Demographic Segments*. Reston, Va.: Newspaper Association of America, 1993.

———. *Newspaper Page and Section Reader: Page Opening and Reading Style*. Reston, Va.: Newspaper Association of America, 1993.

Andersen, Hans Christian. *Andersen's Fairy Tales*. New York: Signet Classic, 1987.

Barnhart, Joe Edward. *The Southern Baptist Holy War*. Austin: Texas Monthly Press, 1986.

Bartlett, Neil. *Who Was That Man? A Present for Mr Oscar Wilde*. London: Serpent's Tail, 1988.

Beam, Joseph, ed. *In the Life*. Boston: Alyson Publications, 1986.

Bechdel, Alison. *New, Improved! Dykes to Watch Out For*. Ithaca, N.Y.: Firebrand Books, 1990.

Berenbaum, Michael. *The World Must Know: The History of the Holocaust as Told in the United States Holocaust Memorial Museum*. Boston: Little, Brown, 1993.

Bergman, David. *The Violet Quill Reader: The Emergence of Gay Writing After Stonewall*. New York: St. Martin's Press, 1994.

Berube, Allan. *Coming Out Under Fire: The History of Gay Men and Women in World War Two*. New York: Free Press, 1990.

Blumenfeld, Warren J., ed. *Homophobia: How We All Pay the Price*. Boston: Beacon Press, 1992.

Blumenfeld, Warren J., and Diane Raymond. *Looking at Gay and Lesbian Life*. Boston: Beacon Press, 1992.

Boswell, John. *Christianity, Social Tolerance, and Homosexuality: Gay People in Western Europe from the Beginning of the Christian Era to the Fourteenth Century*. Chicago: University of Chicago Press, 1980.

Bronski, Michael. *Culture Clash: The Making of Gay Sensibility*. Boston: South End Press, 1984.

Browning, Frank. *The Culture of Desire: Paradox and Perversity in Gay Lives Today*. New York: Crown, 1993.

Butler, Judith. *Gender Trouble: Feminism and the Subversion of Identity*. New York: Routledge, 1990.

Capitman, Barbara Naer. *Deco Delights*. New York: E. P. Dutton, 1988.

Carroll, Lewis. *Alice's Adventures in Wonderland & Through the Looking-Glass*. New York: Signet Classic, 1960.

Chan, Sucheng. *Asian Americans: An Interpretive History*. Boston: Twayne, 1991.

Cohodas, Nadine. *Strom Thurmond: And the Politics of Southern Change*. New York: Simon & Schuster, 1993.

Cook, Blanche Wiesen. *Eleanor Roosevelt*. New York: Viking, 1992.

Coontz, Stephanie. *The Way We Never Were: American Families and the Nostalgia Trap*. New York: Basic Books, 1992.

Coren, Stanley. *The Left-Hander Syndrome: The Causes and Consequences of Left-Handedness*. New York: Free Press, 1992.

Curtin, Kaier. *"We Can Always Call Them Bulgarians"*: *The Emergence of Lesbians and Gay Men on the American Stage*. Boston: Alyson Publications, 1987.

Degler, Carl N. *Place over Time: The Continuity of Southern Distinctiveness*. Baton Rouge: Louisiana State University Press, 1977.

Drake, Gillian. *The Complete Guide to Provincetown*. Provincetown: Shank Painter, 1992.

Drury, Allen. *Advise and Consent*. Garden City, N.Y.: Doubleday, 1959.

Duberman, Martin. *Stonewall*. New York: Dutton, 1993.

Dyer, Kate, ed. *Gays in Uniform: The Pentagon's Secret Papers*. Boston: Alyson Publications, 1990.

Eichberg, Rob. *Coming Out: An Act of Love*. New York: Dutton, 1990.

Faderman, Lillian. *Odd Girls and Twilight Lovers: A History of Lesbian Life in Twentieth-Century America*. New York: Columbia University Press, 1991.

Fairchild, Betty, and Nancy Hayward. *Now That You Know: What Every Parent Should Know About Homosexuality*. San Diego: Harcourt Brace Jovanovich, 1989.

Faulkner, Sandra, with Judy Nelson. *Love Match: Nelson vs. Navratilova*. Secaucus, N.J.: Carol Publishing Group, 1993.

Ferro, Robert. *Second Son.* New York: New American Library, 1988.

Fincher, Jack. *Sinister People.* New York: Putnam, 1977.

Forster, E. M. *Maurice.* New York: W. W. Norton, 1981.

Frank, Barney. *Frankly Speaking: What's Wrong with the Democrats and How to Fix It.* New York: Times Books, 1992.

Fricke, Aaron. *Reflections of a Rock Lobster: A Story About Growing Up Gay.* Boston: Alyson Publications, 1981.

Gallagher, Hugh Gregory. *FDR's Splendid Deception.* New York: Dodd, Mead, 1985.

Giles, Robert H. *Editors and Stress.* New York: Associated Press Managing Editors Association, 1983.

————. *Newspaper Management: A Guide to Theory and Practice.* Detroit: Media Management Books, 1988.

Griffin, Carolyn Welch, Marian J. Wirth, and Arthur G. Wirth. *Beyond Acceptance: Parents of Lesbians and Gays Talk About Their Experiences.* Englewood Cliffs, N.J.: Prentice-Hall, 1986.

Grumley, Michael. *Life Drawings.* New York: Grove Weidenfeld, 1991.

Guest, Judith. *The Mythic Family.* Minneapolis, Minn.: Milkweed Editions, 1988.

————. *Ordinary People.* New York: Viking Press, 1976.

Harbeck, Karen M., ed. *Coming Out of the Classroom Closet: Gay and Lesbian Students, Teachers and Curricula.* Binghamton, N.Y.: Harrington Park Press, 1992.

Heron, Ann, ed. *One Teenager in Ten: Writings by Gay and Lesbian Youth.* Boston: Alyson Publications, 1983.

Herron, Jeannine, ed. *Neuropsychology of Left-Handedness.* New York: Academic Press, 1980.

Hilberg, Raul. *Perpetrators Victims Bystanders: The Jewish Catastrophe 1933–1945.* New York: HarperCollins, 1992.

Juhasz, Suzanne, Cristanne Miller, and Martha Nell Smith. *Comic Power in Emily Dickinson.* Austin: University of Texas Press, 1993.

Karlsen, Carol F. *The Devil in the Shape of a Woman: Witchcraft in Colonial New England.* New York: Vintage Books, 1989.

Katz, Jonathan. *Gay American History: Lesbians and Gay Men in the U.S.A.* New York: Thomas Y. Crowell, 1976.

King, Martin Luther, Jr. *Why We Can't Wait.* New York: Mentor, 1964.

Kiska, Tim. *Detroit's Powers & Personalities.* Rochester Hills, Mich.: Momentum Books, 1989.

Kogon, Eugen. *The Theory and Practice of Hell: The German Concentration Camps and the System Behind Them.* New York: Octagon Books, 1973.

Leonard, Arthur S. *Sexuality and the Law.* New York: Garland Publishing, 1993.

Liebman, Marvin. *Coming Out Conservative.* San Francisco: Chronicle Books, 1992.

Lorde, Audre. *Sister Outsider.* Freedom: Crossing Press, 1984.

Ludlam, Charles. *The Complete Plays of Charles Ludlam.* New York: Perennial Library, 1989.

McCullough, David. *Truman.* New York: Simon & Schuster, 1992.

McNaught, Brian. *On Being Gay: Thoughts on Family, Faith and Love.* New York: St. Martin's Press, 1988.

Miller, James E., Jr. *Complete Poetry and Selected Prose by Walt Whitman.* Boston: Houghton Mifflin, 1959.

Monette, Paul. *Becoming a Man: Half a Life Story.* New York: HarperCollins, 1993.

———. *Borrowed Time: An AIDS Memoir.* New York: Avon Books, 1990.

National Defense Research Institute. *Sexual Orientation and U.S. Military Personnel Policy: Options and Assessment.* Santa Monica: RAND, 1993.

National Gay and Lesbian Task Force. *Pervasive Patterns of Discrimination Against Lesbians and Gay Men: Evidence from Surveys Across the United States.* Washington, D.C.: NGLTF, 1992.

Newman, Leslea. *Heather Has Two Mommies.* Boston: Alyson Wonderland, 1989.

Plant, Richard. *The Pink Triangle: The Nazi War Against Homosexuals.* New York: Henry Holt, 1986.

Preston, John. *Hometowns: Gay Men Write About Where They Belong.* New York: Dutton, 1991.

Ravitch, Diane, ed. *The American Reader: Words That Moved a Nation.* New York: HarperPerennial, 1991.

Rubenstein, William B., ed. *Lesbians, Gay Men, and the Law.* New York: New Press, 1993.

Russo, Vito. *The Celluloid Closet: Homosexuality in the Movies.* New York: Harper & Row, 1985.

Samuels, Steven, ed. *Ridiculous Theatre: Scourge of Human Folly. The Essays and Opinions of Charles Ludlam.* New York: Theatre Communications Group, 1992.

Sedgwick, Eve Kosofsky. *Epistemology of the Closet.* Berkeley: University of California Press, 1990.

Shilts, Randy. *Conduct Unbecoming: Gays and Lesbians in the U.S. Military.* New York: St. Martin's Press, 1993.

———. *The Mayor of Castro Street: The Life and Times of Harvey Milk.* New York: St. Martin's Press, 1982.

Smith, Martha Nell. *Rowing in Eden: Rereading Emily Dickinson.* Austin: University of Texas Press, 1992.

They Risked Their Lives: Rescuers of the Holocaust. Directed by Gay Block. Ergo Media Inc., 1992.

Valentine, Johnny. *The Daddy Machine.* Boston: Alyson Wonderland, 1992.

————. *The Day They Put a Tax on Rainbows*. Boston: Alyson Wonderland, 1992.

————. *The Duke Who Outlawed Jelly Beans*. Boston: Alyson Wonderland, 1991.

Van Gelder, Lindsy, and Pamela Robin Brandt. *Are You Two . . . Together? A Gay and Lesbian Travel Guide to Europe*. New York: Random House, 1991.

Vonnegut, Kurt. *Slaughterhouse Five*. New York: Dell, 1979.

Wilder, Thornton. *Our Town*. New York: HarperCollins, 1985.

Willhoite, Michael. *Daddy's Roommate*. Boston: Alyson Wonderland, 1990.

Williams, Selma R., and Pamela Williams Adelman. *Riding the Nightmare: Women & Witchcraft from the Old World to Colonial Salem*. New York: HarperPerennial, 1978.

INDEX